SOUTH CENTRAL REGIONAL LIBRARY

P9-CQI-906

Miami Branch
NOV / 2011

ATLANTIC OCEAN

. Pierre's Fortress

.Turks
Island

Dominican
Republic

Virgin Islands

Puerto
Rico

Antigua

Death's-Head
Island

Thorne's Caribbean HQ

Mission

Dominica

Martinique

C A

St. Lucia

Rogue's Cay

Sand

Aruba

La Blanquilla

Monastery of
St. Celestine

Grenada

Trinidad

Venezuela

MIAMI
Community Library
MIAMI MB R0G 1H0

Isle of Swords

BY

Wayne Thomas Batson

Thomas Nelson
Since 1798

NASHVILLE   DALLAS   MEXICO CITY   RIO DE JANEIRO   BEIJING

To the Master of Wind and Wave,
I will follow You into uncharted territory.

© 2007 by Wayne Thomas Batson.

All rights reserved. No portion of this book may be reproduced, stored in a retrieval system, or transmitted in any form or by any means—electronic, mechanical, photocopy, recording, or any other—except for brief quotations in printed reviews, without the prior permission of the publisher.

Published in Nashville, TN, by Thomas Nelson. Thomas Nelson is a trademark of Thomas Nelson, Inc.

Scripture references are from the King James Version of the Bible.

Thomas Nelson, Inc. titles may be purchased in bulk for educational, business, fundraising, or sales promotional use. For information, please email SpecialMarkets@ThomasNelson.com.

Interior art and layout by Casey Hooper.

Library of Congress Cataloging-in-Publication Data
Batson, Wayne Thomas, 1968–
Isle of Swords / by Wayne Thomas Batson.
   p. cm.
Summary: A young man awakens on an island, alone and seriously injured, with no memory, and as he searches for his identity he finds himself caught between two notorious pirates battling for a legendary treasure reportedly hidden by monks.
   ISBN-13: 978-1-4003-1018-0 (hardcover)
   ISBN-10: 1-4003-1018-0 (hardcover)
[1. Castaways—Fiction. 2. Identity—Fiction. 3. Pirates—Fiction. 4. Buried treasure—Fiction. 5. Christian life—Fiction. 6. Spanish Main—Fiction.] I. Title.
PZ7.B3238Isl 2007
[Fic]—dc22

                                                          2007005580

Printed in China
07 08 09 10 11 MT 5 4 3 2 1

CONTENTS

Principal Cast

Declan Ross
Red-bearded Scottish pirate; captain of the *William Wallace*.

Anne Ross
Feisty daughter of Declan Ross; longs to be a pirate.

Stede
West Indian sailor, quartermaster, and second-in-command of the *William Wallace*.

Midge
The main carpenter on the *William Wallace*; he has extremely bad teeth and horrendous breath.

Nubby
The cook and doctor on the *William Wallace*; he has a walrus moustache and only one arm.

Cromwell
The bosun of the *William Wallace*; he has a very flat face and wears one large gold earring.

Jules
Deck hand on the *William Wallace*; also acts as Anne's bodyguard. Jules is a gigantic muscular pirate. He has a bristly moustache and wears a black skullcap.

Red Eye
A powder monkey, i.e., one of the quick fellows who sprints down to the hull to get black powder for the cannons. Red Eye is blind in one eye, and his cheek is scarred from an explosion that took place while he was doing his job.

Cat
A young man who awakens on an island, alone and seriously injured, with no memory. Rescued by the crew of the *William Wallace*, he searches for his identity.

Jacques St. Pierre

Former French naval officer turned private businessman;
he has a penchant for fire and explosives.

Padre Domínguez

Priest of the Brethren who travels with the *William Wallace*.

Thierry Chevillard

Bartholomew Thorne's lieutenant; called
the Butcher because of his murderous past.

Bartholomew Thorne

The most notorious—and ruthless—pirate in the Caribbean;
Thorne wants to build a pirate fleet large enough
to control the Caribbean Sea and the Atlantic Ocean.

Mr. Skellick

Bartholomew Thorne's quartermaster.

Scully

Bartholomew Thorne's spy and chief source of information.

Commodore Blake

Young leader of the British naval forces in the Caribbean;
commissioned to hunt pirates on the Spanish Main.

Sir Nigel

Commodore Blake's adviser and right-hand man.

Vesa Turinen

Very old—and very rich—sailor, always ready to make a deal.

Ramiro de Ferro Goncalo

Portuguese shipbuilder; likes to duel.

Nautical Terms

Aft: the back of the ship.

Bow: front of the ship.

Bowsprit: long pole extending forward from the bow of the ship.

Crow's-nest: the highest platform on the mainmast used as a lookout point.

Forecastle: the front of the ship, often where the crew's quarters are located.

Halyard: rope used to pull a sail up.

Hull: The body of a boat or ship.

Jib-rigged: ship's sails that are triangular in shape.

Keel: the structural spine that runs along the bottom of the ship.

Mast: tall pole that supports all the ship's sails.

Poop Deck: rearmost deck of the ship.

Port: if standing on the deck and facing the front of the ship, port is left.

Quarterdeck: raised deck behind the mainmast where the ship's wheel is found.

Spar-collar: (sometimes knows as a gooseneck) a moveable iron collar used to hold horizontal spars to the mast.

Spar: long horizontal pole that a sail is attached to.

Square-rigged: ship's sails that are square in shape.

Starboard: if standing on the deck and facing the front of the ship, starboard is right.

Stern: the back of the ship.

The watch: a four-hour period when a sailor is on duty.

Halyard

Square-rigged

Mast

Jib-rigged

Forecastle

Bow

Stern

Quarterdeck

Poop Deck

Keel

1

A Black Bird in the Storm

Papa, I'm scared!" the little girl cried out as she slid awkwardly across the deck. Before she could regain her balance, she crashed into her father's arms.

"Oh, Dolphin!" he said, shielding her from sheets of rain and sea spray. "What are you doing up here?"

She looked up at him. "I heard a monster out in the sea!"

"A monster? My darling daughter, you heard the thunder and the wind, that's all." He snuggled her in close beneath his coat. "There are no monsters in the sea. It's a storm."

"But it's a big storm!" she whimpered.

"No, not big. Just noisy." But this voice was not her father's.

Dolphin peeked out from her father's coat and grinned. It was Brand, the young ship's mate she'd teased since they left port. *You're my blond monkey*, she'd said to Brand. And most times, he'd laugh, make chimp noises, and scurry up the nearest rope ladder or rigging. Now, the wind whipped his long hair about his face. Dolphin saw him wink and felt her heart flutter.

"I'm still scared," she said.

"It's just a squall," Brand said confidently. "Captain Halifax will see us through. And the *Trafalgar* is the pride of His Majesty's fleet! Now, you mind your father and go back to your quarters 'til it blows over." And just like that, he was gone across the deck.

"There, you see?" said Dolphin's father. "No monsters. Just a storm." He looked down at his precious little girl. Her bright coppery locks were matted against her pale cheeks.

Dolphin stared back, but up beyond her father, following the mainmast through shrouds of rigging, past the crow's-nest, and into the turbulent gray sky. Lightning slashed overhead, and Dolphin ducked again into her father's coat. Thunder crashed, and the entire ship trembled.

"Papa!" she cried. He gave her a brave smile and cradled her head against his chest. He hoped she couldn't hear his heart hammering away. "There, there, my Dolphin. Remember what Brand said. It will all be over soon. Now, let's get you back to our quarters and snug in bed."

"But, Papa, I want to stay here with you!"

"No, you will be much safer below," he replied, a slight edge to his voice. "I have work to do. I'm helping the quartermaster. He's waiting for me . . . see?" He pointed to the grizzled graybeard sailor near the mast. He nodded and grinned at Dolphin. Suddenly, Dolphin clutched her father's leg. She stared, pointing past the quartermaster, past the mainmast, out into the rolling sea. "What's that?"

An enormous ship appeared in the distance. It was tall, with at least three masts, and narrowed sharply at the bow. It knifed through the waves, driving toward them.

Dolphin's father bent low and held his little girl by the shoulders. "Stay here," he whispered urgently. He ran to the quartermaster and pointed out into the sea.

"Pirates," hissed the quartermaster.

"Pirates? In the middle of the storm?"

The quartermaster did not reply immediately. He stared out into the sea. Abruptly, he took in a sharp breath and went very rigid. He grabbed Dolphin's father by the shoulder of his coat and practically dragged him back across the deck. "Get your daughter down below," he said as they drew near the ship.

"Come, my child," Dolphin's father said, his voice taut. "We must go to our quarters."

"But, Papa, the ship . . . who are they?"

"No one to worry about, Dolphin."

"You best not lie to your daughter." The quartermaster's voice was flat, terrifyingly void of emotion. "That ship . . . it's the *Raven*. Bartholomew Thorne."

Dolphin's father felt the blood in his veins turn to ice at the uttering of that name. He whisked his daughter off the deck and raced for the cabins. He banged awkwardly through a door. "I'm so sorry, Dolphin," he managed to say. He could feel her trembling against him. He held her close and continued running. A hundred thoughts raced through his mind: memories, hopes, regrets.

"Papa!" she pleaded as they plunged into their cabin.

He sat down with her on the bed and snuffed the candle in the lantern. As darkness enveloped them, he said, "Don't worry, my precious daughter. It will all be over soon."

And he began to pray.

2
ECHOES OF CANNON FIRE

A cannon shot, deep and sudden, trailed off like a peal of thunder. Something cold touched his fingertips. Another shot. *Run them all out, boys!*

Water trickled over his hand. *She's taking on something awful! Bosun, pitch that leak!* Another shot, nearer still. Water surged into his mouth and nose. A wave partially submerged his head and sprayed his back.

He woke, jerked his head up from the surf, and flailed onto his side. His face, his arms, his back all throbbed and burned. "What happened?" he moaned, coughing up seawater and grinding sand between his teeth. He could not see. *Has someone cut out my eyes?* Hands trembling, he reached up. His eyes were swollen and caked shut . . . but at least they were there.

After several painful attempts, he managed to pry them open. Brilliant white light knifed in. He clutched at his face. His head throbbed, sun blazed mercilessly off the white sand, but slowly his eyes adjusted. He squinted under a cloudless blue sky and saw water. As another wave raced toward him, he rose to one knee. That little bit of movement brought tremendous pain. It felt as if there were shards of glass embedded in his skin.

With another groan, he stood. He reached over his shoulder and, between the tatters of his shirt, felt ripped flesh, sticky and wet. His fingertips came back glistening with blood, and he became light-headed. He swayed for a moment, then steadied himself and looked around. Across a slope of white sand there stood a deep copse of trees—mostly tall palms, surrounded by sea grape and divi-divi trees. He stared at the leaning, gnarled trunks. Divi-divi trees always leaned to the southwest. That meant something . . . he felt sure it did, but he could not grasp what. He looked along the tree line, up and down the shore, and, again, out to sea. "I don't know this place," he whispered.

He grabbed fistfuls of his matted blond hair. His welted face felt foreign . . . like someone else's. A sharp ringing came to his ears. The world seemed to spin. "Who am I? Why can't I remember?"

A flash of green racing across the sand drew his attention, and he turned. At his feet, a large iguana sat gnawing at the leather draw-string of a pouch that lay half-buried in the sand.

Brushing aside the lizard, he picked up the fist-sized pouch. It had some weight to it. "Is this mine?" he wondered aloud. He thought it had to be, but nothing about it seemed familiar. Still, when he loosened the drawstring and began to pour out its contents, he couldn't help but feel a strange gravity weighing upon him.

A sparkling green stone fell into his hands first. It was shaped like an almond, but much larger. The brilliant sun flickered within it as if the stone were alive with fire at its core. Next, a lock of lustrous red hair dropped out and lay in his palm close to the jewel. The hair was a little damp but still very soft. He ran a finger lightly over it, wondering. . . .

The surf raced in and covered his feet, just as the last item—a tarnished silver cross—fell into his palm. Ancient it looked—and not just from the tarnish. It bore strange markings and a script of some design, but he could not read it.

He dropped the three tokens into the pouch. He did not recognize any of these things. Nothing made any sense! His head ached. Weak and confused, he watched as an iguana scurried away and disappeared over the slope. Then he froze, for nearby the lizard's trail was a trail of footprints. They wound away from the trees, down from the slope, almost directly to where he stood. A wave crashed with a sound like a cannon shot . . . or maybe, more like the crack of a whip, and he jumped.

The ringing came back to his ears, and he felt dizzy. As his vision blurred, he looked at the footprints leading up to where he stood. The thought *I am not alone* flashed into his mind before everything around him faded into darkness.

3

THE WILLIAM WALLACE

What is it now?!" bellowed Captain Declan Ross. The pounding on his cabin door had made him knock over his mug. His lightning reflexes had just barely saved the sea chart from the spill. Only one sailor aboard the *William Wallace* would have the nerve to bang on the captain's door like that.

The quartermaster, a West Indian sailor named Stede, threw open the door, blatantly ignoring the custom of waiting to be asked to enter. "This old ship will burst at the very hull—if ya don't find us a place to careen her!"

Ross raised a coppery eyebrow and glared at his longtime friend.

"She's taking on watah below decks, mon!"

"What?" Ross stood. "I thought Midge patched those leaks."

Stede's nostrils flared. "Him did, mon, but it b' gettin' warse. The ship has four days . . . a week tops. B' true."

"I know," Ross replied with a shrug. "You're right. You're always right when it comes to the *Wallace*. Is the wind still light?" he asked, knowing the answer already. He could feel the ship rolling heavily on the ponderous swells of the sea.

"Just a breath," Stede answered, shaking a fist at the ceiling. "I think we may b' on the edge of the doldrums. . . . just b' a feeling."

Ross frowned. Stede's feelings were usually right too. If they were caught in the open sea with no wind and the ship coming apart at the seams . . . he shook his head. "I hope you're wrong. I have no desire to dance with the sharks anytime soon. Come here and look at this," Ross said.

Stede joined him at the desk. "Given the wind and the time you gave me, we might be able to get to this little group of cays."

Stede whistled. "They b' Thorne's isles."

"He can't cover them all!" Ross exclaimed. "He doesn't have enough ships . . . at least not yet."

"Life's hard," Stede said. He whistled again. "So, we'll make the hard choice. But we better pray that we don't get caught ashore by that wicked mon."

Stede left without another word. Captain Ross knew he didn't have to give the command. Stede would plot the course. Sure enough, in just a few minutes, Ross felt the *Wallace* slowly turn to the south.

Another knock—this one more a tap—at the cabin door. The door opened, and there stood a dumpy man with a walrus of a moustache and with just a stump at the elbow to serve as one of his arms. In his one hand, he held a wooden spoon. He stood there waiting.

"Come in, Nubby. What can I do for you?"

"Well, Cap'n, you could get me to port so's I can get some fresh meat! No fish is hitting the nets. We've got nothin' left but hard-tack and some moldy vegetables!"

Ross stared down at his sea chart. "What happened to those dog-sized rats you've been serving?"

"Cap'n, we ate 'em all. All's left is them little boney ones, and the men'll complain if I have to start serving those!" Nubby replied.

"The men will eat what they are served and be glad to get it," Ross stated without looking up from the chart. "And Nubs, cut the rations."

"This'll make the third time, Cap'n."

"Do you see a choice, Nubs?" Ross asked, looking straight at the cook.

"Nay, Cap'n." Nubs frowned dejectedly and beat a hasty retreat.

Declan Ross leaned back in his chair and exhaled loudly. He shook his head. *Let's see . . . the* Wallace *is about to fall apart in shark-infested waters, the only place close enough where we can ground the ship and make repairs is in the territory of the most ruthless man alive, and, oh yes, we're just about out of food. At least it can't get any worse than—*

SLAM!! Ross's cabin door flew open and in stomped a lass with flaming red hair barely concealed beneath a black bandanna. At her side was a silver cutlass. "FATHER!! You have got to let me sign!!"

"We've been through this before, Anne," he replied, rubbing his temples. *So much for it not getting any worse.*

"Well, I don't care what the crew thinks about having a woman aboard! I'm here, aren't I? I've brought no bad luck, have I?"

Ross started to say something about the lack of wind and their diet of rats, but bit his tongue. "What's this about, Anne?"

"It's Henrik and Jules—they follow me around everywhere just so they can give me something to do!"

"Henrik? Jules?"

"This time!" Anne shouted, one hand on the hilt of her sword, the other waving a finger in the air. "Yesterday, it was Red Eye.

Cromwell the day before. Just about every one of the crew—they treat me like some kind of peasant! Even Stede made me go fix him a bowl of lobscouse! You need to let me go on the register—sign the articles!"

"No, Anne," he replied, trying to hold his temper in check. "I promised your mother—"

"But she's not here!"

"Anne, that's enough."

"But I can sail!" she pleaded. Her hazel eyes seemed to turn deep blue as tears flooded in. "I can navigate. I can do all the rigging. I'm better with the sword than almost any—"

"I said NO!!" He slammed his fist on the desk, sending his mug skidding off the side where it crashed on the floor.

Anne's lower lip trembled. She turned abruptly and marched out of her father's cabin. But just before she slammed the door, he heard her mutter, "I'd be a better pirate than you are."

Captain Declan Ross stared at the door. "That's what I'm afraid of, Anne. That's what I'm afraid of."

4
CAREENING

At last!" Ross exclaimed, a smile spreading across his face. He slapped Stede's shoulder and strode across the main deck to the forecastle.

Ross stood proudly on the deck and looked out over the bow. He put his hands on his hips and muttered, "I'm glad we made it. The wind up and quit on us."

"Aw, I've seen us through warse!" Stede called after him.

"Made it?" barked a broom-shaped man who clambered up beside his captain and squinted. "I don't see nothin'."

"Your lights gone dead, have they, Midge?" Ross leaned in close and pointed out over the sea. "Land, you half-blind laggard! The cays. We'll be kissing the sand in an hour. Don't you see?"

Mr. Midgely stared, a dark scowl forming on his stubbly face. Slowly, a wide grin appeared, revealing a set of yellow teeth, most rotten, leaning or poking out of his gums at odd angles. "I see 'em! I see 'em, Cap'n!" Midge exclaimed, breathing each word into Ross's face. "Little-bitty things, they is, but I see 'em!"

"Your breath, man!" Ross exclaimed, ducking quickly away from the carpenter and his rotten teeth. "Worse than usual—oh, that's horrible. What've you been eating?"

"Rats," he replied proudly. "I found a couple of 'em ol' Nubby missed. They were smashed under a barrel, and I—"

"I don't think I want to hear any more," Ross said, moving quickly down the forecastle stairs. It was a vain effort to get the foul reek out of his nose. Ross feared that Midge would one day catch his death from something he ate—which was a shame because the man knew how to fix a ship. "Get your team down to the hold and get whatever lumber you can salvage. And, Mister Midgely . . ."

"Cap'n?"

"At least cook the rats next time."

Ross turned to his quartermaster, who stood at the wheel. "Stede, bring us in slowly!"

"We don't have much choice about that, eh!" Stede called back.

Ross looked up at the sails billowing ever so slightly. It was a wonder they'd made it to the cays at all with such a mild breeze. He shook his head and ran a hand lovingly along the rail of his ship. The *William Wallace* had done them all proud over the years. He'd bought the hundred-year-old brigantine from Ramiro de Ferro Goncalo, an old shipwright in Portugal, for fifty pounds of gold ingots and a cask of salted pork. It was a good deal—for Ramiro anyway. Most pirates would have taken the ship by force, but that's where Ross drew the line. You could take a man's gold. You could take a man's silver. You could even take some of a man's food. But you never took a man's ship.

Next to his daughter, Anne, and his close friend, Stede, his ship was the best thing in his life. The *Wallace* was well armed, fast, and maneuverable. But the *Wallace* was also old. As the ship turned slightly and began his drift run to shore, Ross wondered just how long he could keep the *Wallace* afloat.

"Tie-down!" Ross yelled. Quickly, everyone but Stede and Captain Ross grabbed hold of a rail or a strand of rigging and sat low on the deck. They all braced for the impact of the ship's bow as it plowed into the sandy bottom, waiting to see which new sailor would be cartwheeled overboard during the jolt. But it didn't come. Instead, they felt just a few light bounces, and the *William Wallace* came to rest.

"That's all?" asked Cromwell, the ship's bosun.

Anne laughed. "No wonder, with such little wind."

"Great," Ross muttered. He looked over the bow and saw they were parked still thirty yards from the shore.

"Guess we'll just have to wait until low tide to start unloading," said Cromwell, who never saw a job that couldn't wait.

Stede's gigantic hands clamped down on Cromwell's shoulders from behind. Lifting Cromwell off the deck, he asked, "Permission to throw this outrageous mon overboard, Cap'n?"

"What?" Cromwell's arms and legs flailed helplessly. "Stede, put me down. What'd I do? Put me down."

Ross glared at his bosun being held by Stede a foot off the deck. "You have evidently forgotten that these little cays are Thorne's isles. If you want to wait around for him or one of his friendly mates, be my guest. We will careen the *Wallace* and get out of here as fast as we can. And . . . we will unload this ship right NOW, beginning—I think—with the biggest hunk of dead weight aboard."

"No, Cap'n," Cromwell pleaded. "I just wasn't thinking. You wouldn't take—"

"Mister Stede?" said Ross.

"Aye, sir?"

"Permission granted."

"Nooooo!" In one fluid motion, Stede hurled Cromwell up and over the bow's rail. His arms and legs pinwheeling, he fell like a stone and landed in the turquoise water with a horrendous splash.

The captain turned to his crew. "Anyone else want to wait for low tide to unload?"

Two hours later, the *William Wallace* was nearly light enough—and the tide was nearly low enough—to begin turning the ship on his side to make repairs. Led by a remarkably tireless bosun Cromwell, the crew had secured the hatches and carried most of the stores to shore.

From Ross's vantage point onshore, the cay appeared to be a large crescent. The white sand stretched more than a hundred yards from the surf to the lush copse of palms and other tropical vegetation. The tree line gradually curled toward the sea on the eastern part of the island. Excellent cover—a perfect place to careen a ship. But that worried Ross. He couldn't imagine as clever a pirate as Thorne leaving a cay like this one unwatched for long. "Get a move on, lads!"

Midge was already at work, chiseling barnacles off the exposed sections of the hull. Nubby had discovered an ample supply of iguanas scurrying over the white sands and up the coarse palm trunks. With visions of stew stirring in his head, he flung himself all over the beach after the big green lizards. The captain and Stede busied themselves securing and testing the lines they would use to pull the

Wallace on his side. Everyone seemed to be busy doing something important—everyone, that is, but Anne.

The captain's daughter sat on the edge of a pile of driftwood and carved a piece of yellow coral with a very sharp dagger. She'd always enjoyed that, and she was quite good at it. Rings, bracelets, even figurines—but always decorated with something dangerous: snakes, thorny vines, or sharks. Anne was especially proud of this latest creation: a ferocious Bengal tiger with bared fangs and an outstretched paw. As good as the new carving was, Anne couldn't bear to just sit there while everyone else had pirate things to do.

With an exasperated sigh, Anne stood, sheathed her dagger at her waist, and put the coral tiger in a pouch around her neck. She scanned the activity around the ship and watched how her father doted on his crew. Those scallywags meant more to him than his own flesh and blood. She kicked up a mound of white sand and turned her back.

Her eyes followed the tree line, the palms, the divi-divi trees, and the . . . *wait a minute!* Under the canopy of wide palm leaves, she noticed a familiar shadowy bunch, hanging down like a gray chandelier. *Plantains!*

Anne charged over to Captain Ross. "Father, I think those palms over there are plantains. Can I go look?"

"Plantains?" Ross glanced at Nubby, who was still busy chasing iguanas. "If you're right, you might just save the lives of the whole crew. Go ahead, but . . ." He glanced into the shadows under the canopy of palms. "Take Jules with you."

"I can take care of myself."

"I know you can," said Ross. "But if those are plantains, two of you can carry a lot more back than just one." It was a weak excuse, Ross knew. He just hoped she'd buy it.

Anne frowned at her father. *He never lets me go off alone!*

The dark-skinned giant lightly lowered two barrels from his shoulders and lumbered over. Jules stood a foot taller than the captain. He went about shirtless. With broad, well-muscled shoulders and hands the size of cannonballs, Jules was a fearsome sight.

"Anne seems to have spotted some plantains in the palms over there," Ross said. "Bring as many back as you can carry, and we may yet avoid having to eat Nubby's iguana stew."

"I like iguana stew." But seeing the look on his captain's face, Jules nodded and turned to Anne. "Let's go."

Jules took one step for every three of Anne's. Neither the sand nor the incline slowed him down. Anne could barely keep up. "Red!" he said, a voice like thunder.

Anne grumbled and stomped up the dune after him. "I've told you a thousand times, don't call me Red!" She caught up to him and poked him in the arm with her finger. It hurt—Anne, not Jules.

"What should I call a wench with hair the color of flame?"

"I'm not a wench!" Anne poked him in the arm again. It hurt again—Anne, not Jules. "I certainly won't be fetching you a mug of grog anymore." She poked him one more time to make sure he got the point.

"Why do you keep doing that?" Jules asked. "It must hurt."

His face was stern, and he made Anne feel like a great tree trunk was about to fall on her. But then his moustache quivered, and he broke into a broad grin. They laughed the rest of the way to the tree line.

"I was right," Anne whispered. "Look at them."

In the tops of the palms, nestled beneath wide, shady leaves, were huge barrel-shaped bunches of plantains. They looked like green bananas but tasted more like potatoes until sweetening a little and turning black at their ripest point. Anne snapped a plantain from a squat stalk. Her dagger was out in a flash, and she expertly carved away the green skin on all sides. She took a big bite of the white fruit. "This ought to give us enough food until our next port," said Anne. Grinning mischievously she added, "Or our next 'fat' galleon."

"I still want iguana stew," Jules muttered.

"You can have your green lizard stew," said Anne. "And my portion as well." She drew her cutlass and waded into the forest, jumping, hacking, and chopping. Bunches of plantains fell, and Jules came behind her and hoisted them up on his shoulders.

"You are very handy with that sword, Red," said Jules, taking great pains to stay out of her swing radius.

Anne glared at him and brandished the cutlass. "I told you not to call me that!"

"If you want to be a pirate, a pirate captain even, you need a fearful name."

"And you think *Red* will scare anyone?"

Jules hoisted up another bunch of plantains. "I was thinking *Anne the Red*. Sounds like blood."

"Sounds like some beheaded queen to me." They laughed, but Anne stopped first, becoming thoughtful. Most of the crew knew of her desire to be a pirate, but only Jules knew that her real ambition was to captain a ship herself. Only then could she have the freedom she desired. Freedom to go where she wanted, whenever she wanted. Away from the mainland and the shackles that had fettered her mother and eventually caused her death. Away from the society that looked on her as good for little else than a serving wench or a chambermaid. Away from her father, who loved the sea and admired his crew, but smothered—or worse, ignored—these same traits in his daughter. But Jules was right. If she ever wanted to be a pirate, she needed a name.

Anne went at the plantains with renewed vigor, chopping at all she could reach and venturing deeper into the palms. Jules already carried more than any one man should be able to carry but made no complaint. Still, the weight of the mounds of fruit on his shoulders slowed him down, and Anne found herself well ahead of her chaperone . . . her protector. She winced. She looked over her shoulder. He was pretty far back there.

Then Anne had a thought. It wasn't the first time she'd had this thought, but it was the first time in recent memory she'd had the opportunity. *All I'd have to do is turn a corner and disappear into the trees. By the time Jules realized, I'd be long gone.* Anne thought for sure the island was large enough to hide her. The palms were dense enough, and there might be some caves.

But what would she do next?

Anne hadn't really thought that far. She'd be stranded on one of a thousand cays in the Spanish Main. But . . . hadn't Stede said something about these cays being in Thorne's territory? *Maybe*, she thought, *maybe I could cut my hair . . . stow away on one of Thorne's ships and learn how to be the kind of pirate that people feared.* She leaped and hacked down a huge cluster of plantains.

Or maybe, I'll just get myself killed. She looked back at Jules. He was struggling a little, farther back than before. He wasn't even looking at her. If there was ever going to be a time, it was now.

5

THE BUTCHER

Anne turned a corner around a fat palm and sprinted away. Ducking and swerving recklessly, she smacked through coarse underbrush, tangling vines, and leaves bigger than an elephant's ear. She tripped over a small gnarly divi-divi tree, fell, and lay still.

"ANNE!!" Jules's voice thundered in the forest behind her. Anne leaped to her feet, not knowing which way to run. She ducked under a bough and raced in a new direction. She drove herself on, feeling like her dream of freedom was slipping through her grasp. Two more frantic steps and she burst out of the palm forest and landed facedown in white sand.

She feared she had run in a circle and doubled back to the shore where they had run the ship aground. But as she stood and wheeled around, she realized that it was not so. The island was just larger than she had imagined, and she had raced from one side through the trees and on to another side of the island.

Anne brushed herself off and wondered what to do. There was

something there, on the sand . . . near the water's edge. She glanced
back at the trees. Jules could be getting closer. He could appear at
any moment. Still, she looked at the shape. Something was there, a
dark smudge sprawled across the bright sand.

Squinting and blinking, she took a few cautious steps. As she
neared, the shape became more distinct. It was a person. In spite of
the relentless heat of the Caribbean sun, goose flesh rippled on her
arms. At last she came upon a piteous, crumpled form. *A man. A
dead man.*

Anne wondered where he had come from and what had happened to him. He was covered in blood: some red, bright, and wet;
some caked and purplish; some dried in maroon splotches. His
boots were scuffed and partially underwater. His breeches were torn
and gouged. And his once-white shirt was a mess of bloody tatters.

When she saw the deep, scourging wounds on his back, Anne
knew what had happened to this man. He had been whipped with
a vicious cat-o'-nine-tails. A heavy baton whip with nine cords, each
ending with a jagged piece of metal, glass, or wood—only such a
weapon could do that kind of damage to a man. That was a penalty
doled out only to the worst of criminals or mutineers, but seeing the
damage the cat had done made Anne feel pangs of sorrow. She bent
down and sadly stroked his matted mop of blond hair. *What did you
do,* she wondered, *to deserve thi—*

His head jerked up. Anne fell backward, her heart racing. She
rose to one knee and watched with horror as the man lifted his
head. His face was a swollen mass of bruised and cut flesh. A brief
glint of blue eyes, pleading and desperate, gleamed out from the
mass of hair. His whole body racked with long, wheezing coughs,
and his head fell pitifully onto the sand.

Anne got up and saw that the way his head had fallen had made it virtually impossible for him to breathe. One part of her warning that she should get away, Anne gently but firmly gripped the man's shoulders and pulled. He groaned as Anne flopped him over onto his back. "What am I doing?" she said out loud.

He was breathing, but the breaths were shallow and sounded wet. He was clearly too big for Anne to carry. She looked back toward the forest of palms, and she knew what she needed to do . . . in spite of the consequences. She brushed some hair out of his face. "I'll come right back. I promise."

Anne backed away, careful not to kick up sand. She turned and ran toward the trees. No more than fifty yards into the palms, she smacked into Jules's bare chest. "Thought better of it, eh?" Jules clutched both of Anne's arms below the shoulders and squeezed just enough to let her know that he was not happy about her little stunt.

"Jules, you've got to come!" she screamed. "There's a man . . . on the beach. I think he's dying."

Jules's eyes narrowed. "What is this nonsense? Another one of your adventures?"

Anne grunted and tried to wriggle free. "Let me go, you big oaf! I'm telling you, someone needs help!"

"Show me!" he said, his voice full of warning. Anne sped back the way she had come. Out of the palms and across the sand, they came to the scene of the stricken sailor. Even Jules winced when he saw the condition of the man. Anne saw he lay motionless.

"Oh no!" she cried out and knelt near him. "He's still breathing! Jules, we've got to get him back to the *Wallace*. Nubby will know what to do."

The mountainous pirate did not answer. "Jules?"

Anne looked up and saw Jules staring out into the sea. She turned and gasped. Out past the whitecaps, a menacing ship appeared. It flew black sails on its twin masts and sat low in the water. In spite of the lack of wind, the craft moved with ghostly speed.

"I've never seen a ship like that before," Anne whispered.

"It's a corvette. Two masts, and much faster than the *Wallace*." He grabbed her by the arm and began to drag her up to her feet. "We have to warn the captain!"

"What, why—is it Thorne?"

As they watched the corvette move inevitably from right to left, a blood-red flag rose on the rear mast. "No, not Thorne," Jules said. "Chevillard."

"Chevillard . . ." Anne blinked. She knew all about Thorne's lieutenant. Perhaps not as diabolically clever as Thorne, but easily as ruthless. It was said that a tide of blood followed Chevillard's ship. Thierry Chevillard was known as the *Butcher*.

"If he comes upon the *Wallace* while it's aground . . . ," Jules said.

"I'm faster," Anne said, turning to run. "Jules, carry him, and be careful."

When Anne emerged from the palm forest, she saw the *Wallace* unloaded and half-turned on his side.

"Stop!" Anne shrieked, waving her cutlass frantically as she ran. "Right the ship!" A few members of the crew looked up, but their backs were turned to the open sea. They did not see the corvette with black sails round the bend behind them.

"Stop! Stop now! Right the ship!" she yelled, stumbling across the sand in reckless horror. Still, only a few looked up, most bemused, not understanding. "Father!" she cried at last.

If there was anything in the known world that would get Declan

Ross's attention, it was the call of his only child. He dropped his line and scanned the horizon. "Anne?" Then he saw her, saw her waving frantically and slashing her sword. He heard one word drifting across the sand: "Chevillard!"

Ross turned and saw the prowling corvette and its red flag. The color drained from his face. Knowing it was too late, Ross faced his crew and barked orders. "Right the ship! Right the ship, now! Heave the mast lines! Prepare to fight! We are under attack."

The crew turned in unison, saw the threat on the seas, and transformed into a frenzied cloud of action. Within seconds they began to haul the *Wallace* upright.

Stede strode up to his captain. They both watched Chevillard's advance. He was coming . . . slowly, but inevitably.

As soon as the ship was stable, Cromwell and Midge began lowering the gangplank. Ross looked again at the enemy. *No time. There's no time.* He flew around the bow and yelled, "Midge, get that gangplank up!"

"But, Cap'n, . . . the cannon shot's on the shore. We've got to—"

"Get the plank up NOW!! Then get up in the crow's-nest and keep watch on Chevillard!"

Stede was in his captain's face in a second. "Have ya gone mad, mon? We cannot b' fighting without the cannon shot."

"Quartermaster," Ross said, his words clipped. "We don't have the time to load the cannonballs, and the *Wallace* won't budge with much more weight."

"What ya b' thinking? We cannot outrun a corvette, mon."

"I don't plan to run from Chevillard," Ross said, a maniacal gleam in his eyes.

Stede backed away, grinning. "Yer an outrageous mon, Declan Ross. Ya b' up to something. That b' true!"

"The rascal's cutting us off, Cap'n!" Midge yelled from his perch high on the ship's crow's-nest. The dark ship stayed out of cannon range, but drifted behind them, waiting.

"He's not as dumb as I thought," Ross said. "We've got to get the *Wallace* off this shore, or we're all done." Holding Anne at arm's length, he asked, "Anne, where's Jules? We need his strength."

After Anne explained about the wounded man, Ross turned and looked at the tree line. Jules was nowhere to be seen. He looked back to see his daughter's tears. "You did the right thing, daughter," he said. "No crewman on the *Wallace* should leave another pirate behind."

She nodded, her bottom lip quivering, and joined the others who were lining up on both sides of the bow.

Except for Nubby, who was unaware of the problems and still back in the forest looking for iguanas, the crew of the *Wallace* tried to push the ship back into the sea. Grunts and yells arose as they strained against the massive weight. Unscraped barnacles cut deep into their hands, but they did not stop. They knew that pirates caught on land . . . were dead pirates.

"You look like you could use a little more brawn," said a deep voice from behind. And there was Jules, carrying the wounded man. Ross spun around and grimaced when he saw the bloody mess in Jules's arms. Anne turned as well. Her eyes pleaded, and her shoulders sagged.

"Midge!" Ross commanded. "Get up there and lower the gangplank. After Jules gets this guy down in the hold, pull it back up!"

"Aye, Cap'n!" And like a spider, Midge climbed up one of the mast lines and disappeared over the rail. Once the wounded man was safely aboard, the crew went to work with renewed vigor.

Again, grunts and groans. Sweat and blood flowed. "Chevillard comin' round, Declan!" Stede yelled from the other side of the *Wallace*. Ross stepped away from the bow. Chevillard's corvette had turned and drove toward them. *He's tired of waiting,* thought Ross. *He knows we're stuck, and he's coming to get us.*

"Men!" Ross bellowed. "We need an inch, and the tide will do the rest. Now go for it! All you've got!" This time the effort was eerily silent. They stifled their pain and, with grim determination, laid into the *Wallace*. Breaths escaped in hisses, muscles trembled on the verge of spasming, and hearts pounded so hard the men could feel it in their eardrums. Then they felt it. A shift . . . a subtle bit of motion, but still, the *Wallace* did not break free. "Come ONNN!!!" Ross yelled.

Then Ross spotted Nubby coming out of the forest with a basket of iguanas.

"Nubs, you land-loving lout! Get in here and push!" Ross yelled.

Still not realizing the danger, Nubby argued, "Blast it, Captain, I'm a cook, not a strongman!"

"Get over here now!" Ross bellowed, dizzy with the strain.

Nubby looked beyond the landlocked *Wallace* and saw the looming corvette. The basket of iguanas went flying, and Nubby hit the *Wallace* like he'd been shot out of a cannon. The shift was more pronounced this time. The *Wallace* moved. The salt water flooded into the small crevice that had opened around the ship's hull. And suddenly, the ship was afloat. The *Wallace* slid backward into the surf. "Well done, lads!" Ross shouted. "Now, all aboard! We have a Frenchman to send to Davy Jones's locker!"

As the crew scaled the rope ladders and shimmied up the mast lines, they wondered how they could defeat the Butcher with no gunpowder and no cannonballs.

6

A Desperate Plan

The red flag and black sails of their opponent loomed on the seas before the *William Wallace*. Captain Ross launched a string of commands. "Nubby, get below and see to the wounded man! Anne, you go with him." She nodded and disappeared with Nubby belowdecks.

"Midge, Cromwell, Henrik, Smitty, and Red Eye—meet me by the mainmast!" Ross raised his voice. "Lads, take up every pistol, every dagger, every cutlass, every dirk—anything you can use as a weapon! Be ready for the fight of your lives!"

One man stepped forward. Leathery-skinned with wrinkly slits for eyes, Drake was the oldest sailor aboard the *Wallace*. "But, Cap'n," he said, "you make it sound like Chevillard's going to board us!"

"I mean to let him," Ross said. This announcement rattled the crew, but they followed their captain's orders.

"Stede, take whatever wind we have and steer behind the corvette —out to sea!"

"We can't outrun her!" Stede called back, spinning the wheel.

"No, but we've got to make it look like we're trying to!"

"Care to let me know what ya b' planning, mon?"

"Not now," Ross replied. He drew near to his old friend. "Just keep your thunder gun handy!"

"Got it right here," Stede replied, grinning. He reached into a cabinet beside the wheelhouse and withdrew a short musket with a snubbed barrel that widened drastically at its end.

"At least we have one cannon!" Ross winked. Weaving in and out of crewmen and leaping lines strewn across the deck and open hatches, the captain made his way to the mainmast where a group of bewildered sailors waited. No one was more confused or more vocal about it than Cromwell.

"Shouldn't we be takin' to our station of battle?" he asked.

"You *are* at your station of battle!" Ross said curtly. "Now, speak no more and listen. Cromwell, you and Henrik get to the top of the mainmast, one on the topsail and one on the main. Smitty, take the mainsail on the foremast. Here's my plan."

As he told them, the looks on their faces underwent a marked transformation from shock and horror to roguish grins. Smitty leaped away and scaled the foremast. Each with a boarding axe holstered at his side, Cromwell and Smitty clambered up the mainmast. "Stick close to the mast, lads!" Ross yelled. "Wait for my signal and make a clean cut!"

"What about us?" Midge asked, fingering his own dagger. Red Eye, a powder monkey—one of the many deck hands who shuttled black powder cartridges from the stores below to the gun decks during battle—stood impassively. The left side of his face was scarred and slightly misshapen from a cartridge that had gone off as he loaded it into a cannon. His left eye was blind, the pupil dark red, and the whites permanently colored a sickly pink.

"I have a very important task for you two," Ross said. As he finished outlining his plan, Midge whistled and Red Eye, who almost never smiled, gave a crooked grin.

"What if we get caught?" Red Eye asked. "I don't speak French."

"Just remember," Ross implored. "As soon as Chevillard and the lion's share of his men board the *Wallace*, you two hit the water."

The pieces of his plan all in place, Declan Ross stood on the forecastle waiting for his opponent's next move. He didn't have to wait long. Thierry Chevillard's sleek ship maneuvered across the *Wallace*'s path, cutting off the ship's escape. By Captain Ross's orders, Stede let the *Wallace* drift slowly into the enemy's firing range.

"Declan, I hope ya know what ya b' doing," said Stede.

"Don't I always?" Ross replied. "Second thought, don't answer that." Stede raised an eyebrow, then checked on Chevillard's ship.

"He won't fire right away," Ross said quietly, almost to himself. "He'll wait until his ship rolls on the top of the wave."

"How ya b' knowing that?" asked Stede.

"French tactics. The Butcher sailed for King Louis' Royal Navy before turning pirate. He'll want to fire high and take out our masts before coming to claim his prey—I'm counting on that."

The corvette rolled upward on the swell. A puff of gray smoke appeared on its portside. Then came the report—a muffled boom. "This one will be for range," Ross said. "I just hope he fires long."

Except for the mournful wail of the gulls, the deck of the *Wallace* became silent. The crew crouched—waiting for the broadside to fall. Suddenly, a huge plume of seawater erupted near the *Wallace*.

"He fired short—great. Stede, get us in closer!"

"Closer? That mon will drop a big roun' ball right on top of us!"

Ross took out a spyglass. "Trust me," he said. "Chevillard wants the ship intact. He'll fire high when his ship rolls again. Just get me in there so the shot will go over our masts—not through them!"

As always, Stede turned the wheel at Ross's command, but doubt simmered on his brow, and he glared at his friend. At that moment, he caught sight of the men positioned high up on the masts, and Stede nodded repeatedly. "Oh, ya b' a sly mon, Declan Ross," he said. "It just might wark!" Stede did his best to slide the *Wallace* in a little closer, but the wind—barely a breath now—offered no help.

The corvette lurched back, rolling on the swell. Four of Chevillard's ten portside cannons fired, wreathing his ship in gray smoke. The booms echoed ominously, and Declan grimaced, knowing that he'd doomed the crew . . . if his plan failed. "Ready?!" he shouted up to Cromwell, Henrik, and Smitty. They raised their axes in answer. Ross held his cutlass aloft and scanned the sky.

The first shot landed just short of the bow. The second tore through the rail and part of the roof of the cabins on the stern. The third and fourth shots were high. One cleared the foremast by a foot. The other whooshed harmlessly between the webs of rigging on the mainsail. At that moment, Ross slammed down his cutlass and yelled, "NOW!!"

Cromwell, Henrik, and Smitty brought their axes down on the rigging that secured the sails to the spars and the masts. The sharp blades cut the ropes. The topsail and two mainsails crashed to the deck. The *William Wallace* now really was dead in the water.

7

CROSSING SWORDS

Come on, take the bait. Take the bait," muttered Ross as he watched the sleek corvette rise and fall on the sea swells.

"I don't much like b'ing the bait," said Stede with a nervous laugh.

"I don't like it either," Ross replied. "But I'd prefer a stand-up fight to being blown to smithereens and letting one of Thorne's men pick our carcasses."

"Yer not doing much to comfort me, mon."

"He's got to know something's wrong," Ross argued. "He's seen our sails fall. We haven't returned fire. He's got to come."

The corvette did not fire another shot. At last, it turned and drifted toward the *William Wallace*. "Yes!" Ross clapped Stede on the back. "Arrogant scoundrel! I knew he'd come."

Stede took the spyglass and scanned its deck. "Must b' close to two hundred sailors on that ship! Did ya b' knowing that too?"

"I'd take the crew of the *Wallace* even against four hundred Frenchmen!"

Chevillard's dark ship turned and drifted so close that the crew of the *Wallace* could see the sailors swarming on the enemy deck. The Butcher's men wore black bandannas and had red sashes tied around the waist of whatever surcoat or shirt they had on. They brandished pistols, cutlasses, boarding axes, and many other weapons.

Ross didn't see Chevillard, but that was not a surprise. Chevillard would wait until the battle was well underway before sticking his neck out. Ross had heard tales of the Butcher's famous heavy cutlass stolen from a Spanish master swordsmith. Ross had also heard stories of the plundering of Lake Maracaibo—stories of how Chevillard had lined up more than seventy settlers and personally beheaded one after the other.

"Let's not make this easy on them, lads!" Ross called back to the crew just before the first grappling hook sailed over the railing of the *William Wallace*. Ulrich, one of the gunners, brought his axe down on it quick. The rope snapped instantly, but dozens of other hooks rained down. One skewered Ulrich's shoulder and slammed him tight to the side and dragged him overboard.

As soon as the *Wallace*'s crew appeared at the rails to cut off the hooks, Chevillard's swivel guns opened up. With whoops and shouts, pirates in black and red swung down from the corvette's masts. The first of Chevillard's men to land on the *Wallace*'s deck found himself staring into the wide barrel of Stede's thunder gun. "Yer not welcome aboard," said the West Indian sailor, and he pulled the trigger. The sound of this cannon of a pistol drowned out all other noise.

In an instant, the fight erupted all over the deck. Enemies streamed in across uncut ropes. Pistols and muskets fired all around. Smoke filled the air. Swords clashed, and men from both sides groaned and fell. Cromwell, Henrik, and Smitty leaped from their perches and brought their axes down on several heads in black bandannas. Stede put away the thunder gun—which, while deadly, took far too long to reload. In its place, Stede drew two long machetes from scabbards slung behind his back. He went to work, cutting a swath through the enemy's first wave. Ross's men were better fighters hand-to-hand, but Chevillard's numbers began to overwhelm them.

Ross waited and watched until he was convinced that most of Chevillard's fighting force had boarded the *Wallace*. Then he saw Midge and Red Eye slip over the side unnoticed. That was it. The rest was out of his control. "Now for it, lads!" he yelled, drawing his cutlass. "Give 'em one for Scotland! Give 'em one for old William Wallace!"

He leaped into the fray, rolled, and took down two of Chevillard's men with a long, hard slash across their knees. Ross ducked and, in one brutal movement, swung his cutlass just as a pirate in black aimed a pistol at his head. The pirate's arm—pistol and all—fell at the feet of the astonished sailor. A kick to the midsection sent him flying, and Ross ran to the next fight.

Belowdecks, Anne wiped a moist cloth across the wounded man's forehead. He lay on his side upon a table so that Nubby could treat his back. "These are most grievous wounds," said the ship's cook and doctor.

They heard the cannon shots, the muskets, the shouts, and heavy footfalls. Nubby ignored them and continued his work. Anne grimaced, wondering if at any moment, Chevillard's sailors would crash through the cabin door. If they did, Anne would be ready with her cutlass. But she hoped it would not come to that.

As Anne continued to wipe the dried blood and grime from the man's welted face, she realized that he was much younger than she had at first supposed. He had no beard or moustache, but she hadn't noticed—her attention had been so drawn by the wounds and blood. *How old?* she wondered. *Sixteen, seventeen?*

He groaned and arched his back. "Sorry, lad!" said Nubby. He lifted a cloth daubed in a cranberry-colored paste. "That's just the ointment doing its work."

The lad's eyes fluttered, then opened for just a moment. He looked up at Anne. "I . . . I know you, don't I?" he said weakly before his eyes closed. Anne stepped backward.

"What did 'e say?" Nubby asked. But before Anne could answer, a tremendous crack sounded from somewhere beyond the cabin door.

"Topside!" Anne exclaimed. "They're trying to get down here!"

"Anne," Nubby ordered. "Help me lay 'im on his back—if there's a ruckus, I don't want 'im fallin' off the table!" Another sharp crack. Anne's hand went instantly to the hilt of her sword. "You'll do 'im no good that way!" Nubby barked. "Hide yourself!" Nubby reached into his coat and withdrew a very long knife. Then he ducked into a tall cabinet. "Hide!" he hissed at Anne.

She ignored him and drew her cutlass. "Oh, you're just like your father," he said, and slammed the cabinet door shut. Anne heard boots on the stairs just outside the door.

Declan Ross clambered up to the forecastle deck. The battle still raged, and it seemed the crew of the *Wallace* was holding their own. But to his dismay, Ross realized that Chevillard's men now held the starboard rail. The corvette had drifted closer, and a long gangplank extended the distance between the two ships. A dark shape appeared from this gangplank and strode onto the deck of the *Wallace*. He wore a captain's tricorn hat, but gun smoke hid his face.

Ross watched as this tall enemy swept out a long curved blade. Ross's men, Henrik and Smitty, stood in the villain's way. But they were no match for Thierry Chevillard, the Butcher.

"Nooooo!" Ross yelled, leaping down from the forecastle only to be blocked by a sea of combatants. The crowd twisted and thickened, and Ross could see nothing of his enemy's progress. He made his way at last to the portside rail and grabbed a rope that had been tied off there. He climbed up above the melee and saw that Chevillard was headed toward the stern. He stopped at the door that led belowdecks to the captain's quarters, and slammed a heavy black boot into the center of the door. It shivered. The second kick did more damage. And the third sundered the door altogether.

He's looking for me, Ross thought. He felt a chill. *Anne!*

He began to run along the rail. "I'm here!" he yelled. "Chevillard!" But through the clamor of battle, the French pirate paid no heed to a distant shout from one man. Two of his mates leading the way, Chevillard disappeared through the door.

"No!!" Ross yelled. He raced along the rail recklessly—too recklessly. He reached for a rope to steady himself, but his eyes were trained on the stern. He missed the rope, slipped, and fell. His head banged smartly on the deck. Slowly, Ross got to one knee. *Anne!* he thought desperately. Then he collapsed.

8
Captain's Fall

A pounding came from the other side. The door to the captain's quarters shivered. Anne stood between it and the table where the wounded lad lay. Ignoring desperate whispered pleas from Nubby in the cabinet behind her, she held her cutlass out in front. The wood near the lock cracked, and the door slammed open.

Two sailors charged in, swords outstretched. Anne caught one sword with her cutlass, spiraled her blade around his, and drove it down. With a sudden flick of her wrist, she jabbed the sharp point of her sword beneath the man's crossguard and carved a gash across his fingers. With a yelp, he dropped the sword. Before she could finish him off, the second pirate swept a savage blow at Anne's midsection. She dropped to a knee and drove her cutlass into his thigh. He fell to the ground, clutching his leg.

A man wearing a dark leather tunic and a large tricorn hat ducked under the doorway and stood between the two pirates Anne had wounded.

"Inutile!" Chevillard hissed. He raised a huge cutlass and, with very little effort, killed the two men who had failed him.

Finally, Chevillard turned to Anne. "*Sacre bleu!*" he said, his voice low and gravelly. "*La jeune femme!*"

"Get out of here!" Anne cried out. She glared at him as long as she could, but it was hard to endure his intense menacing gaze. He stood a foot taller than she did. His shoulders were broad, and he was clearly very strong. But there was abject cruelty in his heart-shaped face. A sharply pointed beard bordered his thin, sneering lips. A scar wormed its way across his right cheek and the bridge of his nose. But his eyes were the worst. Black and hard like polished stone . . . cold and pitiless, they stared out from heavy slanted brows.

"Forgive my manners," Chevillard said, now in heavily accented English. He made an exaggerated bow. "But I did knock."

Like lightning, Anne stole the opportunity and thrust at his neck even as he bowed. But Chevillard almost casually dashed away her strike. His second blow tore Anne's cutlass from her hand and sent the weapon clattering against the cabin wall. Chevillard leveled his sword's point at Anne's face and kept it trained on her as she stepped toward her own blade. Realizing she had no chance to retrieve her weapon, she glanced back over her shoulder at the lad who lay on the table.

Chevillard followed Anne's gaze. When he saw the wounded lad, his eyes flickered with fire. "You!" he gasped.

"I'll take fore," said Red Eye. "More men likely to be there. You take aft." Midge heartily agreed. The less fighting the better. They crouched in a narrow space behind a bank of large crates in the corvette's hold. They had come in through an exterior window and found themselves one level above their objective: the gun deck.

"He hasn't moved," Midge said, referring to an armed sailor who stood by the entrance to the stairwell.

"I'll take care of it," said Red Eye. Midge winced. He knew what that meant. Red Eye crept silently out of their hiding place. A moment later, Midge heard a low whistle. He peered around the crate. The guard was gone. Red Eye stood by the stairwell gesturing for Midge. As Red Eye skulked down the stairs into the shadows, Midge hurried after him.

At the base of the stairs, the gun deck spread out left and right. Midge growled under his breath. Chevillard had not left the gun deck unattended. A group of pirates milled about around the base of the foremast. But just as Red Eye had predicted, there were fewer men aft.

"All right," Midge said. "Let's get this over with."

Red Eye grabbed Midge's elbow. "Here," he said. "Take this." He handed Midge a dark ball the size of a grapefruit.

"A grenade?" Midge's eyes narrowed. "How?"

"I was the last one off the cay." Red Eye's grin widened as he removed a dry wick and carefully placed it in the grenade. "I would have gotten more, but Captain Ross caught me, ordered me aboard."

Midge shook his head. "You've more men to take care of. You should take it."

"No." His face darkened. "I won't need it."

Midge didn't doubt it. He took the grenade and spotted a lantern three cannons away.

"Take 'em out quick," Red Eye said. "I'll use the ruckus you make as a distraction."

"Then we turn the cannons," Midge replied. "Remember, down and at the beam, like I showed you."

"Right. Good-bye, corvette." Red Eye moved out.

Midge scuttled away, and then peered around the side of the cannon bay. The two sailors who stood in his way were as far aft as they could be. They gestured animatedly to each other and laughed. But their comic moment was cut short. A dark ball rolled between them. The fuse burned quickly and disappeared, and the grenade exploded. The two men were flung aside like rag dolls.

Midge went right to work. He removed the chocks from behind the last starboard cannon, and he used an iron pike to lever the cannon out of the bay. As it rolled, he tossed a wedge behind the cannon's back right wheel. One wheel stopped, the cannon turned, facing the stern beam. The other wheel chocked, Midge loaded the cannon: powder, cannonball, and at last the plug. He raced to the lantern and lit the cannon's fuse. Then Midge dove out of the cannon's now-open window and disappeared into the dark water.

Chevillard's face twisted in rage. He looked from the prone lad back to Anne as if not sure whom to kill first. He decided on Anne and drove his blade toward her, aiming for her heart. At that moment several things happened in quick succession: Something struck Chevillard from behind, and he stopped short, arching his back and gasping; a pair of explosions rocked the *William Wallace*; and Nubby charged out of the cabinet, raced around Anne, and attacked Chevillard with the kitchen knife.

A knife in his chest and two machetes in his back, Thierry Chevillard—the pirate known as the Butcher, Bartholomew Thorne's lieutenant, and the murderer of countless souls—fell dead.

9
Death's-Head on Sable

Captain Declan Ross awoke to many familiar faces. He stared up at Nubby, Midge, Red Eye, Jules, and Stede. "Anne?" he mouthed.

"I'm here, Father." And there she was. Her scarlet hair was pulled back, and her hazel eyes glimmered with joy in a way that he hadn't seen since Anne was a little girl. She bent over him and kissed him on the cheek.

"Where are we?" he asked weakly.

"Underway," Stede answered.

"Underway?" Ross exclaimed, and he tried to sit up. The moment he did, he felt a pounding in his ears and horrendous pressure near his temples. Nubby and Jules eased the captain back into a prone position. "But . . . the sails?"

"Fixed 'em, we did. We b' heading for Saint Celestine," Stede explained. "Got some fortunate wind back in our sails. Ya slept through most of the trip. One day out now."

"What happened?" Ross asked, his mind awash with memories. "I fell, didn't I?"

"Yes," Nubby answered. "And next time you decide to leap off the rail, try not to make it headfirst!" The group laughed nervously.

"Chevillard?"

"That outrageous mon b' sleepin' with the fishes," Stede said. "I saw him heading for yer quarters. I knew Anne was there. I went after him."

"He saved my life, Father," Anne said.

Ross grabbed Stede's forearm. "That's another lifetime of friendship I owe you."

"That makes four, so far." Stede laughed.

Ross coughed and winced at the pain. "The ship . . . Chevillard's ship?"

"On the bottom," Red Eye said. "Just like you said. We turned her own cannons on her and blew out her backbone."

"But there were survivors, Cap'n," explained Midge. "But knowin' 'ow you feel, we left 'em on the cay."

"That's why we b' hightailing it to Saint Celestine," said Stede. "If Thorne come around the cays and find out what we done . . ." He didn't need to finish. They all knew. Ross shook his head slowly. In defeating Chevillard, he'd just made a mortal enemy of Bartholomew Thorne. The *William Wallace*, and everyone aboard, was now marked.

"We grabbed some provisions from the cay," Anne said. "Plantains and some of the hardtack from the crates."

"And loads of iguana!" said Nubby.

"The ship still needs to be careened something awful," said Midge. "And we lost a lot of men in the scrap with Chevillard. Stede figured Saint Celestine would be the best place to fix the ship."

"Thank God for the monks," Ross said. His head lolled to the side, and he slept.

The next morning dawned glorious and bright as only Caribbean mornings can. Turquoise water glistened as it captured drops of golden sunlight. The sky was a soft purple at the horizon and faded into pure cerulean. Two wisps of pure-white clouds hung over the rising sun like the brow of some great jolly face. Captain Ross stood at the prow of the *Wallace* and breathed deeply of the sea air . . . and freedom. Nothing tasted as good as freedom, especially to Ross, who had for a dark period of his life endured the harsh yoke of slavery.

Ross looked forward to the hospitality of the monks. It had been over a year since the *Wallace* last made port on the island monastery of St. Celestine. It was a place of refuge for pirates, and over the years he and his crew had become friends with the small order, and sometimes brought them spices from afar. The monks there hoped to lead pirates away from sin and into Christianity through their charity and provision. They had huge gardens and orchards. They made the most hearty breads and savory cheeses. And, aside from the buccaneers of Barbados, the monks had the only fresh beef in the Caribbean. They washed it all down with the finest port wine that could be had west of France. This they gladly shared with even the most ruthless of scoundrels. And never once did the monks aid colonial or royal navies in their quest to capture these same pirates. For this reason, it was common fact—even written into most ships' pirate law—that St. Celestine was off-limits for pirate attacks.

So it was an unhappy surprise that greeted the crew of the *William Wallace* when they pulled into port at the holy isle. "Give me the glass," said Ross. Even as he brought the spyglass up to his eye, a cold sweat broke out on his forehead. He scanned the shoreline and saw the statue of Mary kneeling at the water's edge, blessing the sea and all who travel upon it. There were row upon row of wooden stakes attached by gossamer white twine—the vineyards, and beyond them, the orchards and the dark stone of the abbey. But in the foreground left of the monastery, stabbed deep into the sandy shore, was a black flag. Upon its sable field were the white silhouette of an hourglass, a skull over crossed swords, and a raven taking flight.

"It's Thorne," Ross said. "He's put his death's-head flag upon the shore to warn them. He plans to take the island."

"That madman!" Stede exclaimed. "What does that mon think he b' doin'? Attacking the monks is against the code."

"He thinks he's above the code," Ross muttered. "This is no longer a safe haven."

"Welcome, Captain Ross," said Father Raphael Valentia, the chief of the order of St. Celestine. "Your return is an unlooked-for blessing." He glanced behind Ross at the *Wallace*. "Your ship is in need of careening, I see. We will do this for you and supply you with fresh provision."

"Thank you, Father." Ross stood on the deck near the bowsprit. "As always, we appreciate your kindness. But that flag makes me think we won't have the time. When did the death's-head show up?" Ross gestured toward the *Raven*'s flag.

Father Valentia grimaced, and the group of monks gathered there murmured among themselves.

"Captain Thorne's warning defiled our shore before the sun rose yesterday morning."

"That gives you only two more days before he returns and attacks," Ross thought aloud. "Have you made arrangements to get to the mainland?"

"We are not leaving our island," said Father Valentia.

"What?" Ross exclaimed. "You must leave. Do you not realize what that flag means? He's marked Saint Celestine—claimed it as his. He'll kill everyone. Do you understand—EVERYONE!! Father, we are old friends. I'll grant passage to you and the Brothers to sail with us. The Brothers and my crew will be able to quickly prepare the *Wallace*, fill up our barrels and crates with food and drink. We will leave tonight for Santo Magherito. From there you can get to the mainland, far away from the co—"

"We are not leaving, Declan." The monk's face was calm—even peaceful—but resolute. "But we would ask one favor of you."

"Anything, Father," Ross replied.

Father Valentia turned his head and nodded. The group parted, and a hooded monk came forward. He stood by Father Valentia and lowered his hood. His hair was dark, but his eyes were darker . . . sinkholes surrounded by skin deeply tanned but cracked and weather-beaten.

"This is Padre Dominguez," said Father Valentia. "While we remain here to preserve our order, he must escape."

"Must escape, Father?" Ross asked. "No pirate has dared leave a death's-head on this isle, until now. You want me to take him aboard, a monk I do not know, but leave your order here to face Thorne's wrath? Why would this be?"

Father Valentia remained silent.

Captain Ross looked at the black flag stabbed deep into the

sandy shore. Its grinning skull, a menacing intruder to the monastery, nested in the orchard beyond. Ross wiped a trickle of sweat from his brow and looked back at his crew.

Ross turned to face Padre Dominguez. "Do you know what you're asking me, Padre? Your life is forfeit—so is the life of any who grant you quarter! What is it Thorne wants from you?"

The monk's aged, pocked face became so taut that his lips seemed to disappear. He turned to his superior, who nodded. "The Treasure of Constantine," the monk said slowly, as if the words had not been spoken in an age and would bring down a curse upon the one who said them. "I know how to find it."

For a long while, Captain Ross studied the monk's face. "The Treasure of Constantine, Padre Dominguez?" he scoffed. "Every- one knows that fortune was lost in the Bosporus during a squall. All the gold, the silver—even the green diamonds—lay beyond reach in the depths. Next you'll be telling me you know the secret location of El Dorado!"

"Not lost," the monk whispered. "Stolen. Stolen by Spartan marauders in AD 400, but reclaimed by the church and hidden once and for all so that pagan hands would never defile them again."

"Mountains of gold and jewels . . . treasure?!" Ross exclaimed. "What's to defile?"

"You and I define treasure very differently," the monk replied.

"So you say, Padre," Ross scoffed. His head began to pound again. He paused and twisted an end of his coppery moustache between his fingers. "But why would you take me and my lads to this holy treasure? We're just as pagan as any."

"Not so, Captain Ross. The Brothers of Saint Celestine know you are better than that. You and your men were taught to fight at sea by your nations during time of war. When the war ended, the governments left you with a choice between piracy and the starvation of your families. In spite of that—even now—you attack only those who are openly at war with Scotland. And you always grant quarter to—"

"Spare me the benediction, Padre!" Ross exclaimed. "I . . . I can't offer *you* quarter. I can't take you aboard. Crossing blades with Bartholomew Thorne over some legendary treasure—that's just insane!"

Stede jabbed Ross in the ribs. "Think of the treasure, mon," he whispered. "Besides, we already got Thorne trying to kill us and—"

"Not now." Ross spoke under his breath so that only Stede could hear. Then he spoke aloud to the monks. "I'm sorry, Padre, but I just can't risk the lives of my crew without proof."

Padre Dominguez's face saddened. He turned and let his brown robe fall down from his shoulders. And there, tattooed into the flesh of his back, was a very intricate map.

10

HIDE AND SEEK

Late that evening, the crew of the *William Wallace* prepared to sail. On the shore of St. Celestine under a moonless sky, Declan Ross said his farewells to the monks. "Are you sure you won't come with us?" Ross asked. "I've already got one of you aboard. I'm dead anyway. Might as well take you all."

Father Valentia laughed quietly, but it was such a strange, humorless sound that it gave Ross the chills. "Should Thorne come to our island," said the monk, "we will remain hidden in the tunnels beneath the abbey. When he has gone, we will emerge and preserve our order."

Ross was quiet for a long while, then he casually strode up the gangplank. "Mister Stede, nor-noreast, please."

"Aye, Cap'n!" Stede replied. "Nor-noreast!"

Ross would never forget that moment, drifting away. All the monks of the order of St. Celestine remained there on the shore. He could still see their faces in the light of their lanterns. Facing Thorne meant facing torture and death. Few survived his wrath. But they were not afraid. Ross respected that. Not knowing what else to do, he took off his hat and watched until the holy island was devoured by darkness.

From the second-floor balcony of the monastery, Father Valentia watched the dark ships arrive. How many there were, he could not accurately tell. More than a dozen, certainly—more than enough. He watched the tall ships moor offshore and saw them drop launches and cutters into the water.

He lingered a moment looking out over the orchards, the gardens, and the vineyards that had been his love—all things green and growing.

"Father Valentia?" came a hushed voice from the hall. "It is time." It was Father Gregory, a best friend, a true saint.

Father Valentia looked up and smiled. He joined the other monks in the hall. They traveled down the stairs and into the sanctuary. Usually lit by the dancing flames of hundreds of candles, the sanctuary was now shrouded in shadows. The Brothers of St. Celestine gathered there, standing in a wide circle around an enormous mural of the cross inscribed on the floor tiles. Father Valentia moved to the precise middle of the cross and nodded. Four monks stepped forward from the circle. Each walked to one of the four ends of the cross mural. As each man stepped onto the painted tile, there was a faint scraping sound, like stone sliding on stone. The tiles where each of the four monks stood dropped downward an inch.

At that moment, a circular outline appeared around Father Valentia's feet. The hidden platform slowly began to drop below the level of the floor. In a few seconds, Father Valentia was safely in the catacombs beneath the monastery. There, he stepped off the platform and held down the trigger bar that protruded from the wall. This time, the platform rose up past the sanctuary floor. Beneath the circular platform was a wrought-iron spiral staircase. The monks descended the staircase one by one, and when the last one went down Father Valentia let up on the trigger bar. The sanctuary floor returned to normal.

Father Valentia turned to the other monks, his flock, and said, "Father Gregory will lead you to the hidden catacombs—where you will remain until the threat is gone."

As Father Valentia followed behind them, he thought about their elaborate hiding place. Even if Thorne and his pirates entered the sanctuary and discovered the platform, they would never recognize the four pressure plates needed to trigger its movement. Only the monks knew of the catacombs. *Maybe we will survive Thorne's attack*, he thought.

Long white hair and sideburns like silver daggers running down his sunken cheeks made Bartholomew Thorne look like a ghostly apparition as he stood in the center of the sanctuary. His brow bristled and hooded his cold eyes in shadow. He'd sent five hundred men to search the monastery. Scout after scout returned, but no sign of the monks.

"He's got to be here somewhere!" he yelled. Damaged long ago from inhaling smoke as he escaped from a fire, Thorne's voice rasped and grated like a sustained hacking cough. When he grew angry, his breathing could be heard across a room as a low, scraping rumble.

As Mr. Skellick, the quartermaster of the *Raven*, entered the sanctuary, he heard his captain's breath and knew immediately that things went ill.

"What did you find?" Thorne demanded.

Skellick kept one eye trained on Thorne's walking stick. The four-foot-long stave was originally carved from a large white oak bough, but Thorne had a dozen talonlike iron spikes embedded in the wood. The walking stick still leaked sap from the places where the spikes had been installed. For that reason—and others—the crew of the *Raven* called Thorne's weapon the bleeding stick.

"Captain, there are signs of a great gathering at the shoreline," Skellick told him, swallowing back the fear. There was nothing Thorne despised more than weakness, so Skellick gave it to him straight. "A large ship was moored there. A frigate maybe, or a brig."

"Your opinion?"

"It would seem that they heeded your warning," Skellick said. "Boarded a British frigate and fled for the mainland. But . . . I do not believe that is what they did at all. The Brothers of Saint Celestine are nothing if not proud of their lineage and the history of this island. I believe they are still here, trusting in their God to keep them safe," Skellick said.

"Where?"

"I suspect underground or in a cave up in the hills. They may even have some kind of fortified chamber in the middle of this monastery."

"That's why I keep you around, Skellick," Thorne said with a sinister chuckle. "You think like I do. They're still here, all right, but not in the abbey." He was quiet a moment, letting his eyes wander about the sanctuary. He scanned the tapestries, the altar, and paused for several heartbeats on the floor. "Come here," he said. Skellick followed his captain over to a huge stained-glass window. It depicted the apostle Paul's encounter with the risen Christ on the road to Damascus. Bartholomew Thorne lifted his walking stick, smashed it against the window, and stepped out of the way as huge shards of glass fell and shattered on the tile floor. Then, crunching on glass with every step, Thorne walked to the now open window. Skellick joined him, and Thorne pointed up into the hills. "That's where I'd go."

After following the many twists and turns in the catacombs, Father Valentia caught up to Father Gregory at the stair beneath the bell tower. The narrow, climbing steps led to a recessed door hidden behind a tall tapestry in the vestibule.

"Take the others to the bowels of the monastery," Father Valentia whispered. "I will keep watch from the bell tower and will return for you when I know it is safe." Father Gregory did as he was told and led the monks farther into the maze.

Father Valentia made his way up the stairs and paused at the five-foot door. He pulled the lever door release. He pushed on the heavy door, and, with a low crack, it pushed free of the wall. Quietly he closed it tightly, so only the monks could find it. Finally, he left the room and dashed up the steps to the tower room. He pushed open the door. "Good evening, Father," came a strained and raspy voice. "It is time for confession."

11

ILHA DE ESPADAS

"Thank you." The whispered voice startled Anne. She turned. The wounded lad's eyes were open, and for the first time they didn't look like they would roll back into his head at any moment. "Thank you," he said again. "You stayed with me."

Anne felt herself blush and turned her head, trying to make it stop. "I didn't know you were awake . . ." She fingered the coral pendant that hung at the end of a cord necklace. "How do you feel?"

"Like I've been hit by a bull. My head throbs, and I am stiff. I feel like I am lying on broken seashells."

"Those are the scabs. Nubby said they'd be pretty bad. He put some medicine paste on those awful gashes." Anne paused, wondering if she should ask. She grimaced and decided she had to know. "What happened to you?"

The lad turned his head. He did not answer.

"I'm sorry," Anne said. "I shouldn't have—"

"I don't know," he said through gritted teeth.

"What?"

A hot tear escaped. "I don't know what happened to me."

Anne fell silent. She thought about Chevillard, that terrible moment when he entered the room. Anne couldn't be sure, but he seemed to recognize this wounded lad. "Are you . . . are you a pirate?"

"A pirate?" The lad frowned. "Why on earth would you think that?"

Anne stood up. "And just what's wrong with being a pirate?"

"I didn't say there was anythi—"

"For your information, I am a pirate!" she said. "You are a guest aboard a pirate ship. And if it weren't for the *pirates* on this ship, you wouldn't be alive!"

"You are a pirate?" he asked, astonished.

"Yes," she replied hesitantly. "Well, no . . . not exactly. But it's only a matter of time. I can do everything the men on this ship can do. Better than some."

"I'm sorry," he said. "I didn't mean to offend you. It's just that, well . . . most pirates aren't like you."

"I guess you're right about that." Anne softened a bit. "My name's Anne. Anne Ross." She waited for him to respond. He said nothing, but the rims around his eyes became red, and he shook with anger.

"I can't remember . . . I've tried. There's just nothing there. I don't know my name. I don't know what happened to me. I don't know anything."

"It'll all come back," Anne said, smiling bravely for him. "I'm certain it will."

He closed his eyes. Anne wished she could do something to help. From somewhere above came the clear sound of two bells. "Nubby'll be down to check on you soon," she said. "I have watch." He didn't respond. He was so still Anne thought he might have fallen asleep. Anne hesitated, made sure his eyes were completely shut, and then put the leather pouch back on the table near his hand. She thought it was a good thing he hadn't caught her with it. She left the room without another word, wondering about the cross, the lock of hair, and the jewel . . . especially the jewel.

He was not, in fact, asleep. But his mind raced such that he hadn't noticed Anne's final act before she left. No, someone could have fired a cannon at his bedside, and he would have ignored it. For, at last, he thought he had figured something out. The footprints he'd seen on the island. When he'd seen them that day, he'd assumed that someone else had been on the island. But picturing the scene now in his mind, he remembered that the footprints had led up to where he stood. If someone had come out of the palms and approached him while he was unconscious, there would have been a set of footprints returning into the palms. *They were mine*, he realized. *I made the footprints that came out of the palms and across that dune.* And that meant that somewhere on that island there could be other clues to his identity.

"It is called by the Portuguese, *Ilha de Espadas*," said Padre Dominguez. He, Ross, Stede, and Jules sat alone around the captain's desk. Anne, to her everlasting frustration, was on watch and so, not invited. Ross had deftly offered her time at the helm when her watch was over. That defused his mercurial daughter for the moment.

"Isle of Swords, eh?" Ross replied. "That doesn't sound very inviting."

"It is not," said the monk. "The island is a most inhospitable place—a volcanic land mass, wreathed in an ashen cloud. The main-landers believe it to be legend only. A fleeting vision at sea, akin to your Flying Dutchman. Few but the Brethren have set foot on its perilous shores."

"The Brethren?" Jules echoed.

"Those of my order," said the monk.

"Saint Celestine?" Ross suggested.

Padre Dominguez shook his head. "Father Valentia was kind enough to grant me refuge there for a time. And though he knows of it, he is not of my order." The monk weighed a decision in his mind. These men seemed decent as pirates went and would most likely be content with the precious metals and jewels. But could they be trusted? He felt it must be God's will that he work with these men for the greater good.

"The Brethren," he began, "are a small but powerful sect of the church, as secret as we are ancient. Nearly fourteen hundred years old . . . formed during the reign of Emperor Constantine while Sylvester I was pope. Constantine, being a Christian himself, began to collect holy artifacts, priceless items that he added to his already vast treasure. The faithful would travel from throughout the world to view these precious relics of our faith. As you might imagine, oth-ers with very different motives came as well.

"When items began to disappear from Constantine's vaults, and rumor spread that they were being sold off, the Brethren was formed. Utilizing methods not usually condoned by the church, we kept safe Constantine's Treasure."

Ross's mind whirled. He'd never been much for history lessons. "But I thought you said that the Spartans took it."

"Alas, yes, but that is a story I will not openly share. Suffice it to say that we retrieved the treasure. Then we moved this treasure to a location that is . . . more protected."

"Wait," Ross said, holding up a hand and tilting his head. "Are you telling me this Brethren group *stole* Constantine's Treasure?"

"By the time Pope Boniface I began his reign, the Brethren had transplanted many of the church's most sacred relics and artifacts to places of safekeeping."

Ross couldn't believe his ears. This just confirmed everything he'd ever thought about religion. "But isn't there something in that Bible of yours about 'thou shall not steal'?"

"Do you read the Holy Scriptures, Declan Ross?" asked Padre Dominguez. His stare fell cold on Captain Ross. The captain of the *Wallace* lost his smug smile just as quickly as it had come. He stared out of his quarters' balcony window at the whitecaps.

"Uh, no."

"Then do not presume to judge me by them." The monk continued. "The Brethren is a sacred order called by God to maintain the safekeeping of the holy relics of God. The Brethren acts with a pure heart and a clear conscience."

"Whatever you say, Padre," Ross said, relieved to back out of that conversation. He grabbed a handful of nuts from a bowl on the desk. "We're in. So where is this Isle of Swords?"

"In the North Atlantic, some one hundred miles due west of the Azores." Ross nearly spit out a mouthful of nuts.

Stede, who knew the names and locations of every port in the known world, was aghast. "There b' no islands due west of the Azores!"

"Not on your sea charts, perhaps," said the monk, turning to reveal the map on his back once more. "Nevertheless, it exists on mine. And I have been there."

Stede studied the monk's back. "This is one outrageous trip, he b' talking about," he said, turning to Ross. "Three thousand miles, mon."

The captain of the *William Wallace* shrugged. "The Spaniards do it in their heavy galleons all the time."

"And the galleons b' attacked by the likes of us all the time," argued Stede. "Or did ya forget that Bartholomew Thorne's whole fleet b' hunting the seas for us soon?"

The monk grew suddenly stiff. He pulled his robe up to cover his back and turned to Ross. "Even under pain of torture, the Brothers of Saint Celestine would not tell Thorne that I am with you. Thorne should not have cause to chase us in particular."

"Well," Ross said as he ran his fingers through his coppery mane, "actually, that's not quite true. Before we picked you up, we killed Thorne's second-in-command."

"What?" The monk raised an eyebrow.

"We fixed him good, we did," Jules said. "Stede buried his machetes into old Chevillard's back, and Nubby finished him off with about the biggest kitchen knife I've ever seen. We used his own cannons and blew holes out both ends of his ship. Sent her to the bottom quick."

"You killed Thierry Chevillard?" The monk's eyes widened. Ross nodded. "And sank his ship?" Ross nodded again. Padre Dominguez shook his head. "The Butcher will no doubt be welcomed to perdition—vile and bloodthirsty man that he was. Did you leave any survivors . . . any who could tell Thorne?"

Ross lowered his eyes. "Of course you did," said the monk. "For you are not like they are. But Bartholomew Thorne will not let that go lightly. The journey to the Isle of Swords would be treacherous enough without that threat hanging over our heads."

"You mean the storms?" Ross asked. "Padre, I am Scotland-born—the North Atlantic, my old backyard. The Brothers of Saint Celestine did a smart job fixing up the *Wallace*. We can handle the storms."

"More than storms," said the monk. "In the open ocean, there is always the threat of storm. Perhaps worse, the doldrums. But aside from those perils, it is just a long voyage. We will need even more provisions than the Brothers of Saint Celestine were able to provide."

"That's no problem," said Ross. "I have a place in mind."

The monk nodded. "But as we draw within the last one hundred miles of our destination . . . there, the real dangers will begin. The first is an anomaly in the sea—two strong currents collide and form a deceptive perimeter around the island. The turbulent waters will misguide a ship, but the unwary seaman will not discover that he is off course until it is far too late. This is marked by a red dagger on the map, but it cannot be found without the help of the stars. We must make for this point by nightfall and use the stars to pass over the boundary and onto the real course. We will either find the way or become hopelessly lost, wasting precious days seeking the spot where we began."

"This sounds like voodoo, if ya b' asking me," said Stede. "I've sailed that way many times. I tell ya, there b' no island there."

"Voodoo, no," said the monk. "But supernatural, I agree. To my knowledge, there is no other place in all the oceans of the world where this occurs. I believe it is the Almighty's way of keeping the island private."

Stede snorted and crossed his arms.

"Mock if you wish," said the monk, "but I have a suspicion that we will all need guidance from heaven before this venture ends." Stede uncrossed his arms. His eyes narrowed thoughtfully. Jules was amazed. It wasn't often that he'd seen his captain and his quarter-master dressed down in the same afternoon.

"And if we do navigate the stars successfully and find the perimeter where the currents clash, still we must be wary. For a span of seven miles we will ride some of the roughest swells and currents you have ever seen. Worse still—the colliding forces beneath the waves cause deep sucking pockets to open up. One minute you are cresting a wave, and suddenly, a two-hundred-foot chasm opens up off the bow. A ship drawn into the gaping dark mouth in the sea has but moments to live. The currents will slam the chasm shut, crushing any vessel under a mountain of never-ending water."

Stede whistled. Ross and Jules realized they had been holding their breath while the monk spoke. They exhaled together and looked about nervously. Padre Dominguez went on. "We can catch our breath for the next seventy-five miles," he said, winking at Stede, who still looked shaken. "Then we will begin to hear the first beats of the island's molten heart. We'll pass through a shield of mist and volcanic ash, and if the sun has risen, we will see the Ilha de Espadas. The island is shaped like a crescent. The outer rim of the island is sheer and unassailable. The only way to approach it is from the mouth of its bay."

"Let me guess," said Ross. "There's something in the way."

"Yes," replied the monk. "The island is not called Isle of Swords for nothing. Guarding the mouth of the bay is a unique reef formation we of the Brethren call the shards. Hundreds and hundreds of sharp rocks and coral thrust up through the surface like so many daggers. A ship that crashes into one of these is likely to be split and sent to the bottom. There is danger below as well, for hidden spikes of coral lay beneath the waves. There is only one path through the shards, and I alone know this path."

"I don't suppose you'd care to write that down for us," said Ross, already knowing the answer.

"No, Declan Ross," the monk replied. "I will keep that knowledge to myself until we are in sight of the island."

Stede had heard enough. "So, then, we just hurry across that little harbor and fetch all the gold?"

"Alas, no. We must moor in the harbor, and there I must dive for the key."

"Key?" Ross squinted.

"The Treasure of Constantine is locked tight in an impenetrable clifftop castle on the northern end of the crescent. Without the key, there is no way in, unless, of course, any of you can scale a sheer wall of stone some three hundred feet. The only window in the fortress looks out over the ocean, but it is not an entrance."

"And you have to dive for the key?" Ross asked. "Why not just keep the key yourself?"

"A key of such value cannot be entrusted to the possession of a man. A man may change allegiances. A man may be corrupted. A man may get sick and die, and if so, the treasure would be lost to all forever. The Brethren felt that it was best to keep the key within reach of the island, but at the same time out of reach."

"Seawater will corrode the key to naught—given a few years under," Ross said. "I hope you made the key of something sturdy and put it in something watertight."

"The key is wrought iron, tempered by the Brethren to endure the corrosive power of the sea." Padre Dominguez paused, rubbed his bottom lip thoughtfully, and then continued. "The key is encased in wax, sealed in stone, and placed among thousands of like stones. One must know exactly what the stone looks like to separate it from the others. I know this. The key waits for me to dive and retrieve it."

"Why you?" Jules asked.

The monk paused, again wondering how much he could trust them, and also, how much they could possibly believe. "In due time," he said.

"Okay," Ross said. "So, you can do the dive. Just please tell me that once we have the key, we can just go on up and get the treasure."

The monk shook his head once again. "With the key in hand, we begin a five-mile trek from one end of the island to the other. We will enter a network of volcanic caves and sedimentary tubes. From there we emerge in a dense forest. This takes us around the base of Arrojar del Fuego, a volcano that never rests. At last, we are faced with a final climb . . . a mile-long slope that is both steep and perilous. Jags of sharp granite and steps of brittle sandstone at our feet and unusual volcanic lightning overhead. We will make our way to the gate of Boveda de Dios, the fortress that guards both our treasures."

"If all this mon say b' true," Stede said, "then how we b' getting the treasure back down? The slope will kill us, if we b' heavy with gold."

"He is right. It will not be easy," the monk said.

"The window in the back of the fortress, how high did you say it was?" Ross asked.

"About two hundred feet."

"And the depth of the water at its base?"

The monk hesitated. "I do not know for certain, but I suspect there is at least fifty feet of water at the base of the cliff."

"We're going to need woven baskets—and rope, lots of rope." Ross grinned. "I know a man in Dominica. He'll get it for us. That and some other things we'll need."

"I don't suppose he has access to monkey pee, does he?"

The room suddenly went very quiet.

At last, Ross said, "That's kind of an odd request."

The monk laughed. "Yes, I know. Let me explain myself. You see, within the caves and volcanic tubes that we must travel, there lives a species of lizard found nowhere else. They are carnivorous creatures drawn to body heat. One man is not usually enough to draw them out, but given the size of our expedition, they will come at us in dangerous numbers. The monkey pee has a unique smell that wards these creatures off."

"I don' think I want to know what we b' doing with that monkey pee," muttered Stede.

"You're right," said the monk as he turned to leave. "You don't."

"Wait, Padre," Ross said. "One more thing."

Padre Dominguez eyed the captain curiously.

"Why did you—why tattoo the map on your back?"

Padre Dominguez smiled sadly. "There are several reasons," he explained. "It is the largest area of skin without blemish, a kind of canvas of skin. And having the route to a great treasure where one can easily see it would prove too great a temptation, so, again, the back is better suited. But the Brethren's primary reason for having the map inscribed upon our backs is . . . that it is a symbol."

"A symbol of what?"

"Just as Christ bore the cross, we too must bear a burden."

Later, up on the deck of the *Wallace*, the captain and his quartermaster spoke in whispers. "He's hiding something, Declan," said Stede. "Did ya see the way he changed when we told him about Chevillard?"

"Yes," Ross replied, his eyes narrowing. "Almost like he knew the man."

"Yeah, I was thinkin' the same," said Stede. "And, funny how him won't b' telling us the part of the treasure him b' wanting to get fer himself."

"I don't really care what part of the treasure he wants. If Constantine's wealth is half as grand as it's supposed to be, we'll all have enough to get out of this business once and for all," Ross said.

"Declan Ross." Stede clapped his captain on the shoulder. "We both learn the hard way that the sweet trade ain't so sweet."

"No, my friend, it isn't. If the nations we sailed for hadn't cut us all loose, I doubt if many of this crew would have ever turned to piracy! Now, in spite of everything I've done to convince her otherwise, Anne thinks her only lot in life is to become a pirate. I'll burn before I let that happen."

"There b' no need to burn. Anne is smart, like you. She'll come round. And the treasure b' opening doors beyond the lure of the sea."

"I hope you're right," Ross replied, looking out across the waves. But he wondered if Anne was already too far gone.

12
THE CAT'S OUT OF THE BAG

Is there anything I can do to help?" the lad asked.

"Well, look who's up and walking around on deck!" Ross exclaimed. "Don't let Nubby see you out of bed."

"Too late," said the lad. "He threatened to hit me with a spoon." They laughed. The lad stared out on the sea. A low gray mantle of rain clouds waited on the horizon, but there was no land in sight. "Where are we?"

"About a day southwest of Dominica," the captain replied.

The lad nodded absently. He spotted Anne across the deck. She carried a large wooden bucket and disappeared at the forecastle. Uncomfortable silence fell upon them both.

Ross stood at the helm. He had one hand on the wheel. The fingers of the other twirled curly strands of his coppery beard. "Anne told me," Ross said at last. "About your memory, I mean." More silence. "Anything come back?" The lad looked away, rubbed his hand across the diminishing welts on his forehead, and brushed back his hair.

"That's hard, lad," said Ross without a trace of pity in his eyes. "But the sea is hard. I've seen men—good men—take ill and die from a scratch no bigger than an inch. And here's you, near flayed alive. No infection. Nubby says you'll be fine in a week. You got something to live for, and that's a fact."

Ross scratched through his beard to his chin. "For now, you'll be living with us on the *William Wallace*. And as the captain of this old brigantine, I've a mind to accept your offer to help. But . . . I won't be going around calling you lad or boy or some such. If you can't remember your name, I'll give you one."

The lad laughed in spite of himself. This red-bearded pirate with twinkling gray eyes had an odd air about him. Confidence, arrogance, or insanity—the lad wasn't sure which.

"Now we got Nubby, whose real name is William Christopher Jenkins, but we call him Nubs, well . . . for obvious reasons. Then we got Red Eye Bill Scanlon, who had a bit of trouble with a powder cartridge. Some men win a name in combat like Cutlass Jack Bonnet and Musketoon MacGready. But you, I was thinking, you've been whipped near to death, that's plain. And by the look of those wounds, by a cat-o'-nine-tails, no doubt. Not one man in fifty lives through the beating you took. Nine lives you got, or so it seems. So, for now—at least until you remember your rightful name—I, and my crew, will call you Cat."

"Cat?" The lad rolled the name over in his mouth.

"Done and done," said the captain. "Now, you said you wanted to help out, and that's good. Every man aboard must earn his keep. You ever worked on a ship before?" The words were barely out of his mouth when he realized how stupid the question was. "Of course, you don't remember. Right." Cat sighed.

Ross looked out to sea and up and down the deck. "Ah!" he said. He pointed off the port rail. "See that squall line. The wind's going to come at us from the east—a better breeze than we've got now. We'll want another sail." Ross gestured for Cat to follow. They came to the mainmast and stood beneath a vast white sail billowing softly in the wind. But up above the main, another sail was bound, tied to a wide spar. "That's the topsail," Ross said. He pointed to the web of ropes and rigging that stretched from the deck to the main boom. "I'm going to climb up there, untie the bindings, and let the sail loose. . . . When I give you the signal, just hoist away on this rope, and watch."

From atop the forecastle, Anne scrubbed the deck and watched her father. She was amazed at the interest he'd taken in the lad they'd rescued. *Ever since we left for Dominica, he's been hovering over him like a mother hen.* She worked the scrub brush a little harder, its bristles digging into the debris and sediment on the deck.

She'd told her father about the memory loss, and he'd stewed over the name. *Cat.* Anne frowned and scrubbed harder. Little flecks of black and brown flicked off and flew this way and that. She watched her father smile and point at the sails and rigging . . . and smile again. "Look at him," she mumbled to herself. "The first time he's able to walk around on deck . . ." Her words trailed off into a deep growl. She dropped the scrub brush, stood, and scowled at her father.

Declan Ross saw his daughter's glare and wondered, *Now what is she angry about?* He shrugged and turned back to hand the rope to Cat, but . . . he was gone. Ross looked about the deck. No sign. The nearest hatch was still secured. Ross hadn't heard a splash, so he couldn't have gone overboard. *Where in tarnation—*

"Up here!" came a voice from above.

Ross craned his neck, and there, standing on the boom like he owned the ship, was Cat. Ross looked back at the rigging, then back up to Cat. He realized not only had Cat clambered up the rigging in a flash, but he had also untied the bindings and loosened the topsail. Ross mouthed, "How?"

Cat cocked an eyebrow and grinned. Looking out to sea, his eyes narrowed. To the captain's horror, Cat grabbed the top of the rope Ross had been holding and leaped off the boom. As Cat fell, the gaff frame rose to the top of the mast, and the topsail went up. Cat landed softly on the deck next to Ross and tied off the rope. A split second later, an easterly wind barreled into the sails of the *William Wallace*. The ship lurched and picked up speed, and several of the crew cheered.

Anne watched as her father let out a thunderous laugh and grasped Cat by his shoulders. Jules, Red Eye, Midge, and others—all smiles—surrounded Cat and joined in the merriment.

Anne went back to scrubbing the deck.

"He's a sailor," Ross declared in his quarters later that evening. "A pirate or merchant marine."

Stede nodded. "Mayb' British navy?"

"I thought of that," Ross replied. "That would explain his knowledge of the ropes and rigging. But his accent isn't British—at least not mainland British. Reminds me more of the settlements, a hint of the islanders' speech too.

"There's something else . . . something that takes the navy out of the picture. He's got more than the instinct for the sea any good sailor has . . . he's got that flair . . . that pirate risk. Not only did he raise the topsail just as the wind came, but he did it by leaping off the boom—and this, just days after lying near death!"

"That mon b' reckless," Stede said. "But it b' a calculated kind of reckless. Knows what him b' doing so the risks don't matter. I seen it too. This afternoon, I let Cat take the wheel for a spell. I tell you, him's hand was as steady as granite. And b'fore I knew what him was doing, him steered the ship down the backside of a swell and into a gale wind I didn't see."

Ross leaned back so he was no longer visible in the flickering light of the lanterns. "I'm sure of it. Cat is a pirate."

13

An Uneasy Alliance

The *William Wallace* drifted slowly with the current of the Roseau River on the lower western quarter of the island of Dominica.

The early morning sun was already hot. The humid air was thick with motes and tiny insects. Walls of deep green foliage rose up on both sides of the river. And beyond the treetops towered rugged mountains, dark and stony, impassive and ageless.

Sweat glistened on Red Eye's bare chest. He dodged another slash from his opponent's cutlass. A collective gasp whooshed out from the crowd gathered on deck to watch them spar. "Whoa, lad!" Red Eye exclaimed. "That one would've put my head in the river!"

Cat grinned but did not let up. He drove Red Eye back toward the mainmast and peppered him with short jabs. But Red Eye was good, one of the best on the ship. He parried and blocked every one of Cat's attacks. He saw the openings, and, in a real fight, he would have taken Cat down. Still, the kid was pretty solid—better than most—and just shy of amazing for a lad of just . . . what? Fifteen . . . sixteen maybe?

"You're holding back!" Cat yelled. Red Eye just grinned. He sidestepped a heavy slash and spun around the mast. He knew to bring the attack to the kid. His left hand on his hip, Red Eye unfolded a powerful hacking blow that sent Cat reeling to one knee on the deck. But Cat wasn't without a trick of his own. He slapped the flat of his blade hard against the deck. It distracted Red Eye for an instant—all Cat needed. He sprang up like a pouncing lion and struck with such a heavy backhanded stroke that Red Eye nearly dropped his sword. Red Eye growled. *Enough of this!* He moved much faster than Cat imagined. His cutlass became a blur, and Cat found his own sword being battered back and forth with no time for a reply. The next thing Cat knew, his cutlass clattered to the deck, and Red Eye's blade leveled an inch from Cat's chest.

"STOP this nonsense!" a voice rang out. The crowd parted and began to scatter as Nubby stomped through, swinging a wooden spoon. Red Eye lowered his cutlass and, oblivious to the rants of the ship's cook, offered a hand to Cat.

"Well played," Red Eye said as they shook. "Where'd you learn to fight like that?"

Cat smiled weakly. His chest heaved out heavy breaths. His thoughts raced. "I don't know . . . I . . . I just wanted to try."

"What 're ya doin'?" Nubby practically shrieked. To Cat's horror, Nubby lifted the back of his shirt. "Ya trying to open up these wounds again? Ya want to die a gangrenous death?"

"Please . . . don't!" Cat stepped away, hoping no one, especially not Red Eye, had seen. "I'm sorry. I just wanted some exercise."

"Exercise? EXERCISE?!" Nubby's face became almost as red as Cat's. "Ya can find plenty of that without near killing each other!"

Red Eye swallowed back a laugh. He knew that would only make Nubby angrier. He'd felt the wrath of Nubby's wooden spoon before and had no desire to feel it again.

"Well," Nubby went on, "if it's exercise ya want, I think I can manage a bit for ya! At five bells, get ya down below. I have a mountain of potatoes that need peelin'."

Nubby wheeled about, lumbered across the deck, and disappeared through an open hatch. Cat shook his head and reached down for the cutlass he'd been using. When he stood up straight, he felt dizzy. *I'm exhausted*, he thought. *Maybe Nubby was right*. Cat sighed and handed the cutlass to Red Eye. "Thanks for letting me use this."

Red Eye held up a hand. "Keep it," he said. "It suits you."

"No, I couldn't. It—"

"Besides," Red Eye said, turning his back to Cat's protest. "I have a dozen more down below. Probably buy a few when we go to shore. Ha!"

A dozen more swords, he thought. Cat looked down at *his* new cutlass and wondered.

The voices came just as the *Wallace* rounded a bend in the river. After peeling potatoes and eating lunch, Cat had returned to the deck. A massive cliff wall overshadowed the turn in the Roseau. Clefts and nooks in the gray rock gave it the appearance of a scowling skull face. Adding to the effect, wide violent splashes of red surrounded the two cleft eye sockets. Yellow streaks were painted beneath each eye and down from the corners of the mouthlike cave. They made Cat shiver. And then the voices came.

It's looking at me, came one voice, young and anxious.

Do not be afraid, answered a woman's voice, tender . . . loving. *It means we're almost there.*

Cat coughed, fell to one knee on the deck. His ears rang. His vision blurred. He rose, leaned over the rail, and vomited.

Anne watched Cat from her perch in the crow's-nest on the mainmast. She'd been observing him with a mix of anger . . . and fascination. But when she saw him go down and retch over the side, such thoughts were blasted away by worry. She grabbed the web of rigging and slung herself down to the deck. She ran to him and put a careful hand on his shoulder.

"Cat, what's wrong?" she said. "What happened?"

"I heard something," he said, spitting over the side. He didn't know why he was telling her. But somehow, of all the crew he had met so far, he felt a connection to Anne. "There were voices . . . in my head."

"Voices?" Anne leaned over the rail to look at him. "Cat, did you remember something?"

"I . . . I don't know." He coughed, spat again. "I didn't recognize the voices. But . . ." His voice trailed off. He looked up at the skull face of the cliff. "I think I've been here before."

"Absolutely not," Declan Ross said, marching up the stairs from his quarters. Cat was right on his heels. "Not in your condition."

"But, Captain," Cat argued. "You saw me climb the rigging. I can handle carrying a few sacks of grain."

The captain did not turn around but continued striding up on deck. "You'll be strong as an ox when you're well, but I heard what happened today with Red Eye. Nubby said you looked like you were about to pass out. And it won't be just sacks of grain. We're talking hundreds of pounds of rope, barrels of black powder, and crates of cannon shot. This is heavy stuff."

"But, sir," Cat said, and he made the mistake of grabbing the captain's arm. "I—"

"Don't!" Ross turned around and brushed off Cat's arm. "Don't ever do that again. I am the captain of this ship." He saw the crestfallen look in Cat's eyes and wished he hadn't been so abrupt. He softened. "What on earth has you so on fire to visit the shores of Dominica anyway?"

Cat glowered. "I recognized that face in the cliff."

Ross looked up at the scowling rock. "That?" He pointed. "That's an old warning talisman. Carib Indians painted those rocks years ago to warn the English—and the French—not to come any farther inland. Scary folk, those Carib. Even today, it's best not to mess around in the forests up north. You've seen this place before?"

"I'm not sure," Cat replied. "But I think if . . . if I go ashore, I might start to remember."

Ross felt like something had a grapple-hold on his heart. Cat couldn't remember anything. Not one thing. Here was a chance that he could maybe trigger something, bring his identity back. And yet, Ross knew he had to say no. The thing that really troubled him: He couldn't tell if he was saying no purely because he was worried about Cat's health.

"I'm sorry, Cat," Ross said finally. "We've a lot to do, in a very short time, and we cannot take the risk of you getting yourself hurt.

Besides, the British navy has been known to make port here. If we need to make a hasty exit, we can't risk you falling behind."

Ross joined a group of sailors by the rail. They began lowering a cutter into the river. Cat watched and wondered if he'd ever remember who he was.

Cat lay cramped in a hammock slung between two ceiling planks only three feet apart. He figured he should be happy with the accommodations in Stede's wardroom. He was alone while most of the crew slept in very crowded quarters on the lower gun deck. And the rest of the crew had their hammocks hung with just eighteen inches between them.

The landing party had been gone for several hours. Cat stayed busy for most of that time, but it drove him crazy to see the shores of Dominica and not be able to explore them. So even though there were still many hours of daylight left, he had made his way belowdecks to Stede's quarters. But sleep did not come, not a hint of it. He swayed gently in the hammock, held his leather pouch on his stomach, and wondered about the contents. *The green jewel has to be worth something,* he thought. He wondered if he could use it to hire someone to take him back to the island where he had been found. *Probably not,* Cat decided. He didn't even know where that island was or what it was called. He didn't really want to lose the jewel anyway. It might have belonged to him, might be a clue to his identity. *Might be.*

The tarnished cross with the strange markings was even more puzzling. He'd studied it and discovered that on the long end it was serrated, tiny jags and grooves cut into the metal—almost as if it had been placed in some sort of holder or stand.

But of the three items, none was more vexing than the lock of red hair. It was lush and soft and brilliantly crimson. But whose was it? The thought occurred to him that Anne's hair was red like that. But she didn't know him. They'd just—

There came a knock at the door. It was faint and subtle, but Cat was sure there had been a knock. Who? Stede wouldn't knock. Cat slid out of the hammock and dropped quietly to the ground. His muscles protested. The sparring in the morning had worn him out. Wounds in various places throbbed dully, reminding him that he wasn't quite well.

Cat quickly put his leather pouch behind a large conch shell in Stede's cabinet, the only hiding place he could find. He ambled over, crouched, and put his ear to the door. Another knock, this one a little louder, jolted Cat backward a step. A whispered voice, "Cat?"

He opened the door a crack and peeked out. "Anne?" He stood up and opened the door wide.

"Hurry up," Anne barked under her breath. She barged past him and shut the door and locked it.

"Anne, what are you doing?" he asked, feeling awkward and somewhat suspicious. "What's with all the sneaking around?"

"You want to go ashore, don't you?" she said. He looked at her quizzically. "You said you wanted to go ashore, that you might remember something, right?"

"Y-y-yes," Cat stammered. "But Captain Ross forbade me. To go would be mutiny."

"For me, yes," she replied coolly. "But not for you. My father has no right to keep you on this ship."

"Your father—"

"Is not someone I like very much right now," Anne interrupted. "He doesn't know you. For all he knows, Dominica could be your home. He's keeping you captive against your will." Anne didn't mention that he'd done the same to her ever since her mother died. But Anne's face was red, and her smoldering eyes carried the unspoken message: Do you want to go or not?

Cat hesitated. Seeing the Carib stone face had brought back something, really the first memory of anything. And he longed to investigate Dominica. Still, Captain Ross and the crew had welcomed him aboard, healed him, fed him, gave him quarter—it seemed like betrayal. *But . . . what if this is my only chance?*

"Come with me, Cat," Anne said, seeing his reluctance. "Look, we'll just go for a bit, have a look around, and be back before nightfall. With all the gear and supplies they're looking for, my father won't get back to the *Wallace* until late—maybe tomorrow morning. No one will ever know."

Cat was desperately intrigued by the possibility, but something still troubled him. Anne seemed different. Gone was the tenderness he'd seen in her before. Now, she seemed spiteful or . . . indifferent.

"Yes. I want to go," he said at last. "But how will we get off the ship without anyone noticing?"

"Can you swim?"

Cat wondered. "I think so." He truly had no idea, but earlier he didn't think he knew what to do with a sword either.

"Good. We'll drop into the river from the balcony window in my father's quarters." She opened the door and motioned for him to follow.

"Anne?" He put a hand on her shoulder. She turned. "For what you're doing, thank y—"

"Don't thank me," she said, turning away from his touch. "I'm not doing this for you."

14

MAGNIFIQUE JACQUES ST. PIERRE

"Saint Pierre's can't be much farther," Ross said, hacking through the overgrown rain forest path's foliage with his machete.

"How can you be sure this man will have all that our journey will require?" asked Padre Dominguez.

"If there's anyone in the Spanish Main who will have even the most obscure items or equipment, it's Jacques Saint Pierre," Ross said. "I brought you along because I know the goods we'll need for sea travel, but you've been to the Isle of Swords. You know things we'll need that I'd never think of . . . things like monkey pee." This earned chuckles and guffaws from Jules, Red Eye, and the twelve other crew members who followed behind the monk.

"This Saint Pierre, can he be trusted?" asked the monk.

"He's one of the few Frenchmen I know who can be," Ross replied with a grin over his shoulder. "I just hope he accepts our offering."

"What?" Padre Dominguez blurted out.

"You'll see," said Ross. The crew chuckled some more.

At last, the landing party broke out from under the rain forest canopy. They entered Misson, a surprisingly large town that meandered on both sides of a serpentine road at the base of Mount Macaque. Shops and cottages lined the road, and a huge church made of gray stone sat above the foothills. The sun glistened off its wide stained-glass window, and Padre Dominguez marveled at the sight. Ross led them along a back alley on the side of town that backed up to the mountain. The British navy rarely ventured into Misson, but the French navy certainly did. Ross didn't want to meet up with either.

They heard the sound of rushing water before they turned the corner to St. Pierre's mill. White water cascaded down the side of the mountain, traveled down a long wooden chute, and poured into a massive churning wheel. Ross led them around the back of the building. They traversed under the water chute and entered the base of the mill building via a marvelous stone archway. "Jacques built this whole place himself," Ross said.

Everyone, even those of the crew who had come to the mill with Ross before, gasped as they entered. The place was positively amazing. It was stuffed with every manner of merchandise. Hand-carved furniture, glittering metalwork, barrels full of swords, sacks of grain, and casks of every size and shape littered every square foot of the building. Other items—lanterns, coils of rope, bundled-up sails— hung from the low rafters. There was very little room to walk.

"'Scuse me, Captain," said Red Eye. "You mind if I stay behind a bit and look at these here pretty swords?"

Ross stopped. "What do you need another sword for?"

"You can never have enough blades," Red Eye replied. He held up a cutlass with a jagged blade. "Besides, there's more than the standard cutlass here. Knives, daggers, rapiers . . ." His voice trailed off as he became lost in sword lust.

Ross shrugged. "After we see to our supplies, you can enjoy yourself," he said. "But you'll be carrying what you buy, and that only if we have enough hands to bring the rest of the things we NEED back to the *Wallace.*"

Reluctantly, Red Eye left the barrel of weapons. Ross led the rest up a narrow corridor lined with barrels stacked one on top of another. The other end was lit with soft orange light. This was the part Ross hated, for he knew that these barrels were filled with black powder. And Jacques kept a mighty forge just around the corner.

Ross's party exited the corridor and found Jacques St. Pierre hammering away at some white-hot piece of metal on an enormous anvil in front of the forge. He was a short man with wildly curly dark hair, but his wide-brimmed hat overshadowed his face. In spite of the heat generated by the forge, St. Pierre wore a heavy frock coat over a frilly white shirt. Aside from his sleeves, which were rolled up, he looked every bit the courtly gentleman and not in the least like a smith or shopkeeper.

He slammed the hammer down, sending a fount of orange sparks flying. At last, he lifted his head and noticed his visitors. "Oho, mon capitaine!" he announced. Using tongs, he tossed the glowing piece of metal into a barrel of water. "At last you have returned!"

He strode over to Ross and clasped his hand with a grip like iron. "Hello, Jacques! Looks like you've been busy. Waterwheel is still working, I see."

"Like clockwork, mon ami, like clockwork."

Ross glanced back up the barrel corridor. "You, uh, sure you want to keep those barrels of black powder so close to your forge?"

Padre Dominguez looked back at the barrels. *Black powder?*

St. Pierre grinned and twisted his thin moustache. "You pirates worry too much about explosives!"

"Easy to do," said Ross. "When you've seen what one of those going off can do to a ship."

"Nonsense!" St. Pierre replied with a dismissive flick of his wrist. "I do not drop hot coals into the barrels. And my barrels do not leak. It is safe. Absolument!"

"But why would you take the risk?" Padre Dominguez muttered, still staring at the barrels.

St. Pierre peered around Ross and looked the monk up and down. "Père, you should have more faith," he said. "I have no wish to die, but there are many who hunt for me and would see me hung. There will be no criminal's death for Jacques Saint Pierre. Should an enemy come in numbers too great for me to fight by hand, should they be so bold as to surround my mill, then . . . and only then, I will shove a white-hot poker into the barrels. I may die, but I will take them with me."

St. Pierre cackled aloud and smacked his knee. Then his face became serious and he turned to Ross. "Declan Ross, you did not come to trifle with me about my personal safety. You have need of my mercantile?"

"We are sailing the North Atlantic," Ross replied. "We'll need cannon shot, black powder—"

"Plenty and to spare," said St. Pierre.

"And rope, lots of rope."

"I have miles of it!"

"We'll need foodstuffs. Plenty of grain, salted beef, fresh fruit."

"You know that I have these supplies, Capitaine!" St. Pierre said.

"We'll also be needing some, uh . . ." Ross glanced at Padre Dominguez, "other things."

"I am sure I can meet all of your needs!" St. Pierre clapped his hands. "I even have a few special items I have collected and set aside just for you. Now, did you bring me what I asked for?"

Ross looked hesitantly back at Jules. The burly sailor brought forth a large, oddly shaped bundle. St. Pierre raised an eyebrow and asked, "Well, did you get it?"

Ross nodded to Jules. Jules unwrapped the bundle, revealing a large ship's wheel.

"What is this?" St. Pierre exclaimed. "I asked you for ten pounds of English bacon, and you bring me a wheel I could make in my own woodshop in a day?!" The Frenchman grabbed a hot poker and held it up menacingly.

Ross held up both hands. "Jacques, wait! Let me explain."

"No, Capitaine Ross, I have already waited. Two years I have waited for that savory meat. And when I saw you, my mouth started to water. But no! You have not brought me the bacon!"

"But this isn't just any ship's wheel."

"I don't care. I cannot eat it for breakfast."

"This is Chevillard's wheel."

"I don't care if it is the King of Engl—what?" St. Pierre's mouth shut.

Ross knew immediately he had made a worthy offering. "We salvaged this before Chevillard's corvette went to the bottom."

St. Pierre's look of shock vanished, and his smile broadened so wide that the fire from the forge reflected off his large white teeth. "This is Chevillard's wheel?" he said. "You sank the Butcher's ship?"

Ross nodded.

"And Chevillard?"

"Dead."

St. Pierre threw his hot poker into the barrel of water. He leaped a foot off the ground. "Oh ho, Declan Ross! This is joyous news indeed!"

"So you don't care about the bacon?"

"Oh no. I still want the bacon," he said with a wink. "But this is magnifique! At last, that wretched man is dead. I will make a short table out of his wheel and put my feet upon it to watch the sun set behind the mountain! Oh, what a gift! Declan Ross, for this, I will open up my special room! Extraordinary things for your ship . . . and weapons. Oh, I have so many things to show you!"

St. Pierre led them on a spiraling route through his mill until finally arriving at a massive vault door in the basement, where he held up a torch. The flickering light illuminated bulky locks from floor to ceiling—padlocks, bolts, latches too. "Got enough locks?" Ross asked.

"I told you," Jacques said, placing the torch in a wall sconce. "It's my special room." He fished out a crowded key ring and began unlocking and unlatching. The last bolt slid free, and the door opened with a low, straining groan. "Wait here," he said. He took the torch and disappeared inside. When he returned, he said, "There are many torches inside. I needed to light them all . . . to make your first glimpse all the more spectacular!"

With a mighty "Ha-ha!" Jacques threw open the door. His grin broadened at the collective gasps and whistles from Ross and his team. The light of ten torches danced upon gold, silver, brass, and copper. Tables on the left were littered with saws, clamps, sextants, and all manner of devices and instruments. The table on the right, to Red Eye's astonishment, held an assortment of swords and blades much finer than the ones he had seen aboveground.

"How . . . how much for one of these?" he asked, a tremor of excitement in his voice.

Jacques replied, "What role did you play in Chevillard's demise?"

Red Eye grinned. "I blew out the hole that sent his ship to the bottom."

"Then, for you, take any three that you like."

Red Eye almost laughed—he was so overjoyed. While Red Eye sifted through the swords, St. Pierre encouraged the others to look around and choose something that caught their fancy. Then he took Ross by the arm and led him deep into the room. They came to a set of six enormous cannons, three on either side of the narrow aisle. "What are these?" Ross asked. "Ten- . . . twelve-pounders?"

"These, mon ami, fire sixteen-pound cannonballs."

"Sixteen?!" Ross was skeptical. He studied the long barrels, black cast iron inlaid with bronze and housed in dark wood carriages.

"Yes, I know, these cannons look too light for those kind of ship-killing cannonballs. But I found this woman in Portugal who casts with iron and bronze to make the barrel smooth, but relatively light. She claims that they will fire a sixteen-pound ball accurately over six hundred feet."

Ross was impressed.

"As a token of my appreciation, take two of these for the *Wallace*."

"How will I get them back to—"

"I will have them delivered," St. Pierre explained. "You still anchor in your usual place, at the bend on the Roseau?" Ross nodded. "Good. My servants will bring them when you leave."

By the time their shopping trip into St. Pierre's special room was over, Ross and his men had acquired a spectacular array of goods, instruments, and weapons. Jules even came away with a bag of Mediterranean spices for Nubby to add to his iguana stew. It needed something to make the rest of the crew like it. Red Eye had three swords. Ross picked out a new navigation device St. Pierre called a backstaff for Stede. "That should just about do it," said Ross.

"Except for the monkey pee," said Padre Dominguez.

"Oh, right . . . that," said Ross.

"And one more thing," said Jules, handing the captain a small, cloth-wrapped package.

"What's this?" Ross asked.

"It's blue coral for Anne," Jules replied, looking away. "She should have something, don't you think?"

"Right . . . uh, thanks, Jules," said the captain. "She's probably still mad that I didn't let her come."

Later, as the sun began to set, Ross, his landing party, and dozens of St. Pierre's hired servants carried loads of supplies as they made their way back through the rain forest. "I don't understand," said Padre Dominguez. "Why was he so happy about Chevillard's wheel?"

"Thierry Chevillard once attacked a merchant ship sailed by Saint Pierre's brother Vincent," Ross explained. "Chevillard forced Vincent and his crew to become pirates. When Vincent refused to burn a settlement to the ground, Chevillard had Vincent drawn and quartered."

Padre Dominguez made the sign of the cross.

15

GHOST TOWN

Cat dangled from the frame of the balcony window twenty feet above the water. Anne impatiently treaded water beneath him. "Just let go!" she whispered.

Easy for you to say, Cat thought. *You know if you know how to swim!* But unwilling for Anne to think him afraid, Cat held his breath and plunged into the blue-green water below.

The first few moments under the water were the worst. Cat's heart hammered at his ribs, and his lungs screamed for want of air. It seemed like he sank forever, down into the murk. But his descent began to slow and reverse. He did not struggle or flail, he simply let himself float upward. When Cat surfaced, his ears rang. He opened his eyes to a blurred vision of sun shining in a young woman's red hair. *Kick your feet,* a voice said. *There, just like a little shark.*

"What did you say?" Cat asked as he spluttered and shook his hair out of his face. He kicked his feet and began to paddle his hands back and forth. His vision cleared, and there was Anne swimming beside him, looking at him strangely.

"I said, 'Swim, Cat. Kick your feet.' You looked like you were about to sink back under."

"I guess . . . I guess I know how to swim," he said, and he smiled weakly.

"There's a lot you seem to know how to do," Anne said. Cat smiled, thinking it was a compliment, but Anne's gaze was full of resentment. Anne stared at him for a moment more before saying, "Come on. Stay right behind me. We need to stay on the *Wallace*'s stern."

Anne emerged from the water and disappeared across the thin shore into the lush rain forest foliage. Cat followed. He felt wretched, soaked head to foot like he was. And he wondered if he had been foolish, leaving his leather pouch and its mysterious contents on the ship.

The forest looked ominous, dark, and alive. Strange sounds—warbles, trills, and distant screeches—emanated from green depths. The smell, at least, was inviting. Lilac, honeysuckle, and other sweet floral aromas mingled with the mulchy smell of the forest floor.

"We'll make our own way for a bit," she said. "We need to get on the main path out of sight from the *Wallace*."

As they hacked their path through the rain forest with their cutlasses, Cat noticed little orange crabs scurrying out of their way. There were other creatures as well: colorful frogs, violet-colored butterflies, and an occasional emerald green tree snake. Once, Cat noticed a pair of large brown eyes peering out at them from one of the treetops, but whatever it was disappeared around the trunk.

When they came to the main path, Anne made sure the way was clear and then gestured for Cat to follow. "We're making for

Misson," Anne said. "It's a town at the base of the mountain." She pointed up through the treetops. Cat saw the gray-green stone of the mountain rise steeply into the deepening blue sky.

"If you have been here," Anne continued, "if you saw the Carib's mural, Misson's most likely the place you went. We'll have to stay away from the mill, though. That's where my father went. But there are alleys and paths I know that can keep us mostly out of sight. Hopefully, you'll see something that you'll remember."

Cat nodded. But there was still something odd in the way she spoke to him . . . a distance, a chilly detachment. He wanted to tell her about the voice he heard when he came up from the water. "Anne?"

She turned. "What?" She looked annoyed.

"Nothing."

They walked the forest path in silence, always climbing. Cat's legs, back, and neck ached, and his head began to throb. When they passed the jagged stump of a huge fallen tree, Cat felt his skin prickle. The hair on his arms stood up. Not knowing why he did it, Cat looked suddenly to his left. There, just visible beyond the leafy branches, a narrow path forked.

"I know this," Cat whispered. Anne didn't hear. She kept on walking.

"Anne," he called. "I know this."

She turned around just in time to see Cat dart off the main path and plunge into the forest. "No, not that way!" she yelled. "Cat?" But Cat paid her no heed. If anything, he increased his speed. With a grunt, Anne ran after him.

Cat was fast. Anne couldn't believe it. The way he'd been walking behind her, stumbling over roots and getting whacked by branches, she'd just figured he wasn't much in the woods. But now he pulled ahead, and it was all Anne could do to keep sight of him.

Driven by impulses he could not explain, Cat sprinted up the path. Everything felt familiar now—every root, every large tree, every bend in the way. The path split once, and Cat didn't hesitate. He flew up the trail on the left. The path forked again—this time three ways—and, without a glance at the other two, Cat drove himself up the middle way. Then he disappeared around a wide bend in the path. When Anne turned the corner, she stopped short. Cat was nowhere to be seen.

Seeing him gone, Anne felt a sudden sense of loss. This was her fault. If he ripped open his wounds on a jagged branch, if he made a wrong turn and fell off a cliff, she'd never forgive herself. "Cat!" she yelled, even as she charged ahead. The path snaked left and right and up a gradual hill. Anne crested the hill. The down slope gave her too much speed. She ran on, unable to stop herself, stumbled awkwardly through a curtain of whiplike branches, and nearly ran smack into Cat. He stood beneath a natural archway of trees and stared out at a small town Anne had not known existed.

One- and two-story buildings—some white, some pastels of green, blue, and pink—lined both sides of a once-well-trodden road. The sun beat down upon loose shingles and patched-up roofs. Windows were broken out, and some of the buildings were blackened as if by fire. There was no sign of anyone on the road, no sign of life inside any of the buildings, no sounds but the teeming rain forest that surrounded this place. The town was abandoned.

"What is this place?" Anne asked.

"I don't know," Cat answered. "I mean, I know I've been here before. But . . ."

"You ran that path like you'd run it a hundred times."

"It's hard to explain." Cat rubbed his temples. "How can I know this place, every house, every detail—but still not know it? It's like peeking at something through a crack in a door—you know that you know what you're looking at, but you don't see enough of it for it to come clear in your mind."

"Well, there's a way to fix that," Anne said. "There's no one here. Let's go take a look around."

Cat nodded, and they slowly marched along the empty road. They walked up the creaking stairs of the first building on the left-hand side of the road and pushed open the door. Flakes of chipped paint fell at their feet, and a vile smell—half the stale, clothy odor of mold and half the sickly sweet scent of decay—greeted them as they entered. Flies buzzed, and rats scattered from the half-eaten carcass of some unidentifiable dead thing in the center of the floor.

As Cat stepped inside, his foot brushed an empty dark brown bottle. It spun slowly on the floor among broken shards from countless others. Three barrels rested against the wall in the back of the room. Cat kicked one of the barrels with the heel of his boot. It clattered onto its side. "They're empty." Cat shook his head. "I don't remember anything here. Let's go to the next one."

None of the next several houses turned up anything at all. But when they came to an odd one-story building in the middle of the town, Cat felt the skin on his arms prickle. Something heavy weighed in his stomach. He stopped and stared up the cracked stone walk, up the wide steps, between the sturdy columns, to its dark door.

"What is it, Cat?"

"I don't want to go in here," he replied. He backed slowly away.

"But if you feel something out here, maybe going inside . . ."

The chill on his arms quickly spread. Cat found himself short of breath, but still he could not take his eyes off this strange building. The only two windows—both broken out—stared back like empty sockets. "I have a terrible feeling about this place," he said. "But if there's something inside . . . something I might remember, I've got to look, don't I?"

Anne nodded. Cat's reaction to this house made her feel uncomfortable. She scanned the empty buildings on both sides of the road. The place was so quiet—so empty. Anne swallowed and nodded again. The place was a ghost town.

The stairs creaked as Cat and Anne ascended. The floorboards of the porch trembled, and each footfall gave an empty thud as if there might be some empty space beneath them. Cat stood at the dark door for several seconds before finally reaching out and turning the knob. It was unlocked, but the door protested as Cat pushed. It came free, and swung slowly into a shadowy twilight.

The smell hit them first. It was a hundred times worse than the first house. The odor of decay and death drifted out of the darkness. Cat covered his mouth and nose with his arm and took a cautious step inside. There was little to see in the two rooms: a few more empty barrels, some wood scraps, and an odd hook-shaped piece of metal that was embedded into the plaster of the wall. Anne coughed and stepped in beside him. "Maybe you're right," she said. "Maybe we shouldn't be here."

As their eyes adjusted to the shadows, Cat went forward and saw that the wooden floorboards gave way to stone in the back of the building. In fact, the narrow hall between the two rooms extended farther back than he'd thought. With Anne right behind him, he stepped onto the stonework and followed the hall. They came to a large door. The horrific odor was much stronger here. Cat opened the door, and the smell of rot became nearly overwhelming. They both looked down at the floor of the closet. Recessed into the stonework of the floor was a dark disk of metal. There was a tiny divot on the side of the disk. It was big enough maybe for a finger or two to slip in and pull up the disk.

"Do you think we should?" Anne asked.

Cat tried in vain to remember something about this place. "The smell . . . I don't know. I think we should leave."

Anne frowned. She wondered if he really did remember something—something he didn't want anyone to know. She put two fingers into the hole and pulled. The metal didn't budge. She pulled again with all her strength, but the disk would not move. "It's too heavy or rusted shut," she said.

Cat shook his head. Without a word, he left the building.

"Cat?" Anne called after him. "Cat, wait!" She caught up to him and grabbed him by the arm. He immediately shrugged her off. "I'm sorry," she said. "I should have listened to you. I just thought tha—"

"It's not that," Cat replied. He slumped to the ground and put his head in his hands. "It's this place. It's all of it. I feel like years of my life have been stolen away. Years, ha! I don't even know how many."

Anne knelt beside him. "I know this isn't the same," she said. She found it hard to meet his gaze, so she stared at the ground. "But I know how it feels to have life stolen away from you. When my mother died, my father changed—at least he did toward me. He stopped treating me like a daughter, stopped letting me play and explore. Now, he keeps me on a leash." Anne wondered what he was thinking—if he thought she was crazy or mean. She'd wished before that he could remember his identity so she could be rid of him. Now she wished only to comfort him. "I can't make you remember," she said. "But I'll help you any way that I can. And I guess, I just want you to know . . . that you aren't alone."

As Cat started to turn his gaze toward her, he spotted the side of the strange building they had just left. There, illuminated in the grass by the last rays of the afternoon sun, was a pair of storm doors. He was on his feet and at the doors in a heartbeat. Anne stood beside him.

"This place . . . it . . ." Cat clutched his head. An echo of a desperate scream, long and shrill, burst into his memory. The scream grew louder, more desperate, and then vanished. "I've been here."

That was all Anne needed to hear. In spite of the fear that lurked in the corners of her mind, in spite of the smell of decay that permeated the area, Anne grabbed the handles and threw open both storm doors. A cloud of flies swarmed out, and the smell of decay became so intense that Cat and Anne gagged. The swarm had gone, and they could see into the basement room. Anne caught her breath, and they both staggered backward. They ran recklessly into the street—and sprinted past building after building. They came at last to the foot of a stair before a two-story house. Cat dropped to his knees and wept. Anne dashed into a patch of tall grass and vomited.

16
GLT

What they had seen in that basement room did not bring back any memories for Cat. In fact, both he and Anne wished many times afterward that they both could forget what they had seen.

"Who would . . . who would do that?" Cat asked moments later as they sat on the warped steps of a boarded-up cottage.

Anne bowed her head. "Pirates," she whispered.

Cat looked across the road. His left hand wandered over the scars on his back. He turned back to Anne. "Why?"

Anne shrugged. "Maybe they were stowaways . . . or mutineers. I don't know."

"But why would pirates bring them inland just to torture the—"

"I said I don't know!"

"Your father wouldn't do that."

"My father is no monster," Anne said. "He has his vices—but unlike so many others in the sweet trade, Declan Ross grants quarter when quarter is justly requested. When he conquers a ship, he does all that he can to spare the lives of the crew and passengers. What we saw . . . that kind of horrible torture . . . is the work of a soulless villain . . . someone like Edmund Bellamy, Thierry Chevillard, or Bartholomew Thorne."

Cat shook his head. There was nothing he could do to rid his mind of the images he'd seen in that basement. Hanging inverted, visible through the bars of their iron cages, were more than a dozen bodies. The sun's light had mercilessly revealed flesh, torn and rotting; skeletal limbs; and grinning skulls. Anne and Cat had stumbled onto a chamber of horrors. And worst of all for Cat were the echoes of screams he'd heard. Had they come from the victims left to rot in that dank basement? And if those screams came from a memory of his past, what did that mean?

"Come on," Anne said. "Get up. We need to get out of here."

"But I haven't seen the rest of the town."

"Haven't you seen enough?" The question hung in the air.

Cat stood. "Something drew me here. You said it yourself, it was as if I'd run that path a hundred times." Anne wasn't sure she wanted to see any more, but she nodded . . . for his sake.

The sun had at last dipped behind the mountain, and a gray twilight fell over the abandoned town. In the shadows, Cat and Anne missed a turn in an alley and wound up in a part of the town they had not seen before. The buildings were taller and seemed to be in better repair. Cat spied a large house up ahead. It was two stories, and, with its small belfry on top, it almost looked like a church. At that moment, a strange sound came out of the forest behind the row of houses. It was a thin, rising bird's call, but the bird could not be seen. Cat stopped walking and stared. The air grew cold. *Keeee-wic, keeee-wic, keee wic, wic, wic.* The call came again.

"That's a black ani," Cat whispered.

"What?"

Cat's skin prickled. He squinted. He could hear a woman's voice echoing within his head. It was as if she were calling from up ahead. *Come inside. Leave the birds alone.* And all at once, it all became familiar: the bird's call, the alley, the silhouette of the two-story building. Cat flew up the alley.

"Cat!" Anne, a step behind, called. "Cat, not again!"

It's getting late, came the woman's voice. *Come inside this instant or I'll fetch a switch!* Cat's mind flooded with images: a porch swing, a steep narrow stair, a curving room at the end of a hall, and a ladder. And suddenly, he was there—at the two-story house. It had a wide porch with a rail. The porch swing was gone, but two chains dangled from the ceiling where it might have been. Cat threw open the front door and raced up the narrow stair. There were three rooms upstairs, but Cat ignored the first two and went straight for the room at the end of the hall.

Leery of what she might find, Anne followed Cat into the building. He was already gone up the stairs when she entered. She glanced left and right and then climbed the stairs as well. Anne searched the first two rooms and found nothing. "Cat?" she called as she approached the room at the end of the hall. The last room seemed to be empty as well. "Cat?" she called again.

"Up here!"

Anne found that the room's outer wall curved to the right, creating a small alcove. On its far wall, a ladder dropped down from a square opening in the ceiling. Anne scaled it quickly and emerged in the belfry tower overlooking the dusk-shrouded town.

"Look," Cat said. He pointed to a beam that extended horizontally from one post to another like a kind of safety rail. There was something carved into the beam. At first she could not tell exactly what, but she came closer and stooped.

"GLT?" Anne traced her finger across the coarse lettering.

"I carved them," Cat said excitedly. "I must have. I heard a voice calling me from this house."

"A voice?"

"I know it sounds crazy, but several times since we made port in Dominica, I've heard a woman's voice in my mind. And I've caught glimpses of images—like when I saw the path and the face on the rock wall. I somehow knew this house the same way—I saw the porch, the stair, this room, and the ladder. And I knew I'd find something up here."

"Initials . . . ," Anne said quietly, thinking. "Your initials? What do they stand for?"

Cat shook his head sadly. "I don't know." Despair crept over his face.

"No, Cat, this is incredible!" Anne said, standing and taking his hand. "GLT . . . you could be a George, a Gabriel . . . a Gregory!"

Cat looked out over the shadowy town, and hope began to bubble up inside. At last he had something more to go on. Not much—mere letters—but they were letters to a name . . . his name. All he needed to do was consider the possibilities. *How many "G" first names could there be?*

The smile disappeared from Cat's face and he stood stock-still, staring out over the town. "What?" Anne asked, suddenly alarmed.

"Shhh!" Cat urged. "Look." He pointed into the massive dark forest past the far end of town. Here and there, tiny orange lights flickered.

"Torches," said Anne.

"Who?"

"I don't know." Anne watched more and more tiny torchlights appear. She turned and started down the ladder. "We've got to get out of here—get back to the *Wallace*."

"Wait!" Cat grabbed her shoulder. "Look there." The torchlights were now no longer confined to one area. Cat and Anne turned and looked from one side of the town to the other. Everywhere in the woods, torchlights shone. Hundreds, maybe thousands. It was as if the little abandoned town were surrounded by a swarm of angry orange stars. And the stars were closing in.

"What do we do?" Cat asked. "They're everywhere!"

"I don't know. Hide, maybe."

"What if it's the pirates, the ones who—"

"Don't say that!" But as quickly as they appeared, the torchlights began to blink out. The forest around them was once again dark. But there was a heavy feeling in the air. They both knew the danger had not passed.

"Get down!" Anne hissed. She pulled Cat's sleeve. He stooped down near her, peering just above the rail. From every forest wall surrounding the town, dark figures emerged. Dozens and dozens of them scurried out, disappearing for a moment at one building and then dashing silently to the next. Anne turned and saw more of them emerge from the forest just a hundred yards behind the building in which they stood. So many, too many to count, they closed in from every angle.

"We've got to hide!" she whispered urgently. Cat started down the ladder, but Anne stopped him. "Too late. Pull up the ladder. Close the trapdoor."

Cat did as she suggested, wrenching the ladder up and leaning it against the rail. He and Anne lifted the heavy door on its rusty hinge. Trying desperately to keep it silent, they lowered the trapdoor gently into place. Then they turned and waited. A slice of the moon had risen. The rooftops and alleys were bathed in gray blue. Suddenly, they heard soft footsteps. Many footsteps. Anne and Cat hunched down as low as they could, but each peeked above the rail.

"Soldiers," Cat whispered.

Anne nodded. In the moon's light, they saw dozens of pale faces beneath dark hats. They clutched long, dark objects in their white hands—muskets. Their razor-sharp bayonets gleamed. The alley below filled silently with soldiers. Cat and Anne held their collective breath and slumped down, their backs to the wall. Anne turned to Cat. "We're trapped."

17

ROOFTOP HOPPING

"Commodore Blake, we've searched every building," came a heavily accented voice from below. "The town is empty."

"British," whispered Anne.

"It would seem that our information was a bit . . . dated," said another voice. This one only lightly accented, but deep and rich with confidence. "Perhaps a little light will see us through. Kindle the torches and search every building from top to bottom. If there is anything, anything at all that could tell us where they've gone, we must find it. And, Mister Kent?"

"Yes, sir."

"Take a brigade back to Tarou Point. Bring word to Commodore Ainsworth to mobilize a third of the fleet to scour the southern ports, especially Roseau and Soufriere. Our quarry may have departed long ago, but if any have lingered, we will snare them at night when they are sleeping—or drunk!"

"Yes, sir!"

Anne clutched Cat's hand. "Roseau!" she whispered. "The *Wallace* is moored just up the river from there. We'll be cut off. We've got to get to the ship."

"What about your father . . . the landing party, are they even back from Misson yet?"

"I don't know," Anne replied. "But it doesn't matter. If the British take Roseau, we're all done for."

Cat reached for the iron ring of the trapdoor. "No, wait!" Anne exclaimed. They both fell silent when they heard movement in the room beneath their feet. "They're down there." She looked frantically around the belfry. There was nothing. No rope, no tools, no escape.

"The roof," Cat whispered. Anne looked over the rail. "We could climb over the rail and creep along the roof. Then we can leap across to that little cottage. If we can drop down somewhere behind the troops, we can disappear into the forest and make our way back to the river."

"Are you crazy?" Anne looked away. "That's ten feet across if it's an inch!"

"Yes, but we're leaping down. We could make it."

"And break our legs!" Anne complained.

"No, just roll when you hit the other roof—that'll spread out the blow."

"How do you know that—oh, never mind! Even if we make it unharmed, the whole British navy will hear us."

"You have a better plan?" Cat asked.

"No."

Before she could think of one, Cat stealthily slipped over the rail and onto the roof. Anne gritted her teeth and followed. They crept along the rooftop until they came to within a yard of the edge. The gap between buildings wasn't quite ten feet, but it was close.

"Come on!" Cat urged. He backed up a step and was about to run for it.

"No way," Anne said. "I'm going first."

"No, we go together," he replied, the moonlight glinting fiercely in his eyes. "If we go one at a time, and the troops hear us, some-one is going to be left behind. We have a better chance if we leap together."

Anne looked at Cat with new respect. "So what do we do when we hit the roof down there—that is, of course, if we don't kill our-selves in the fall?!"

"We run," said Cat. "Run behind the chimney in case they start shooting. Once we're there, leap again to the next building. But keep up with me and head toward the woods. I think that's our only way." Anne nodded.

"Ready?" They both sped to the edge of the roof and leaped. The night air whooshed by, and they tumbled to the cottage's rooftop. They landed with an enormous thud but rolled. To Anne's amazement, they both survived unharmed. But a great commotion arose in the alleys below.

"What was that?!" a voice yelled.

"There!" came another. "Up on the roof!"

"Fire!"

Cat and Anne heard the sharp reports of rifles being fired. They ducked behind the chimney just in time. Musket balls smacked into the roof, sending shattered shingles flying in all directions. Another blast hit the chimney near Cat's elbow. "Ow! We can't wait here!"

He tugged Anne behind him, and they leaped straight across to the next building. They landed awkwardly this time, stumbled, but were not hurt. Alert to the shouted commands below and the musket balls whizzing by them in all directions, Cat and Anne raced from rooftop to rooftop. Finally they came to the last building before the woods.

Anne looked down. It was a decent height. "How do we . . ."

"Watch me," Cat said. He agilely spun round, dropped to his stomach, and slid over the edge. He hung by the strength of his hands and arms and dropped lightly to the ground. Anne shook her head and attempted to do the same. But when she slid over the edge, she could not hold her grip, and she fell backward.

Cat was there to break her fall, but Anne didn't even have time for a thank-you. He took her hand and yanked her into the woods. They had barely gone ten yards into the forest when they smacked right into dark blue uniforms. They fell backward, stunned.

Anne rose to her feet first and drew her cutlass. Cat rose and did the same.

"Drop your weapons!" one of the soldiers commanded. Cat and Anne looked around. There were a dozen men, each leveling a rifle in their direction. More soldiers poured in behind them.

Reluctantly, Cat and Anne lowered their swords and let them fall from their hands. The troops moved in.

Cat and Anne were led roughly back up the alleys and out into the main street. They were shoved to the ground before a tall man. He wore black boots, dark blue breeches, and a breasted white vest under a blue frock coat. Gold was embroidered upon his lapels, and he wore a wide black tricorn hat trimmed in silver.

"Lieutenant Crowley," said the man, stooping and taking Anne's hand. "Are you in the habit of manhandling a lady?" He gently lifted Anne to her feet and bowed slightly to her, all the while glaring at his subordinate.

"No, sir, Commodore," he replied. "But . . . she's a pirate!"

"Really?" the commodore asked. "Has she a sign upon her back?"

The other soldiers laughed. Crowley went red in the face. "Well . . . no, but she has that look about her. They both do. Why, they've got to be—"

"Of course they are pirates!" The commodore became suddenly fierce. "This town is a pirate stronghold! Nonetheless, she is still a lady. And under my command, we will treat her civilly, do you understand?"

Crowley winced and nodded. "Yes, sir."

The commodore fixed his gaze upon Anne. "I am Commodore Brandon Blake, of the British Royal Navy," he began. "I apologize for your treatment, but you must understand, we are in pursuit of as ruthless a band of killers as the seas have ever known. If you cooperate with us, tell us where they've gone, I have the power to pardon your offenses. And that goes for your friend here as well."

Cat stood and brushed himself off. Anne said nothing. She was confused, angry, and acutely aware that the seconds were ticking away. If the British navy cordoned Roseau, the *Wallace* would be trapped.

"I shall ask you again," said the commodore. His green eyes were fierce, penetrating. "Where have they all gone?" Still, Anne did not answer. "Come now, you cannot have much loyalty to that villain. After all, you've been left behind."

"Commodore!" a man called. "Commodore Blake!" He ran up and spoke in breathless huffs. "We found something . . . there's a basement . . . fifteen corpses. Sir, they were tortured, left hanging upside down. It's a bloody mess down there, sir."

The commodore stared hard at Anne and then Cat. There was a power in his gaze that made them both feel like he could see right through them. The commodore continued to stare but said, "Mister Beckett, how long have the bodies been there?"

"Nigh on a week," Beckett replied. "Maybe more. It smells something horrible."

"A week," the commodore echoed. He was thoughtful a moment. He looked more intensely at Anne and Cat. "You know about the bodies," he said to them. "I can see it in your eyes. But what I don't know—" He drew a long silver cutlass and held the point a few inches from Cat's chin. "What I don't know is if you had something to do with it."

"Leave him alone!" Anne shouted. "He didn't hurt those people!" In spite of the sword, Cat stared at the ground.

"He looks guilty to me," said the commodore, his brow lowering and his jaw set.

"No!" Anne cried out. "Cat's innocent! We had nothing to do with it!"

"Innocent?" The commodore frowned. "I doubt that either one of you is innocent. But I am inclined to believe you did no harm to those we found in the basement. You see, we've come across such piteous scenes many times before."

Cat and Anne stared at each other, then back at the commodore. "Now, listen to me," he said, lowering his sword. "I am making you a very merciful offer. Just tell us what you know and you can be free. Otherwise, our court will have no recourse but to charge you with piracy—charge you even with the murders of those we found in the basement. You will hang from the gallows. You will—"

Anne blurted out, "We don't know anything. We just found this place and—"

"Enough!" The commodore's rage spilled over. "Tell me where Thorne is!"

"Thorne?" Anne echoed.

"Bartholomew Thorne!! This was his hidden camp. You must know where he has gone!"

Anne chose her words carefully. "I know who Bartholomew Thorne is, but we aren't part of his crew. We came to Dominica for supplies."

"Then how did you know about this place?" Commodore Blake threw up his hands. "This is pointless. You had your chance. Mister Crowley, put the lad in manacles and leg irons."

"Yes, sir." Crowley hesitated. "Uh, what about the girl?"

"Have you not yet learned my customs? No, so long as she remains ladylike, we will let her walk with us unbound."

Another man, dressed similarly to the commodore but with quite a bit less gold on his lapels, leaned over and said to the commodore, "Sir Brandon, are you sure that's wise? She seemed awfully willing to raise a sword."

"Wise or not, Sir Nigel, we will allow her to walk unbound," the commodore replied. "But to be sure she will not escape, why don't you walk behind her. Mister Crowley will walk in front. With two such capable escorts, we have very little to fear from this young lady."

18
A Coral Tiger

"Where are you taking us?" Anne asked. The British troops under Commodore Blake's command had completed their search of the abandoned town and now walked briskly along a wide path through the dark Dominican forest.

"To Misson," replied Sir Nigel from behind. "There are a few people there the commodore would like to question. Plus, there's a nice little cell where we can put you two for a bit."

Misson? Anne cringed inwardly. It just kept getting worse. A fleet of British ships would soon be hunting the southern ports, cutting off the *Wallace*'s escape. And now hundreds and hundreds of British troops were about to descend upon the town where her father and many of the crew were shopping for supplies. She looked up at the moon through the canopy of trees. She had no idea how late it was or if her father was still in Misson. Still, what could she do? They'd taken her sword. They'd taken her dagger. Cat was chained at the wrists and ankles. And she was surrounded on all sides by numerous soldiers. She needed a plan.

Anne glanced back at Cat. Their eyes met for just a moment. "Face the front, my lady," said Sir Nigel, each word coated with contempt. Anne looked away. She began fingering the coral tiger hung from her necklace. Their caravan began to slow a little. Anne looked ahead and saw why. The path narrowed, forcing the ranks of soldiers to thin at the bottleneck. Anne looked back at Cat again, wishing she could ask him what he thought.

"I said, FACE FRONT!" Sir Nigel waved his torch in Anne's face. She flinched back and did as she was told. Lieutenant Crowley looked back over his shoulder and laughed. That made Anne furious. She squeezed her coral tiger so hard that the jagged edge at the bottom of the carving pricked her finger. She put her finger in her mouth and tasted blood. . . .

Blood. The plan came together in a rush. Anne looked again at the steadily narrowing path. It was so tight, the troops had to walk through single file. In a few moments, the group of soldiers near her, including Crowley, Cat, and Sir Nigel, would all have to line up to pass through.

Anne again looked up at the moon through the canopy of trees. She had always had a very good sense of direction. She was fairly certain that they had been traveling northeast for almost the entire hour since they'd left the town. That would mean the path back to the *Wallace* was off to the right. She thought of Cat. If her plan were to work, it had to happen fast—with the element of surprise. There would be no time to free Cat from his bonds. And with those chains on, there was no way for him to run. There was no choice. She'd have to leave him.

At last, they came to the bottleneck in the path. As she figured, the soldiers in front and behind narrowed to single file. Anne waited until dozens filed in behind them, and they were all hemmed in on both sides by the lush forest. Slowly she pulled the coral tiger from the neck-lace. She held it firmly in her fist with the jagged point sticking out like a very small dagger. She looked back over her shoulder at Cat, defying Sir Nigel and hoping to arouse his anger. When Cat looked up, she mouthed, "I'm sorry." He looked at her questioningly.

"Here now!" Sir Nigel growled. "I thought I told you to— keep—your—eyes—forward!" He started to lift his torch like before, but Anne surprised him. She kicked backward with her left foot, pushing the torch toward Sir Nigel's chest. The flames leaped up his beard. He howled. Lt. Crowley turned around again, but Anne was already moving. She planted the sharp coral into his upper thigh. He cursed and clutched his leg. Anne disappeared between two large trees and fled into the forest.

"Come back here!" Sir Nigel bellowed, still patting out the flames from his beard and chest. Several soldiers opened fire, but they had been walking in the torches' light. Their night vision was gone. Anne instantly faded into the darkness of the forest.

"Don't waste another shot!" someone shouted from far up the line. "After her!"

By the time the troops stopped shooting and raced into the woods, Anne had a huge head start. But she had to be careful. Her night vision wasn't much better than theirs, since she too had been staring at torches. And the footing was horrible. If she ran into a tree or fell into a ditch, it would all be for nothing. As her eyes adjusted, she made a sharp right turn and ran as fast as she could through the branches, brambles, and bracken. After careening recklessly through the forest without stopping for what seemed like an eternity, Anne froze in place. She waited for her heart to stop pounding and listened intently to see if anyone was in pursuit. The only noises she heard were the welcome sounds of the tropical forest at night.

The forest flew by in a grayish blue blur. Anne found herself bounding over stumps, roots, and fallen logs. Her legs burned from the exertion. Suddenly, she burst through a row of feathery ferns and landed in a narrow hollow. She stopped herself just before she would have smacked into a gnarled tree root that protruded from the bank of the hollow.

The path! It had to be. In the pale light, she saw a well-trodden passage snaking its way through the forest. Anne turned around, wondering if she'd thought things through well enough. To turn right would take her south to the *Wallace*, her original plan. She had to get to the ship to warn them about the British convoy so that they could—do what? Put to sea to escape the coming trap? But she knew they would not set sail if her father and the landing party had not yet returned from Misson. To turn left would take her to Misson. If her father was still there, he needed to be warned. But it was too late for that, wasn't it? Anne knew she could never get there before Commodore Blake and his British troops. And what if she ran all that way only to discover her father had already returned to the *Wallace*. How would she attempt to rescue Cat? Anne couldn't keep all the possibilities straight in her head.

She sighed and turned to the right. She needed to get to the ship. Someone on the *Wallace* would know what to do. As she began to run south on the path, her stomach churned. Her little excursion plan for Cat had become a disaster. And one way or the other, she knew that it was all her fault. She just hoped that Cat wouldn't pay for her foolishness with his life. That fear in mind, Anne drove herself down the path. In the dark, she had no idea how far away the

Wallace was. She stumble-stepped most of the way, stopping once to catch her breath. Then something flickered up ahead.

Anne skidded to a stop and crouched. The path wound like an "S" in front of her, and at the top of it, around the second curve, torches appeared. Ten, twelve maybe. Anne froze. Could Commodore Blake have guessed her intentions? Had he sent a regiment south to cut her off from the main path?

Anne saw them approach the first curve. She needed to get off the path and fast. She looked up. No climbable trees near enough. She could see there were at least a dozen or more. Not knowing what else to do, she dove off the path into the foliage and hid.

They spoke in hushed voices as they approached. Anne ducked, practically lying facedown on a bed of dirt and dead leaves. She peeked up through the leaves. The torches were passing by. She couldn't see if they were wearing uniforms, but they were definitely armed. Torchlight illuminated the barrels of several muskets. They continued to pass, and Anne thanked her lucky stars. She had thanked them too soon.

Something grabbed her by the wide leather belt she wore and lifted her clean out of the bushes. A rumbling deep voice said, "I found her, sir!"

19

ROSS'S PLAN

You have a bad habit of running off, Red," the huge man said.

"Jules?" Anne couldn't believe it.

He hoisted her up, carried her like a handbag, and put her down lightly on the path . . . directly in front of her father. Even in the flickering light of the torch, she could see the vein bulging on his forehead, the tendons taut on his neck. Anne started to speak, but didn't even get out a syllable.

"You betrayed me, Anne," Declan Ross said. "You betrayed us all."

His words felt like knives. Tears started pouring down her cheeks. "Father, I didn't mean for—"

"Don't!" he said. "Your intentions do not matter here, Anne. You abandoned the ship. Some might even call it mutiny." Anne cringed. She knew what the pirate's code said about mutiny.

Ross continued. "And you took Cat with you! Why do I feel so confident that this was all your idea?" His blazing eyes bored into her. "What kind of sense is that, daughter? He's a wounded man! You put his life in danger." Ross looked into the woods behind her. "Where's he hiding anyway? Cat, you can come out now!" Declan called out into the forest. There was no answer.

"Where is he, Anne?" he asked.

Anne fell to her knees and sobbed so hard she choked. Her words came out between wet breaths and gasps. "I'm so sorry, Father."

Some of Ross's ire melted away, and he knelt and lifted Anne's chin. "What happened?"

She told him all of it. From their discovery of the abandoned town to Commodore Blake's order to send his ships to scour the southern ports to their eventual capture. She even explained how Commodore Blake had refused to put chains and leg irons on her, treating her like a lady.

"I wouldn't have escaped otherwise," Anne said.

Ross was thoughtful a moment. "How long ago did this Commodore Blake send his ships south?" Ross asked.

"I don't know exactly," Anne replied. "No, wait, it was near sundown. I remember. The sun had just gone behind the mountains."

"Sundown," Ross echoed. "His men had to get to their port. The ships needed to be made ready. Sailing time, Stede?"

"That b' about an hour," he replied, shaking his head. "We might b' making it before those outrageous navy ships show up—if we b' going straight to the *Wallace* and put to sail right away. But . . . we ain't doin' that, are we?"

Ross grinned, and in the torchlight, he looked wild. "I won't—not until we get our newest crewman back."

Red Eye appeared at the captain's side. "I'd like to volunteer for this little expedition, if I may."

The captain nodded. "I'll need your special talents," Ross said. "Jules and Midge too. But that's all. Stede, you and all the others will take my daughter back to the *Wallace*. I want you to sail with all speed around the southern tip of Dominica. Make for La Plaine. If our luck holds, we'll see you there in a couple of days."

"Ya have a plan, mon?" Stede asked.

"Part of one. We can't match this Blake's numbers. But he won't be expecting us, and I probably know Misson better than he does. But for this to work, we're going to need a distraction . . . a big distraction." Ross scratched his furry beard a few moments. "I wonder if he would . . ." Ross muttered. "He doesn't think much of the British either. Yes . . . I think he just might."

"Ya have that look again," Stede said. "I don't mind telling ya, that worries me, mon."

"You just worry about the ship," said Ross. "Get the *Wallace* out of here. I'll see you in La Plaine."

Ross led Jules, Midge, and Red Eye again under the stone arch behind St. Pierre's mill at the foot of Mount Macaque in Misson. On the other side, Ross found a heavy wooden door with wrought-iron hinges and a sturdy-looking black lock. Ross raised a hand to knock and heard an ominous click.

A man holding a pistol stepped out of the shadows near the door. "Bonsoir, Englishman!" whispered Jacques St. Pierre.

"Jacques, you're very lucky I'm a nice guy," answered Ross. "Men from Scotland such as myself have killed for less."

"Ah, pardonne, mon capitaine!" St. Pierre lowered the gun and embraced Ross. "You will forgive my insult, but there are many

English soldiers about. They make me, how you say, discomfortable? So I have been making preparations . . . just in case."

"So they are here," said Ross.

St. Pierre made a sour face. "They came creeping in not long after dark," he said. "Like cockroaches, they scurried all over Misson. But where are my manners? You are not such insects. Come inside and we will talk. I am guessing that you have not come back to shop more, eh?"

St. Pierre produced a large iron key, worked the lock, and led them inside. They passed the wall of black powder barrels, the forge, and the stairs to St. Pierre's special room. He welcomed them into a study and seated them in big leather chairs among stacks of books.

"Can I get you something?" he asked. "Wine, maybe? A biscuit?"

"Yes, please," said Midge. "That would be right lovely, it would."

"No, we don't have time," Ross declared, scowling at Midge. Midge's shoulders slumped. "Jacques, it's the English I've come to see you about. They took one of my men. Any idea where they would put a prisoner?"

"The hospital," he replied. "There are two cells there. A man named Julliard keeps the peace—mainly when pirates are in town. Ha!"

"I need to get my man out of there," Ross explained. "And I've got to do it fast. The British navy is on the way to cordon off the southern ports."

"I see," said St. Pierre, the wheels of his mind already spinning away. "But getting a man out of this place will not be easy. The soldiers are like roaches, I tell you. So many!" St. Pierre looked at Ross and his men. "But no, you did not come to fight them. No, that would be tres stupide!"

"I have a plan," Ross said. "I'm going to need your help. And I'm going to need a lot of your black powder." Ross explained his plan to Jacques St. Pierre. The Frenchman's grin grew wider and wider as he listened.

"What you ask will probably bring the English here," St. Pierre announced when Ross was finished. "Everyone in Misson knows I am the man to see about things that go boom! Ha-ha! But, for the man who brought me Chevillard's wheel, I'll do it! And as to the location of this diversion? Dutchie's barn, I think. He has always wanted a new place anyway."

Ross and Red Eye were hidden in the woods outside of a long, low stone building on the northern edge of Misson. They sat on either side of a small brown barrel.

"Can you see, Midge?" Ross asked.

Red Eye waited to make sure none of the British guards were passing by, then drew his cutlass. It was one of the swords St. Pierre had given him. Its blade was wide and unmarred. Red Eye tilted it, changing the angle of the blade several times. He stared in the direction of the stone fountain near the main road. Nothing. Red Eye signaled again with his sword, two flashes in rapid succession. Then, finally, from the fountain came two answering flashes. "He's ready," Red Eye said.

"Good," Ross replied. "You put the fuse in the barrel?"

"Yes," he replied. "Ten seconds' worth, like Saint Pierre said. You sure this little barrel will be enough?"

"Jacques said so," Ross replied. "Besides, we want to break Cat out, not blow him to kingdom come. Now, the question is, which cell? Keep an eye out for guards. And Red Eye . . ."

"Yes, Captain?"

"I know you're itching to try out your new dagger, but don't come out unless you're sure one of the guards has seen me." Red Eye sneered in response, and once again Declan Ross was glad Red Eye was on his side. Ross left the refuge of the forest and sprinted up to the building. Small trees and bushes provided some cover—but if a curious guard came by, Ross knew it would all be over. The first window he came to had no bars and was not a cell at all. He was about to pass it when he heard voices.

". . . sleeping now," said one heavily accented voice. "Can't say as I blame 'im. I could use a rest myself."

"Still nothing to say?" asked a second voice. Ross was about to move on to the next window but froze when he heard the rest.

"Sir Brandon, I'm disposed to think he's mute. Did you see the scars on his back, the welts healing on his head, his arms—just about everywhere else?!"

"I saw them," said the second voice. Ross peered over the edge of the window and saw two men in dark blue uniforms sitting at a table near a large cabinet full of canisters and jars. The man speaking took off a dark tricorn hat bordered with silver. He had blond hair and sideburns that nearly reached his chin. "It is clear that this man took a beating that could render him mute," he said, taking a long sip from a glass.

"But I'm not convinced that it did in this case. There is cleverness in this lad's eyes. The way he studies his surroundings reminds me of a doctor I once knew. When I first put him in the cell, he seemed to be analyzing every inch of the place. I'm quite certain he was trying to devise a way to break out."

The other man, older, less fit, with dark hair and a thin beard, laughed. "Not much chance of that happening. Ha! Not unless he can knock down walls with his bare hands."

A third man entered the room. He wore a similar dark blue uniform but was clearly younger and of lesser rank. "Commodore Blake," he said, addressing the man with the long sideburns. "We've found no trace of Thorne or his men. But a man in the tavern said that pirates come to Misson often to do business with the man who lives in the mill on the other side of town."

Commodore Blake stroked the brim of his hat. "Perhaps he'll recognize our guest. What say we gather a few of the lads in the morning and pay this miller a visit, eh, Sir Nigel?"

"I quite agree," he replied.

Ross's stomach tightened. He wondered what offenses St. Pierre had committed against the British. If nothing else, there'd be a lot of explaining to do about the events that were about to transpire. Ross hurried to the next window, the first with bars. It was completely dark in the room. "Cat!" he whispered, conscious of how close the room was to Commodore Blake's. No answer.

"Cat?" he whispered again, just as a group of soldiers rounded the corner. Ross dropped down behind the bushes and began to draw his sword. He stopped and watched through the foliage. There were five soldiers. Only one had a lantern. That was fortunate. They walked somewhat casually but came to a stop right beside the bushes where Ross lay hidden.

"Hey, Osbourne, not a bad place to work, eh?" said the guard with the lantern. He swung it about in a slow circle. "Just look at all the foliage."

"You're right about that, Jarvis," said another. "Wouldn't mind getting a place of me own here—me and the missis, that is." There was a general laugh. They seemed happily oblivious. Ross was glad about that, but he sure wished they would move on.

"No tellin' when this'll all be done," said a third soldier with a sigh.

"When Bartholomew Thorne's hung from the gallows at New Providence, that's when," said Jarvis. "Like as not."

"There are other pirates," said Osbourne.

"Yeah, but Thorne's the worst."

"And for the commodore, it's personal."

At last the soldiers began to drift away. But suddenly, the guard named Jarvis swung round with the lantern and came back over to the hedge near Ross. He stooped a bit and squinted. "Here now, what's this?"

Ross tightened his grip on his sword. He felt like the guard was staring right at him. The other soldiers gathered round. The guard handed the lantern to one of the others and leaned closer to the hedge. Ross tensed, ready for action.

In the forest nearby, Red Eye already had his cutlass in one hand. He drew a long dagger with a serrated blade. He knew this wasn't the way the captain wanted it to go, but the British were getting too close for comfort. Things were about to get ugly.

Jarvis took something off his belt and began to reach toward Ross. "Well, look what I found hidin' over here."

20
Raid under Cover of Darkness

Ross let his blade slide slowly the rest of the way out of the sheath and slid the sharp point into the shrub. He was ready to thrust the weapon through the bush and straight into the Englishman's gut.

Red Eye emerged from his hiding place and, without a sound, crept up behind two of the British soldiers.

"Surprised to find you here," the British soldier named Jarvis said as he reached over the hedge. He moved slowly, cupping his hand. Suddenly, he struck. His hand moved faster than Ross expected. Ross reacted. He shoved his cutlass, but it caught in the crook of a branch.

The Englishman stepped back from the bushes and held up a large bluish moth. *"Adscita globulariae!"* he said. "A brilliant specimen."

Ross exhaled. Red Eye dove back into the forest.

"Normally you find such a creature on the trunk of a conifer where it blends in. How odd to see it just sitting there on the building. Beautiful, isn't it?" He held it up to the other soldiers.

"You're an odd one, Jarvis!" said Osbourne. The group of soldiers walked off, laughing hysterically.

Ross shook his head. *A moth? I almost killed him over a moth.* As soon as the troops were out of sight, Ross sprang up again. He knew the longer he waited, the more likely someone would discover him. He rose up to the barred window and called again, "Cat! You in there?" Still there was no answer.

Ross checked for soldiers and then hopped through the bushes to the next window with bars. "Cat?" he whispered. This had to be the right place. "Cat?"

A face suddenly appeared at the window. Ross was so startled he fell backward into the bushes. "Captain Ross?" It was Cat.

Ross stood, looked both ways along the building, and motioned to Red Eye. "Cat, listen. We don't have much time. Go to the other side of your cell. I want you to get as far away from this wall as you can."

"Why?" Cat asked. At that moment, Red Eye appeared with two items: a small hooded lamp and a barrel of black powder. He placed the explosive barrel by the wall beneath the window. Cat said, "Oh."

Ross nodded. "When this goes off, we should be able to get you out."

"What about Commodore Blake and the other troops?"

"We have a plan for that," Ross said. Cat looked at him quizzically. Ross winked and said, "Let's just say, the biggest boom will get their attention."

Cat disappeared from the window. Red Eye ran back to the woods and signaled with his sword. He waited for the signal back.

There it was—three flashes. Red Eye waved to Ross. Ross uncovered the lantern and lit the fuse. Praying that St. Pierre had cut exactly ten seconds of fuse, Ross dove out of the bushes. He sprinted across to the woods and crashed next to Red Eye.

Red Eye and Captain Ross stared back and forth between the barn on the other side of the fountain and the fuse burning by Cat's cell window. The fuse on that small barrel of black powder must have been a little short. It went off first with a boom and a flash of orange light. But a split second later: FOOM!!

A thunderous shock wave shook the town of Misson. Orange, yellow, and white light flashed and bathed the area. A great cloud of fire and debris rose from the ground where the barn once stood. A gust of hot, sulfurous wind swept over them.

Red Eye smiled. "That Jacques sure knows how to celebrate!"

They watched from their refuge as British troops streamed out of the hospital and ran to the scene of the great explosion. Then the two of them drew their swords and ran through a drifting cloud of smoke to the wall of Cat's cell. The black powder had breached the wall. Ross and Red Eye began to kick at the loose stones. Small flecks and chips broke free and skittered away. From behind, Midge, Jacques St. Pierre, and Jules appeared. "You didn't put enough powder in that barrel," Ross growled.

"Pardonne, Capitaine," Jacques replied angrily. "I assumed you wanted your man whole and alive—not scattered in the air like so many burning pieces!"

"Move!" said Jules. He took one long stride and slammed the bottom of his boot against the stone. An enormous chunk of rock broke free. Another kick, and enough stone caved in for Jules to enter. Midge waited outside while the others rushed in. They found Cat huddled in a ball near the other side of the cell. He was unharmed—though still clutching his ears. He jumped when Ross put a hand on his shoulder.

"On your feet, Cat," Ross said. "Unless, of course, you'd like to spend the night with the British."

"Uh . . . Captain?" Midge said through the opening. He sounded worried.

"I take it you were not satisfied with our hospitality," came another voice from behind them. They turned. Standing outside, just a few paces back from the hole they had made, was Commodore Blake. Midge backed into the cell. Red Eye handed Cat a sword. Ross and St. Pierre already had theirs unsheathed. Jules stood at the ready. "So you were responsible for the fireworks this evening. An impressive display. It almost worked."

Ross stepped forward. "Stand aside," he said.

Commodore Blake drew his own sword. "I think not. This man is our prisoner, and after your efforts tonight, so are you."

"This man," said Ross, gesturing to Cat, "is just a lad. And until you unlawfully took him—and my daughter—prisoner, they were crewmen."

"She is your daughter?" Commodore Blake's brows rose. "I see where she gets her spirit. Just crewmen, eh? So, I suppose you are just merchants with commerce in Dominica."

"That's right," Ross said. "I am a merchant sailor out of Scotland. We had business in Misson with Mister Saint Pierre, here."

"Is that right?" asked the commodore. Ross nodded. "Now, why do I not believe you are telling me the truth? Is it the fact that your daughter and this lad were found roaming around a notorious pirate hideaway? Or is it that instead of coming to the door and seeking to explain your case, you decided to blow up half the town? No, neither of those. I think the reason I do not believe a word from your mouth is because I know exactly who you are. You are Declan Ross, captain of the *William Wallace*. And you, sir, are a pirate wanted by my country, and heaven knows how many others. And though I was hoping to catch Bartholomew Thorne, I will happily settle for you."

"The odds aren't in your favor, Commodore," said Ross, and he took a step forward.

"Oh? I suspect they are a little better than you think," he replied with a nod. From the left and the right, more than a dozen armed soldiers marched out and stood behind him.

21
STALEMATE

It doesn't have to go like this," Ross declared with a subtle shake of his head.

"I quite agree," said Commodore Blake. "Put down your swords, and I promise you a fair trial."

"Fair?" Ross snorted. "If you mean the six of us doing the hempen jig on the gallows at New Providence, no thanks. I like my neck just the way it is. I suggest a better plan. You put down *your* swords, *your* guns, and let us pass. If you do, I promise you will all live."

Blake's eyebrows shot up. He glanced left and right at his men. "I do not think you understand your circumstances. Clearly—"

"Commodore!" Ross shot back. "Look at your men. They are barely out of boyhood. I can see the fear in their eyes—and it is well that they should fear. The men I have assembled here are the fiercest warriors of the open sea. Take Red Eye, for instance." Red Eye stepped forward, brandished his cutlass, and opened his bloody eye for the British to see. Ross continued. "The only reason he hasn't killed anyone yet is because he honors my command. I need but say the word, and he will suddenly be among you, swift and silent as a ghost. Your men will begin to drop to the ground before they realize the danger!"

Commodore Blake was not shaken. But the same could not be said of his troops. They began to shift in place and exchange nervous glances. "And this massive man beside me," Ross went on, gesturing to Jules. "Did you notice he bears no sword, no pistol? That is because he needs none! Jules has killed more men with his bare hands than the lot of you have killed with all your weapons combined." Jules flexed the muscles of his massive barrel chest. He cracked his knuckles and gave the British his "prowling wolf" grin. Cat looked up at the men of the *William Wallace*. He had no idea if what Ross said was true, but looking up at them now, he found it hard to doubt.

"You may have such seasoned and treacherous men in your charge," Blake said. "But we need not scrap with you on your terms. You have put yourself between the devil and the deep blue sea. Iron bars behind you. And this narrow opening is your only escape. But if you make to charge through it, we but need to wait for you to emerge and shoot you one at a time. And every moment that passes, time works to our advantage. I have sent for more of my men. They will leave your diversion and swell my ranks. You are caught, Declan Ross, like a mouse in a trap."

Cat marveled at the two commanders. In their glares, a battle of wills raged like two tall ships, side by side, firing relentlessly but refusing to sail out of harm's way. Blake, at last, broke the stalemate. "Drop your weapons, Declan Ross," he said. Looking directly at Cat, he added, "Perhaps there are some among you who need not be hanged as pirates."

Cat shrugged away the commodore's glance. Ross and the crew of the *Wallace* had taken him aboard when they could have left him to die on that island. And they had risked all to come back to Misson when they easily could have just left him in the hands of the British. For better or worse, Cat had thrown in his lot with the men of the *William Wallace*. He raised his sword and stilled the uncertain quiver in his stomach.

St. Pierre suddenly stepped forward. The British soldiers shifted. One or two raised their muskets. Jacques looked at Ross, shook his head, and sheathed his cutlass. Misunderstanding St. Pierre's action as a gesture of surrender, Blake smiled. He now wore the prowling wolf grin. But not for long.

Surrender was the farthest thing from St. Pierre's mind. He sheathed his sword only to get his hands free. From one pocket he withdrew a smooth round object about the size of a fist. A short fuse stuck out of the top. In a split second, Jacques flicked something in his left hand, and the fuse was lit. He tossed the object through the breach in the wall, and it rolled at the feet of the British soldiers. "Grenade!"

Commodore Blake and his men scattered. The grenade exploded a second later, a thunderous blast that left a huge roiling cloud of dark smoke. Ross yelled, "Through the breach, men!" He led the charge, followed directly by Red Eye and St. Pierre. Jules and the others came right after. They found themselves in an odd orange twilight. Dawn was at hand, and the inferno from the exploded barn raged on. Black smoke and ghostly morning mist swirled. Blake's sailors were disoriented for just a moment, but when they turned to stand their ground and block the escape, they found they had lost their advantage. A soldier lifted his musket and fired over Ross's head. Ross felt it go by. The soldier braced his weapon against his shoulder and charged at Ross with his bayonet. Ross slashed the bayonet aside and threw his shoulder into the sailor's chest. Stunned, he fell away and lay still.

Three British came at Cat. He parried the first attack with a sudden upward slash. Then he spun out of the way as the other two charged by. They ran directly into Jules. One of their bayonets jabbed into Jules's upper thigh. With a grunt, Jules grabbed the Englishman's rifle, withdrew it from his leg, and broke it into pieces over his knee. Jules grabbed the two soldiers by the gold buttons on their chests and flung them aside like rag dolls.

"This way!" They all heard the voice from up ahead. It was Red Eye's voice, but no one saw him. "Get moving, louts!"

Ross gathered his men and led them in the direction of Red Eye's voice. As they ran along the tree line, Ross wondered what had become of Commodore Blake. Had he been wounded or killed by the grenade? Ross somehow doubted it. Blake had proven much too savvy for such an ignominious end. Still, he couldn't just disappear.

The huge basin of the fountain loomed up on their left, and before Ross and his men could clear it, a rank of British soldiers charged in. They immediately formed a line and barred the pirates' way. One of the British soldiers unleashed a shrill blast on a whistle. Ross would have rather had these men open fire with their muskets. The whistle, Ross knew, would summon reinforcements. Ross knew they had to move—and move fast—to avoid the cloud of enemies that would no doubt descend upon them soon. He raised his cutlass and took a step toward the British, but suddenly, Red Eye darted out of the trees behind the enemy.

He swooped past them, raking his sharp blade along the backs of the enemies' knees. The entire line buckled, falling to the ground without firing a shot. Ross and the others leaped past the wounded enemy. As they began to run, Ross slapped Red Eye on the back. "Proud of you," he said. "You didn't kill anyone."

"Give me time," Red Eye replied.

Ross stopped and turned around suddenly. *Where was Cat?* He had been running behind Midge just a moment ago. "Midge, where's Cat?"

"I dunno, Cap'n," Midge replied, slowing to a trot. He looked around with genuine surprise. "He was right there beside me— leastways until the fountain."

"Jacques, take the men," Ross said. "We'll meet at your mill. If I'm not there in a few minutes, can you lead them on the east road to La Plaine?"

"Oui, mon capitaine," he replied.

Jules started to protest, but Ross said, "I'll find him! He can't be far. Go on, before the reinforcements show up and catch us all. Follow Jacques." Jules nodded, but his glance betrayed much worry and doubt. In a moment, they were gone into the shadows.

Ross ran back past the writhing soldiers at the fountain. Panic beginning to rise in his throat, Ross scanned the woods—every crook and alcove. But there was no sign. "Captain, look out!" It was Cat, but the warning was too late. Something hit Ross hard on the right side of his face. He staggered a few steps and hit the ground. When he looked up, he saw the outstretched blade of Commodore Blake. In his other hand, he held a pistol, leveled at Cat's chest.

"Get up," said Blake. "Slowly!"

Ross rose to one knee. He held out his hands in a calming gesture. "I'm getting up . . . just like you said."

"Drop your sword!" Blake barked. He looked back and forth between Ross and Cat.

"Okay, okay! Just easy with that pistol." Ross let his sword fall to the ground.

Blake looked at Ross quizzically. "Is this lad your son?"

Ross shook his head. "Then tell me," said Blake, "who is he that you would risk so much to save him?"

"I already told you," Ross said, trying to hold the commodore's eyes with his own. "He's one of my crew."

"Really, Captain Ross?" Blake said with contempt. He started to look back at Cat, but too late. "No pirate that I've ever heard of—" Cat's heavy boot slammed into Blake's hand, sending the pistol flying. Blake grunted and wheeled his saber toward Cat, but Ross had snatched his cutlass from the ground and was there to block.

"Run, Cat!" Declan yelled. But Cat started to run the wrong way. Blake pushed away Ross's sword and attacked. "No, the other way!" Ross yelled, repeatedly blocking and dodging Blake's swift blade. "Follow the tree line—argh—to the big church. Then—ah!—head south to the mill with the big waterwheel. I'll meet you there if I can!"

Cat sprinted away just as rays of the morning sun began to cut through the overcast and streamed red through the mist and smoke. Ross and Commodore Blake dueled back and forth beside a barn. Blake was good with a sword—not Red Eye good—but good enough to hold his own for a while. But Ross was stronger and more experienced. He studied Blake's attack and began to predict each move as it came. Soon, Ross pressed his advantage and caught Blake off balance. It was then that Declan Ross revealed the unique talent that had allowed him to best his enemy in almost every previous duel.

In the blink of an eye, Ross switched hands with his cutlass. Now, using his left hand and powerful backhanded slashes, Ross slammed

Blake's sword up against the side of the barn. Ross pinned Blake's weapon there and snapped his right arm, back-fisting the commodore across the cheek and jaw. Blake's saber clattered to the ground, and he staggered and crashed onto his back. The commodore shook his head, spat, and wiped blood from his lips. He started to reach for his pistol, which lay just a few feet from his outstretched hand. But Ross was there and kicked the gun away. Then Ross drew his own pistol and pointed it at Blake. He did not fire. He hesitated, looked at the cutlass in his left hand and back to the pistol in his right.

"What's the matter?" Blake asked. "Can't decide which way to kill me?"

Ross lowered his cutlass and laughed. "Funny Englishman," he said with a snort. "No, I have no desire to kill you. In fact—though my da would roll in his grave if he heard me say this—I rather like you. You're smart." Ross lowered the hammer of his pistol and bent over to meet Blake's eyes. "And you treated my Anne like a lady. For that, you live to fight another day. But, since you probably won't tie yourself up . . ." Ross slammed the end of his pistol against Blake's head. He groaned and slumped to the ground.

Ross put his pistol back into his belt but did not sheathe his cutlass. Hoping desperately not to run into Blake's reinforcements, Ross sprinted away. As he followed the path he hoped Cat had taken to the mill, he realized his mistake. In telling Cat how to get to the mill, he had told Commodore Blake where to find them. Ross could only hope that his British enemy wouldn't regain consciousness until he and his crew were long gone.

22

RACE FOR THE MILL

"Wait! Don't shoot!" cried Midge. He knelt next to a prone Jacques St. Pierre on the balcony on the second floor of his mill. St. Pierre stared down the barrel of a long rifle at a man running frantically toward them from the alley near the church. "Put the gun down, Frenchy! That's Cat. That's our boy!"

Midge slapped Jacques on the shoulder before disappearing down the wrought-iron spiral stair. "You almost made me shoot him," St. Pierre muttered. "Rat-breath idiot!"

They found Cat breathless at the front gate. "Where's the cap'n?" Jules thundered.

"On the other side," Cat huffed. "Not far from the cells. He's fighting Commodore Blake."

"And you didn't stay?"

"He ordered me to go," Cat explained. "I didn't know what else to do—" Jules opened the gate and hauled Cat inside. He began to lift Cat off his feet.

Red Eye was there in an instant. He put a hand on Jules's big forearm. "Easy, Jules. The cap'n gave the lad an order. Cat did the right thing."

"Now, you brawny giant," said St. Pierre. "If you are so anxious to lift things, get back to the task I gave you. The arrangement is good, yes? But not nearly enough barrels. Keep going, eh?"

Cat turned and noticed rows of barrels stacked two and, in some cases, three high all around the perimeter of the mill. Some were hidden behind short palms and other trees, but many more were in plain sight. "What are you doing?"

"I am, how you say, preparing for guests?" St. Pierre replied with a wink. "It is only a short matter of time, I think, before they will arrive." St. Pierre laughed. "Now, if you will excuse me, I have a few more things to make ready."

The Frenchman trod quickly away and disappeared with Midge into the mill. "What's in those barrels?" Cat asked. Jules just laughed and walked away.

Ross rounded the bend and saw the church. The rays of the morning sun had turned golden and splashed the enormous stained-glass windows with light. Ross knew the image emblazoned upon the glass, Christ being taken down from the cross. He'd seen it before in artwork and etchings the monks of St. Celestine had shown him. Something about this version, however, penetrated Ross with a horrible, aching sadness. Maybe it was the deep and somber colors upon the glass. Or maybe it was being so close to the large image—the sun shining, making the wounds so visible. His nail-scarred hands and feet, the crown of thorns, his pierced side—it reminded

Ross of Cat when Jules cradled his limp body on the day they fought Chevillard. *That must be it*, Ross thought as he left the church behind him. He did not look back.

Ross was careful to stay in the alleys and in between buildings whenever he could. He had no idea how many soldiers Blake had in Misson. Anne had said there were a lot . . . hundreds. So Ross ran on and stayed hidden. But there was one place, he knew, just before the mill, where there were no back alleys and no tree cover. He'd have an open sprint of two hundred yards where he'd be as visible as a cardinal in a bare tree to anyone in the central market of Misson.

It was coming up soon, but Ross's view of the marketplace was obscured by the very buildings and trees he'd used for cover. Then he saw a break between buildings up ahead, and he surged ahead for it. He could see the mill, but it seemed a hundred miles away. For as Ross broke free from the cover of the structures and foliage, he saw a huge mass of dark blue marching out of the marketplace toward the mill. British soldiers, more than he could count.

"It's him!" Midge exclaimed.

"Are you sure?" St. Pierre asked. They stood at the balcony and looked back and forth between the army of British soldiers advancing on the mill from the west and a lone man sprinting wildly in from the north.

"Don't you see his coppery beard?" Midge asked. "Y'know, you have bad eyes."

Not as bad as your breath, thought Jacques.

"It's Captain Ross, all right," said Jules. "But will he make it?"

"He had better," said St. Pierre, a sneer curling on his upper lip.

"The capitaine told me I should lead you to La Plaine. I will be furious if I waited here for nothing!"

Jules looked at the advancing army. "That is a lot of soldiers."

"All of you, go now to my study and wait," Jacques commanded. "I will go to the gate for Declan and meet you. We will make our stand by the forge. Ha-ha!" St. Pierre raced out of the room. The others heard his frenzied cackles from the stairwell, and he was gone.

"He told the lad to make for the mill," said Commodore Blake, pointing ahead with his saber. He marched at the front of his men. His head throbbed ferociously from the knot Ross had given him. And he very desperately wanted to settle the score.

"Do you think we will arrive in time?" asked Sir Nigel beside him.

"I do not know how long I was unconscious," Blake growled. "But we will descend upon that mill like locusts. And for the love of king and country, we will find Captain Ross and his men!"

"Look, there!" yelled one of his men. And then they all saw it. A man had raced out of the trees up ahead and seemed in an awful hurry to get to the mill.

"That's him!" cried Commodore Blake. "Now for it, lads! Do not let him get to the mill!"

"I hate not being able to see what's going on!" Cat said as he paced in St. Pierre's study.

"I feel the same," said Red Eye, sheathing a dagger at his side.

"But we've got to be ready. Arm yourself better than that, lad." He picked up one of the pistols on the wide table and tossed it to Cat.

"Wait," said Jules. "No guns."

"What?" Midge looked up. He had four pistols and room for two more in a bandolier across his chest.

"Saint Pierre said no guns," Jules explained.

"I'm keeping them," said Midge, patting the weapons. "They're my babies. Besides, the blasted British will have guns, like as not."

"Yeah, Jules!" said Red Eye. "Why would he tell us not to use our pistols?"

Jules shook his head. "I don't know exactly," he said, though his eyes were bright with suspicion. "I think it has something to do with those barrels of black powder he had me stacking all over the place since we got back."

Midge's eyebrows shot up. "Uh, say, Jules," he said. "'Bout how many barrels of powder you think he's got stacked up round here?"

"More than a hundred," Jules replied.

"Oh." Midge hurriedly removed all his pistols and tossed them on the table.

St. Pierre stood at the wrought-iron gate and waved madly at Ross. "Dépêchez-vous!" he cried. "They are almost upon you!" He looked to the left. The British closed rapidly. The sun gleamed off their bayonets and sabers. But Ross was closer.

The captain of the *William Wallace* charged through the gate, yelling, "Shut the gate! Shut the gate!" as he skidded to a stop beside St. Pierre. "Jacques, what are you still doing here?" he asked.

"Pardonne, mon capitaine," St. Pierre replied. "I could not abandon you to this fate you seem to desire. And I will not just abandon my mill to the British for their looting pleasure. No!" He glanced at the storm of Englishmen approaching. "Now, mon capitaine, are we so polite as to hold the door for our enemy?"

Ross shook his head vigorously.

"Follow me!" St. Pierre led an astonished Declan Ross quickly past a wall of barrels and through the heavy wooden door into the mill. This he closed, locked, and barred.

"That won't hold them for long," Ross said. He turned and started to say something else, but saw the stacks of barrels now on both sides of the hall. "Jacques, what are you doing?"

Jacques St. Pierre did not answer. He knelt by the barrel closest to the door, tugged for a moment, and yanked out its stopper. Black powder immediately began to pour out onto the floor. St. Pierre went methodically from one barrel to the next, pulling out their plugs and letting the powder spill out.

"Jacques, what are you doing?" Ross repeated, his voice growing high and edgy.

Thump. Thump! THUMP!! Sudden, sharp banging at the door made Ross jump. He skidded in the spilled black powder and almost fell. "Ah, our guests are here," said St. Pierre.

"Open up in the name of the British Royal Navy!" came a voice.

Ross grabbed St. Pierre by the shoulders. "Have you lost your mind, Jacques?"

"A long time ago, my friend. Ha-ha!" He looked down at the floor. From the door, halfway to the forge, it was covered in black powder. "Let us get the others, and we shall see if the English have the stomach for my little game."

St. Pierre ran down the hall with Ross hollering behind him. "Jacques, we can't play games with black powder!"

"I can!" he called back. St. Pierre slammed open the study door. "Gentlemen, it is time!"

"Where's the captain?" Jules demanded.

"Right here," Ross said, appearing in the doorway. More shouts came from the other room, muffled by the door at the end of the hall.

"Open this door or we shall break it down!"

"Captain, what do we do?" Midge asked.

Ross looked at St. Pierre. The Frenchman winked, fished out yet another key from the ring that hung on his belt, and opened a cabinet. He quickly took something out, jammed it into a large inner pocket of his surcoat, and winked again.

Ross watched him shrewdly. "Jacques has a plan."

St. Pierre nodded, gestured for them to follow, and hurried out of the room. He led them to the forge, a three-foot cube of gray and black masonry. He opened its heavy cast-iron door, illuminating himself in an angry reddish-orange. Then he lit a torch from the glowing embers inside. He closed the forge and held up the torch for all to see.

"Now, we wait," he said.

23

THE END OF DECLAN ROSS

Hours earlier, while Ross and Red Eye were in Misson trying to spot Cat's cell, Stede stood at the wheel of the *William Wallace* and bade farewell to the scowling Carib face painted high on the mountainside.

"Douse the lights!" Stede ordered as soon as they were underway. Cromwell and several others went from lantern to lantern, snuffing the wicks within. It was probably all for naught, Stede knew. The sun would be up by the time the *Wallace* approached open sea. If the British were there, they'd see the *Wallace*. And all would be lost.

But when the morning sun was already climbing into the sky and the *Wallace* made its final turn in the Roseau River, Stede began to think they had escaped after all. "They're not here," he whispered.

Padre Dominguez lowered his hood. "Well done, Quartermaster!"

The *Wallace* surged into the Caribbean Sea. Stede navigated around the shallower waters and began to swing the ship to a more easterly course. "Look!" Cromwell pointed off the stern.

"Oh no," Stede mouthed as he saw four British warships coming swiftly toward them from the west.

"Can we outrun them?" Padre Dominguez asked.

Stede shook his head. "The frigates, maybe. But they got two schooners, mon. They'll b' on us before we can blink."

At the mill, St. Pierre and the others did not need to wait long for Commodore Blake and his men. Something heavy crashed into the other side of the door. The door shivered. A second strike, and they heard a loud crack. A dusty beam of sunlight shone in for just a moment. With a horrendous ruckus, the door burst open. Several British soldiers carrying a hunk of lumber the size of a tree trunk stepped aside. In walked Commodore Blake and his men.

"Stop!" Jacques St. Pierre commanded. He alone emerged from behind the forge. He held his torch aloft and said again, "Stop! You are trespassers here!"

Blake held up a hand to halt his men. "Frenchman, you have already signed your arrest warrant! Who are you to stand in the way of British military business?"

"I am Jacques Saint Pierre," he replied. "And you have no business here. I do not fear England, I do not fear you, and as you will see . . . I do not fear death!" Ross and his crewmen stepped out and stood beside Jacques. The Frenchman smiled, raised an eyebrow, and glared at Commodore Blake.

"Jacques Saint Pierre?" Blake said. He turned to the man standing next to him. "Sir Nigel, why do I know that name?"

The dark-haired man stepped forward. "Jacques Saint Pierre is wanted for trading goods with known pirates, for high thievery against the East India Trading Company, and for sabotaging the HMS *Surrey* on the Barbary Coast."

"Aw, that last one was never proven!" exclaimed Jacques.

"Be that as it may," Blake said with a wry smile. "There are certainly enough charges to justify your arrest. And after your deeds early this morning . . ." Blake raised a pistol. "I do not care whether we take you dead or alive."

"Commodore," St. Pierre said calmly. "I would not fire that pistol in here, if I were you."

"Why not?"

St. Pierre pointed at the commodore's feet. He and the other British soldiers looked down and saw the black powder. The color drained from their faces. "I apologize for the mess," Jacques explained. "You see the barrels stacked head high on either side of you? I am afraid they are leaking their black powder, and I have not had time to sweep."

Commodore Blake's mouth hung open as he looked at his pistol and understood St. Pierre's implication. "A stray spark," Jacques continued, "from the flintlock of that pistol might just fall into the powder, mon ami. And that would be the end of us all."

Blake and most of his men immediately holstered their guns. Blake unsheathed his saber and said, "Be it by gun or by blade, it matters not. You are all under arrest. If you choose not to cooperate, you will all die here." Commodore Blake came forward.

"I would not take another step, Commodore," said St. Pierre. He waved the torch back and forth and feigned tossing it toward the British soldiers. "If you do, I will throw this torch into the powder at your feet."

"You'll all be killed as well," said Commodore Blake with a nervous laugh. "You're bluffing."

"Am I?" St. Pierre reached into his surcoat pocket and took out a small round object.

"Not another grenade," Blake muttered.

"Yes," said Jacques. "And so that you know I am not bluffing . . ."

St. Pierre held the torch to the grenade's fuse, and the long fuse was lit. The flickering, sparking fire began to hungrily crawl up the winding fuse.

"You're mad!" Blake cried. "You'll kill yourself!"

"Jacques!?" Ross whispered urgently behind him.

St. Pierre ignored Ross and explained, "You see, Commodore, I took a vow a long time ago never to be captured alive. And these men behind me would rather go out on their own terms than endure a trial and a hanging."

"Jacques!" Ross whispered. St. Pierre ignored him again. The fuse continued to burn. It was a quarter of the way gone.

"Come now, Saint Pierre," said Blake nervously. His men shifted uneasily behind him. "You are a bargaining man, right? Perhaps I could arrange for all of the charges against you to be dropped. Just hand over Declan Ross and his crew. And for heaven's sake, put out that fuse!"

"Ah, mon ami," St. Pierre said with a sigh. "It is a temptation, for I almost feel like I could trust you, but no, I have thrown in my lot with Declan Ross. And even if I wanted to put out this fuse, I could not easily do so. It—like the grenade—is special. It is waxed hemp strands filled with powder and then wrapped like a snake around an iron cord. You cannot cut this fuse, pull it out, or put it out—not unless you could drop it into a barrel of water. And alas!" He kicked over the barrel nearest the forge. "My water barrel is now empty."

"You fool!" Blake yelled. He looked at Ross. "Captain Ross, do something!"

Ross, who thought he understood what St. Pierre was doing, said, "What can I do? Like he said, better to die quick than jerking around on the end of a rope."

"You're all mad!"

"At last you understand," said St. Pierre. "Now, Commodore, unless you wish to join our little au revoir, I suggest you and your men depart. And you no doubt noticed the barrels around my mill? They too are filled to bursting with black powder." Jacques looked at the fuse. It was nearing halfway gone. "You have about thirty seconds to get as far away as you can before everything within fifty yards gets blown to pieces!"

Commodore Blake's face contorted into a kind of snarl, but he knew when he was beaten. He ordered his men to retreat, and they fell back quickly, tearing out the door they had broken down and fleeing en masse at top speed.

A few moments later, with just a quarter of the fuse left, Ross grabbed St. Pierre by the shoulder and said, "Jacques, that was great!" Red Eye and the others gathered around the Frenchman. "You sure scared Blake!" Ross continued. "Ha! Remind me never to play cards with you! That was the best bluff I've ever seen!"

St. Pierre's expression turned solemn. "I wasn't bluffing."

Ross's grin vanished. "What?" He laughed nervously. "Very funny. That fake grenade really had them going. It even had me going!"

"It's not fake," said Jacques. The fuse continued to burn.

"What do you mean—Jacques, put it out!!"

"I am afraid I cannot." Jacques St. Pierre looked grimly from eye to eye and said, "I redirected the water troughs from the mountain. The English might have tried to flood the mill and ruin my plans. You see, they are outside—at a distance, yes, but they are waiting.

As I told the good commodore, I will not be captured. Now, gentlemen, it is time to say our good-byes."

The British schooners closed rapidly, but, other than their speed, they made no aggressive movements.

"Why don't they fire?" Padre Dominguez asked.

"Maybe they want to get closer," Stede whispered aloud. "Maybe they—" A flash of orange lit up the ship. Stede leaped to his feet and looked up into the sky over Dominica. The sound that followed was so loud and sudden that Stede and the crewmen of the *Wallace* dove for the deck or ducked. But this was no cannon fire.

When they finally managed to stand, they could see that beyond the foothills, in the direction of Misson, a huge roiling plume of dark smoke and angry red flames was rising into the sky. Stede took advantage of the distraction and sailed the *Wallace* around a bend.

Stede looked back over his shoulder at the rising fireball. "Oh, Declan . . . what have you done?" Just then, Anne stumbled up onto the deck. She stood next to Stede in silence, staring into the sky. Tears welled and spilled down her face. She fell to her knees and wept.

Commodore Blake and his soldiers were a hundred yards away from St. Pierre's mill when the entire structure—the two-story house, the stone base and arch, the waterwheel and framing—was vaporized by an explosion unlike anything they had ever experienced.

Blake coughed and pushed himself up from the dirt. He stood awkwardly. His mouth was agape, and he stared at the inferno, which, a moment ago, had been St. Pierre's mill. The commodore blinked, shook his head, and thought about Declan Ross. He remembered the loyalty this pirate had shown to his crew, risking his life twice just to bring one man back. Blake remembered their duel and the result. "He spared my life," Blake muttered. He looked up at the fireball climbing into the morning sky. "You fool." When Blake said it, he wasn't sure whom he'd meant: Declan Ross for choosing certain death over capture, or himself for driving a decent man into a corner from which the only escape was the grave.

24

GRAVEROBBERS

Clouds gathered over Dominica, casting a pall on the stained-glass window of the church in Misson. Brother Jerome, one of the monks who helped Father Espinosa care for Misson's faithful, wiped the sweat from his brow and continued sweeping the stone walk that divided the graveyard behind the church. Father Espinosa, of course, had gone to help fight the fires that sprang up all around what remained of St. Pierre's mill. And that left Brother Jerome alone in the graveyard. Not that he was afraid to be there alone. After all, Jerome was in the prime of manhood, strong and confident. And it was, in spite of the new cloud cover . . . daytime.

Brother Jerome stopped sweeping a moment and adjusted the collar of his brown robe. The stone walk before him stretched over a hill and followed the graveyard down into a semi-wooded hollow. Brother Jerome swallowed. Wisps of smoke had drifted down into the low-lying areas and now curled slowly around the skeletal trees, the ever-staring statues, and the looming monuments. "Ah! Ridiculous pagan superstition!" he scoffed aloud, finding the sound of his own voice a little bit comforting. "It is nothing. Smoke from a dozen little fires being put out."

He continued sweeping, whistling a favorite hymn, as he worked his way over the hill and down into the hollow. It seemed to grow quieter as he descended. The gloom deepened as well as he worked his way down the stone walk that wound under the canopies of trees and ended near the shadow of the higher hills. Brother Jerome looked back up the hill to the church, which suddenly seemed a hundred miles away. Feeling as if someone were watching him, he spun around. But the only thing there was a stone angel. She guarded a gravesite with outstretched wings. Her large blank eyes made Jerome shiver. *Calm yourself! You've been down here a thousand times,* he told himself.

Then he heard a short scraping sound—like stone grating against stone. Brother Jerome wheeled around, holding up his broom like a weapon. He looked at a large stone sarcophagus just ten feet away. The name engraved there identified the deceased as Jourdan Sebastian Prewitt. Born 1659. Died 1712. *Dead only a few years*, thought Jerome. The inscription along the side of the stone coffin was in Latin. Thanks to the expert teaching of Father Espinosa, Jerome could read Latin very well. Just this once, he wished he hadn't been such a good student. The inscription read: *Venio cum gladio de mortuis.*

I come with sword from death. Jerome started to shake. He heard the scraping sound again. This time longer. And he noticed the slab lid of the sarcophagus had shifted. Then he heard an otherworldly voice, spoken from far away and yet, still near.

". . . waited long enough," said the voice, heavily accented in French. *Jourdan Sebastian Prewitt*, thought Brother Jerome. *That is a Frenchman's name!*

The stone lid began to move. He could now see a dark gap where the slab had moved away. Tendrils of dust drifted out and curled like fingers around the sarcophagus. "Time to escape this foul tomb," said the voice. "Time to rise . . ."

The stone lid seemed to move on its own accord. It slid across the tomb and fell with a crash at its side. Rivers of gray dust flowed over the edges of the now open grave. Brother Jerome dropped his broom. He felt frozen in place. His heartbeat thundered. Slowly, a pale figure shrouded in the swirling dust began to rise up. He wore a wide-brimmed hat from which wild, curly dark hair fell like a veil and an old frock coat. In his hand was a menacing silver sword. As he rose, he turned and saw the terrified monk. Brother Jerome, at last overcome by the appearance of this apparition, fell unconscious to the ground right next to his broom.

"Who is that?" Ross asked, emerging behind Jacques St. Pierre.

"One of Father Espinosa's faithful," Jacques replied. "Jerome, I think, is his name."

"Did he recognize you?"

Jacques shook his head and hopped over the edge of the tomb. "I do not think so. The way he passed out like that . . . I think he thought I was a fantôme. Eh, how you say . . . a ghost."

Ross laughed. "We might have all been ghosts!" he said as he followed St. Pierre. Jules, Red Eye, Midge, and Cat emerged immediately after. "Jacques, I thought you'd killed us all."

"In truth . . . ," said St. Pierre, thoughtfully stroking his thin moustache, "I would rather die on my own terms, certainly not at the hands of the British!"

"How long'd it take you to dig that tunnel?" Jules asked, seeing the Frenchman in a whole new light.

"Moi?" St. Pierre snorted. "Even if I had muscles like yours, it would have taken twenty years. But I am friendly with the Carib. We trade goods often. For three years, they helped me with the tunnel and to excavate my special room. Alas! It is gone now. But what I had stashed away in the mill is only a drop in the bucket!"

"You mean . . . you have more?" asked Midge.

"Of course," Jacques replied with a dismissive wave. "I have other caches all over the islands. But before I say another thing, Declan, I have a favor to ask of you."

"Name it," Ross replied.

"What you have done for me," Jacques began. "What we have done for each other . . . it makes us more than just trading partners. It makes us brothers. I wish to sail with you on the *William Wallace*. I wish to join your crew. Will you have me?"

"YES!!" answered Jules, Red Eye, Midge, and Cat simultaneously.

"Gladly," Ross said, grinning. "You can sign the articles the moment we get on board."

"Merci beaucoup, mon capitaine!" said Jacques. He grinned and shook Ross's hand repeatedly. "Then I will tell you, I have a grand fortification on the Caicos Islands. There we will gather a dozen of those cannons you like so much. And anyone who dares oppose the *William Wallace* on your—on our—journey, will be sorry. Ha-ha!"

Brother Jerome moaned softly and began to stir. "Now, Capitaine Ross, we need to get moving lest the British discover our ruse. The Carib have shown me the quickest paths, but it is still six miles to La Plaine."

"Let's go," Ross replied. St. Pierre led the way and set a quick pace. All the while, Ross wondered if Stede and the *Wallace* would be there when they got to La Plaine.

25

THE LOCKET

In his cabin on board the *Raven*, Bartholomew Thorne scraped a thin knife through the barbs of his walking stick. He always kept it with him, and, after use, he always kept it clean. But now he scratched and scraped and gouged—much harder than he needed. Flecks of dried blood, even pieces of wood fell away. Harder and harder he worked, his breathing deepening to a phlegmy growl. Finally, he pushed the knife against the wood with such force that it stabbed into the meat of his right palm.

He didn't yell . . . he didn't feel it. The fire-scarred flesh on that hand would never feel pain again. Thorne removed the blade and absently watched dark blood ooze out of the new wound. *A little payback from beyond the grave, Father?* Thorne did not smile at the thought. The monk had endured more pain than Thorne ever thought possible. But when, at last, his old, stubborn will was broken, Father Valentia had uttered the last name Bartholomew Thorne had ever expected to hear: Declan Ross.

Ross had taken the map—correction—the human map, Padre Dominguez. *Why?* Thorne wondered. *Declan knows better than to cross me. He'd had enough room on that old brig of his to take all the monks. But he didn't. He only took Padre Dominguez.*

The most obvious answer was the treasure. Like any pirate, Ross would be drawn to the promise of legendary wealth. Still, there was plenty of gold to be had from the fat Spanish galleons that sailed the Caribbean. Thorne stabbed the knife into the top of his desk. Of course, Ross could be seeking vengeance at last for old debts . . . but why now? Why after all these years? No, Thorne decided, Ross wasn't the vengeful type. He wouldn't put his life, the lives of his crew, in danger just to right such long-buried offenses from the past.

Thorne leaned back in his chair and looked out the aft windows. He couldn't see Scully's little sloop from this angle. Only the endless turquoise of the sea and, of course, the white sand and swaying palms of the island. This small patch of hilly land in the middle of the Caribbean had once been called *Isla Aves* for the myriad of tropical birds found there. But after Bartholomew Thorne claimed it and made it one of his central ports of operation, it became known as Death's-Head Island.

Thorne got up and went to the starboard window. There it was, Scully's ship, bobbing in the water, dwarfed by the other ships of Thorne's growing fleet. Scully wasn't much good in a fight, but his sloop was fast, and the man had a way of getting information. Thorne shook his head. *Scully's warning saved us in Dominica.* The British had come too late.

Thorne had never asked Scully who his source in the British navy was, but as long as the information kept coming, he didn't really care. Scully would have news. He always did. Thorne expected his quartermaster, Mr. Skellick, to come down any minute with much to tell.

Thorne went back to his desk and sat down. Feeling uneasy, he reached, as he often did, to the upper drawer on the left. It slid open easily. Bright afternoon sun from the aft windows glistened on an oval silver locket. Thorne picked it up and held it in his scarred hand. Ironic, really. He'd hated it when she gave it to him. *A pirate doesn't hold to such dainties!* he'd said. Now, he held this locket the most dear of all his treasures. He had been a fool to attack the British port at Southampton. Their trap had been well set, and their cannons had wrought havoc on the *Raven*. So many lives were lost that day. But only one was real to Thorne. In the fire, he hadn't been able to save her, but he still had the locket.

He opened it slowly and gazed down upon a small painted image of his first wife—his only wife, really. The others were nothing, distractions or parasites. Only Heather mattered. He ran a finger over the paint, lovingly tracing the outline of her heart-shaped face.

The color of her hair in the painting wasn't quite right anymore. It was too dark, absent the crimson fire that shimmered when Heather stood on deck in the sunlight. But the eyes were definitely right. Almond-shaped, deep green like a stormy sea. It was Heather. But as he stared at her eyes in the picture, they seemed to change. There was anger there now, and, worse, disappointment. Within him, an ache began to pulse, and he could feel his throat constrict. The hand holding the locket began to tremble. His heartbeat raced. *What's wrong with me?* he wondered. He'd lost the map, and he'd lost it to Ross—that was it. But Heather's eyes in the locket . . . how they seemed to accuse . . .

Thorne snapped shut the locket. "No!" he rasped. "It's not my fault!" With an enraged growl, Thorne raked the top of his desk with his right arm, sending the knife, a mug, and a lantern crashing to the floor.

What is the matter, my darling?

Bartholomew Thorne froze. He'd heard a voice. He looked nervously around his quarters. His eyes fell at last on the silver locket. "Heather?" he whispered. His quarters became deathly quiet. Thorne shook his head.

Ross will not get far. You will hunt him down and take what is yours.

"NO!" Thorne yelled, placing the locket in the drawer and slamming it shut. He stood up, knocking over his chair. "I can't hear you! You, you're dead!"

"Sir?" Thorne looked up, and Skellick stood in the doorway. He did not speak. He looked pale and shaken.

"What's wrong?" Thorne rasped.

Skellick swallowed. "Uh . . . nothing, sir. Well . . . I thought I heard—"

"What did you hear, Quartermaster?" Thorne's breathing became audible.

"N-nothing, sir. I came to tell you. Scully's brought word."

"The cays?" Thorne asked. Skellick nodded. "Chevillard?" Skellick nodded again. "What's he done now?"

"Well, sir, it's not so much what he's done—"

"Out with it, Mister Skellick," Thorne commanded, his voice thick and raspy.

"He's dead, sir. A week ago . . . Chevillard and many of his crew. His ship was sent to the bottom near Rogue's Cay. Scully picked up the survivors—'bout forty in all."

"What happened?"

"They were tricked by another pirate."

"Who dared come to my cay?" Thorne tightened his grip on the bleeding stick and ground his teeth audibly. "Who?"

"Declan Ross."

A wave of hate overwhelmed Thorne. He began to tremble. He clenched his fist so hard that blood ran from his wounded hand and dripped onto the barbs of his bleeding stick. His thoughts churned like a cauldron of lava. It didn't really matter why Ross had ignored the death's-head he had left on St. Celestine. It didn't matter why Ross had gotten between him and Constantine's Treasure. And it didn't matter why Ross attacked Chevillard. Declan Ross and his crew would have to die.

"Skellick, get word to the other ships: A king's ransom in gold for the captain who finds the *William Wallace*. It is an old brigantine—not especially fast, not especially well armed. Ross tends to hunt the shipping lanes from the north coast of Venezuela up to the cays near Port Royal. Find the ship, kill the crew, but Ross has a priest aboard. A monk named Dominguez. He is not to be harmed. Is that understood?"

"Every word, Captain," replied the quartermaster.

"And tell our resourceful friend Mister Scully, as he makes his usual rounds among the British, to find out anything he can about Ross. Scully will meet us . . ." Thorne looked down at his sea chart. "Isla Mona, the rocky eastern coast—in two days. Advise Scully not to be late."

"Aye, sir."

"Good," Thorne said as he stood. Thinking he was dismissed, Skellick turned to leave. "And Mister Skellick . . ."

"Yes, sir?"

"You said that forty men survived the battle with Declan Ross?"

Skellick nodded. "Some wounded in varying degrees, sir, around forty."

"Once we are out to sea again, have the wounded thrown overboard. Then send the others to me one at a time, five minutes apart."

26
WRITTEN ON HER HEART

How long will we wait?" Cromwell asked. He leaned over the rail on the portside of the *Wallace* and gazed into the dark tree line of La Plaine on Dominica's east coast.

"Suppose it b' ya out there," Stede replied. "How long would ya want us to wait, eh?"

Cromwell edged away from the quartermaster. He had no desire to be thrown overboard again.

On the forecastle deck, far from Stede and the others, Anne sat in a dark nook between two barrels. She had her head bowed into the palm of one hand and anxiously twirled a long lock of her crimson hair with the other. How had it all gone so terribly, terribly wrong? All she'd wanted to do was help Cat find out who he was, to take him ashore just long enough to get the clue that he needed.

Who am I kidding? Anne chided herself. *I just wanted to get rid of him.* She stood up and began to pace the deck. She paused each time at the port rail and strained to see the flicker of a torch, some sign that her father, the others—and Cat—were returning safely. But a weight in the pit of her stomach told her otherwise. She'd seen the towering fiery plume surge high above the island. She knew one way or the other that her father had been involved. Anne couldn't keep from imagining scenes of his death . . . and all because of her. With each lap back and forth, her despair—and her anger—grew.

Her skin suddenly prickled, and she felt a presence behind her. Drawing her dagger, she wheeled about. There stood a dark, hooded figure. He loomed menacingly over her, and she struck. But deftly, the shadowy being moved. Anne felt a pain in her wrist, and the dagger slipped from her hand. Anne clutched at her throbbing wrist and looked up. Her blade was now in the hands of her attacker. He held the dagger out and came toward her.

"Commodore! Commodore Blake!" came a loud voice from behind.

Standing in the still-smoldering ruins of St. Pierre's mill, Blake turned and saw that it was Father Espinosa. The gigantic monk did a kind of waddle-run. His cheeks were red and bulged like pink grapefruits, and he breathed heavily. There was another monk with him.

"Commodore Blake!" yelled the large man. He yelled, in spite of the fact that he stood now only a few feet away.

"Yes, uh . . ." Blake looked up and saw the long brown robes. "What can I do for you?"

"Nothing, I suppose, but perhaps I can do something for you." He gestured to the other monk. "This is Brother Jerome. He has found something I think you should see."

Something in the way that he said it . . . something in the look on Father Espinosa's face made Blake feel uneasy. "Sir Nigel!" he called.

"Yes, sir?" answered the slender, dark-haired soldier.

"Bring ten of your best. Make sure they're armed."

Brother Jerome led them north to the church and down into the graveyard. "I was just sweeping the walk," he explained. "A mist or maybe smoke began to creep in, and it became very quiet." Brother Jerome led them down the cobblestone walk into the hollow. The mountain's shadow had deepened. "I stopped just up ahead," he said, gesturing. "I heard a strange sound." He led them to a large stone sarcophagus. "The tomb opened, and someone . . . someone came out of the grave!"

Father Espinosa led them over to the edge of the tomb. "As you might understand," he said, "Brother Jerome was overcome by the, uh, startling appearance. When he came to, he bravely looked into the tomb . . . and found this."

Blake and his men drew near. "Stairs!" he said aloud.

"Should we follow them?" asked Sir Nigel.

"No need," Blake replied. "I already know where they will lead." He was quiet for a moment. "I am afraid I have vastly under-estimated Declan Ross and his men. Sir Nigel, once we finish help-ing with the cleanup at the mill site, we will return to the fleet. I've had enough of fighting on land. Let us take to the sea and challenge Ross to elude us there."

"What about Bartholomew Thorne?" Nigel asked.

"I have not forgotten Thorne," Blake replied. "But his trail has gone cold. We shall take our fleet and form a sea net. We will drag the Caribbean north and east of Dominica and see what we catch!"

The dark, hooded figure now had Anne's dagger. "You should be more careful with such weapons," he said, returning her dagger to her as he lowered his hood.

"Padre Dominguez?" Anne's mouth remained open as she sheathed her dagger. "I could have killed you."

"No," he replied. "I do not think so."

Anne still felt a slight throb in her wrist from when he had disarmed her. "How did you do that?"

"I wasn't always a priest," Padre Dominguez said, but he did not elaborate. He stood very still and did not speak for several moments. He seemed to be waiting. All the while, she could feel him watching her.

Anne had marveled at his dark eyes that first day in St. Celestine. Even in the bright sunlight, they were as black as pitch. But the darkness there was not the color of emptiness. No, if anything, Padre Dominguez's eyes were too full—full of knowledge, full of history, full of wisdom.

"I climbed the ladder and stood here on the forecastle deck," he said, breaking the silence at last. "I watched you pacing. I thought you knew I was here."

Anne looked away and shook her head. "I'm sorry . . . I was just lost in thought."

"So I noticed," he said. "You are troubled."

It hadn't been phrased as a question. Anne shifted uneasily from one foot back to the other. When she looked again into his eyes, she found there was compassion and more than that . . . peace. Peace, like a still lake on a moonless night. Anne felt as if a cork had been removed from her heart. Everything just spilled out.

"My father, Cat, Jules—all of them—they are dead!" she cried. "And it's my fault!"

"We do not know they are dead," he said.

"But if they are, it's my fault. Father told me I couldn't go on the island, but I didn't listen. I was angry, and when I saw how badly Cat wanted to go, how Father was keeping him prisoner too, . . . well I . . . I just had to do something." Anne blinked and looked away. "I know Dominica well enough," she said. "I just figured we'd go look around a bit and be back on the *Wallace* before anyone knew."

"But you had other motives."

Anne felt her throat tighten. "How, how did you know?"

"You are a passionate person, Anne Ross," he said. "You are moved to action by these passions, and when these actions cause harm, you bear the guilt . . . and rightly so. But there is something else, I think. You also have the writing of God on your heart."

"What?" Anne almost laughed out loud. "Writing of God? But I don't even believe—" He cut her off with a wave of his hand.

"Beneath your passions," he said, "there lives a powerful sense of justice, something that weighs and measures not only what you do—but why you do it. This is the writing of the Almighty."

Anne quietly rocked back and forth on her heels.

Padre Dominguez continued, "The Scriptures say 'the law of God is written on their hearts.' I am convinced, it is written on yours."

"Padre Dominguez," she replied, shaking her head. "I . . . I don't know what you're talking about."

"Do you not?" he asked, his eyes penetrating. "Tell me, the pain you feel now . . . would you still feel it as intensely if you had acted solely out of charity?"

Anne did not answer.

"If you had done all this because you honestly thought it would help Cat—and no other reason—would your sorrow be the same?"

Anne began to tremble. What was with this priest? He seemed to see right through her, and every word he said peeled her open like a plantain. She rushed to the rail and began to sob. "My father," she cried, "just welcomed Cat aboard, just accepted him, made him part of everything. I'm his daughter. I'm his flesh and blood! And he hardly even talks to me—except to say no. I wanted to get rid of Cat. Not kill him, I mean . . . I just wanted him off the ship. Back in his own life."

Padre Dominguez put a light hand on her shoulder. "Your father loves you, Anne. In my short stay aboard the *Wallace*, I have seen it. He watches you with great pride. He talks of you often. But he is a man of many responsibilities. And in the midst of them all, he is afraid . . . afraid that he can no longer protect you as he should."

She turned around, wiping away tears. "But he doesn't have to keep me in a cage. He . . . can't keep me in a cage."

"No . . . no, he cannot. And I suspect that he knows this, and it gnaws at him every moment he thinks of you." The monk put up his hood, but before he turned to walk away, he said, "Your father is the captain of a ship, a man used to making decisions, directing others—having the answers when others fail. But with you . . . with you, he does not have the answers. You will have to show him. And it will begin when you learn to read what is written on your heart."

He descended from the forecastle and disappeared somewhere on the main deck. *A strange man*, Anne thought. *One minute he took away my dagger like I'd never held one before, and the next, he's reading my mind.*

No one had ever spoken to her like that before. He seemed so supremely confident . . . and peaceful. Anne pondered his words. She didn't know what to think about all this "God writing things on your heart." She hadn't really given God much of a thought since her mother died when she was about four. She had vague memories of her mother taking her to church. She remembered the nice vicar with rosy cheeks. He used to press a sugar stick that tasted of peppermint into her little hand as she passed through the receiving line after the service each week. But after her mother died, Anne went to sea with her father. And many things changed for Anne.

It wasn't that she blamed God for her mother's death. It was all too common for people to get sick and die in Edinburgh on the windy east coast of Scotland. But her father, a man who admittedly never darkened the door of a church himself, only mentioned God in brief rote prayers before dinner.

Anne put her head down on the rail and drifted off into thought. She did not see the small flickers of yellow light in the trees on-shore. She didn't see the small band of men leave the trees and board the cutter Stede had left ashore. But when Declan Ross and the others came aboard, she heard them. But even as her heart surged with gratitude and joy at their return, another part of her wondered about what the monk had said.

Anne climbed down from the forecastle and walked through the shadows of the main deck. She had directly disobeyed the captain of the ship . . . her father. And because of that, the lives of many had been put in danger.

"You have much to account for, daughter," Ross said. "But that must wait. We need to put to sea. I want to get as far away from Dominica as we can by morning. For now, you and Cat are confined to your quarters." That was the only thing Anne's father had said to her.

She twisted and turned in her bed and listened to the waves slap the ship. One after another. *Smack . . . smack . . . smack.* The sea was restless. Anne was too. As the daughter of the captain, and the only female on board, Anne had her own quarters. It was small, just a closet, really, but it had never felt so small and confining as it did this night. Anne closed her eyes and wondered if there was anything, anything at all, written on her heart.

27
MOSES'S LAW

The next day was dreadfully hot. The crew of the *William Wallace* stood in a circle around the mainmast on the steaming deck. The ship was well out to sea, en route to St. Pierre's stronghold in the Caicos Islands. But, by Ross's command, they'd lowered all but the smallest sails and slowed considerably.

Ross stood at the wheel. His back was straight, his shoulders thrown back. But to every sailor gathered there, he looked miserable. His eyes that usually sparkled with energy—and mischief—were bloodshot. His effervescent grin was gone, replaced by a morose scowl. He stood at the wheel while Stede prepared to read from the articles of the *William Wallace* concerning the charges against Anne and Cat.

As quartermaster, Stede was in charge of maintaining discipline aboard the ship, but even he had trouble choking out the words. He knew the code. He knew what the code required. But he didn't want to see justice done this time. *Too young, they are,* he thought.

He cleared his throat and did his duty. "For missing yer appointed wark shift and making others take up the slack . . . five lashes." At the mention of lashes, Nubby's head turned abruptly. He stared at Cat and swallowed.

"B'ing off the ship without leave," Stede continued, "five lashes." The crew murmured. Red Eye shook his head.

"For recklessly endangering the lives of the crew"—Stede grimaced—"ten more lashes." Tears spilled down Anne's cheeks.

"But above all charges held against ya, stands this one: directly disregarding the law of the captain's command . . ." Stede looked away and at last whispered, "mutiny. For this the punishment is marooning on a solitary isle or . . . death."

The crew knew the consequence for mutiny, but still, hearing it levied against Anne and Cat caused an uproar. Opinions became more and more enflamed. A fistfight broke out between Drake and one of the younger crewmen. Jacques St. Pierre tried to break it up, but a dagger was drawn—

BOOM!! Stede fired his thunder gun into the air. The deck went silent. Smoke encircled the quartermaster's head, and he glared at the crew. "Now shut yer mouths, all of ya! I don't like it any more than the rest. But beating each other to a bloody mess won't help."

"But, Stede, they're just kids!" Red Eye exclaimed.

"The law is hard," Stede said. "But the law b' the law."

"Aw," complained Midge, "it's not like they joined up with Bartholomew Thorne or . . . showed the British where we are! A dumb choice, yes, but no more'n that! Cap'n, can't we cut 'em some slack?"

"Yeah!!" many others of the crew yelled. Cat stared impassively out to sea. Anne looked up at her father.

Declan Ross had made many hard decisions as captain of the

William Wallace, but none weighed on him like this one. "The articles of the *William Wallace* are very clear on this point: the captain's word must be followed. If the chain of command is violated and nothing is done to set it right, then we have nothing to keep this crew together. Nothing to keep us sane. Each of you went on the register. Each of you signed. There's no way around—"

"They didn't sign." A deep voice came from the crowd. Jules stepped forward.

Stede looked at him sideways. "What?"

"Cat and Anne . . . ," Jules said. "They never signed the articles."

No one spoke. The sun seemed to grow hotter still. The crew exchanged nervous glances. Stede, whose face had been a mask of concentration for a few moments, broke into the broadest grin possible. "This b' true!" he yelled. "If they didn't sign the articles, they ain't really members of the crew, right, mon?" He looked up at Ross.

"Perhaps," muttered their captain. "Perhaps we cannot punish them as we would one of the crew."

"I say we let them off!" said Red Eye. "They've learned their lesson."

"But, Captain!" shouted Drake. The graybeard stepped into the circle made by the crew. "Maybe they didn't sign. But we can't just excuse their deeds. They willfully turned against your own command and in so doing betrayed us all!" Some in the crew shook their head. Others agreed with Drake.

"They must be whipped at least!" someone shouted.

Someone else cried, "Give 'em Moses's Law!"

"Vote on it!" Jules thundered above all other voices.

Stede looked at the captain. He nodded. "Vote on it, we will!" said Stede. "All those who'll call Cat and Anne mutineers and see them be hanged or marooned, say so now!" A wave of relief washed over Cat and Anne—and Declan Ross too—for no one, not even Drake, raised a hand.

Stede went on. "Those in favor of letting them off altogether, cast yer vote now."

Red Eye's hand shot into the air. Midge's came next, followed by Jules and Cromwell. It was the first time the two of them had agreed on anything. Anne and Cat looked around, but no other hands went into the air.

Stede sighed. He knew already what the crew had decided. "Moses's Law?"

One by one, hands went up, until it became clear that a majority had been reached. "Moses's Law it b'," whispered Stede.

Stede went to the mainmast. The canvas bag bound there was hung high to make it very visible at all times. In this way, men knew what punishment awaited if they failed in their duties. Stede reached in and pulled out a thick wooden handle covered in a coarse leather sheath. From one end of this thick segment slithered a long tapering strand of braided leather.

"Moses's Law," said Stede, holding up the whip so all could see. "That be forty lashes lacking one. I choose to divide it twenty lashes for Anne. Nineteen for Cat." Alarm bright and urgent in her eyes, Anne looked at Cat.

"You can't do that!" Nubby burst out of the crowd. "You saw the condition Cat was in when we got 'im. The wounds are just now beginning to heal. You start whipping 'im again with that torturous weapon, and . . . you'll kill 'im!"

"I'll take his lashes," came Anne's quiet voice.

Padre Dominguez looked up. He nodded.

Cat turned and scowled at Anne as if she couldn't possibly have uttered anything more horrible. "Anne, no! I must take the punishment due to me."

"You wouldn't be due any punishment at all if I hadn't put the idea in your head and led you overboard!" Anne's face reddened. Her eyes pleaded. "Please . . . ," she said. "I am to blame for this."

For Declan Ross, the misery that pounded his heart like storm waves on a sandy shore abated suddenly—replaced by an altogether different feeling. Anne seemed to change right before him. The willowy little girl, all dimples and attitude, a mischievous pixie with red pigtails—she was still there. But now there was also a steadfast young woman. Ross looked away and nodded to his quartermaster.

"Very well, then," said Stede. He went to Anne, took her hand, and led her to the starboard rail. He gently placed her hands upon the rail. Then he whispered something in her ear.

She looked back suddenly. "Do you think he'll allow it?" she asked.

"He'll have to," Stede replied. He turned away and marched ten paces across the deck. He looked one last time up to Declan Ross. Stede silently willed his captain to put a stop to all this. But he knew Ross couldn't. To go against the vote of the crew, to show favoritism to his own kin, and to ignore the ship's articles would invite irreparable problems and perhaps . . . real mutiny.

Stede turned and faced Anne's back. He lifted the flail weapon and drew back his arm. Knowing that this whip would fall thirty-eight more times, he let fly his first stroke with much less force than he would have normally. Still the whip snapped upon Anne's back, and she let out a sharp cry. It had not cut through the material of her shirt, but Anne felt the warm sting of a new welt across her shoulder blades. Stede aimed the second stroke much lower. Anne arched her back and swallowed the pain.

"This isn't right!" Cat yelled. "I am just as much at fault." He took a step forward but was hauled back in by Jules's iron grip. Cat struggled, but it was no use. The third whip stroke fell. Anne grunted.

"Let it be, son," Jules said. "For just a moment more."

Cat relented, and Jules released him. Cat turned and looked up at the gigantic pirate. *What did he mean, 'for just a moment more'?* Jules glared at Red Eye as the fourth stroke fell. A thin red trail spread across Anne's shirt. Red Eye's mouth hung open—his face betraying an unspoken question. Stede nodded, and Red Eye ran forward into the center of the circle.

"Hold that whip, Quartermaster!" he commanded. A mixture of puzzlement and anger on his brow, Ross looked at Red Eye. Stede turned around.

"Don't ya b' interrupting the discipline, mon," Stede said. "Unless ya wish to earn some lashes for yerself."

"That is exactly what I mean to do," said Red Eye. "Anne's felt the sting, she's paid her debt, but we have not paid ours!"

"What are you talking about?" the captain called down.

"Anne was wrong to leave the ship," Red Eye explained. "But if it wasn't for her and Cat, we might all be shackled guests in the hull of a British brig." The crew murmured.

"I'm listening," said Ross.

Red Eye smiled mischievously. "When Anne and Cat got themselves captured," he continued, "they acted as spies, really. Found out Commodore Blake's plan, they did. Blast! We didn't even know the British were on the island! If we hadn't heard it from Anne, hadn't moved the ship round east when we did, we'd have been cut off."

"That doesn't change a thing," Drake said. He approached Red Eye. "The crew voted Moses's Law—that's got to be paid!"

"And paid it shall be," said Red Eye. "Thirty-five lashes left, by my count. I for one will gladly take a lash or two to show gratitude for our freedom—which we owe to Anne and Cat. Now, which of you will share in the pain?"

One by one, crewmen came forward. Even Drake himself volunteered. He walked slowly by Cat and whispered in his gravelly voice, "The law is the law. No hard feelings."

"What do you say, Captain?" asked Red Eye. "We'll take the remainin' strokes and consider the debt paid?"

"Put it to the vote," Ross said, trying to keep his relief from being obvious.

"Wait!" Stede exclaimed. "B'fore we vote, I think we should add something to make sure there b' no more confusion over their punishment in the future. After the whipping's done, let Anne and Cat sign the register."

Ross felt like he'd been hit in the gut by a cannonball. The eyes of all the crew were on him, but none weighed more heavily than Anne's. He knew she was old enough, and he couldn't deny Anne's recent display of responsibility. Still . . .

"Shall we put it to a vote?" Stede asked. Reluctantly, Declan Ross nodded. "What b' the will of the crew? Shall we accept thirty-five strokes of the whip on our own backs to pay Anne and Cat's debt? And shall we swear them in as full members of the crew of the *Wallace*?"

Hands went up—almost all. Drake wanted it made clear that he would accept the lashes, but had no desire for Anne to sign the register. "Bad luck," he muttered over and over. But in spite of his misgivings, it was decided.

Red Eye went first. Gritting his teeth, he took two strokes. Jules went next. The first lash hit his broad back with a strange muffled snick. "Too weak, Stede!" Jules complained. "You can do better than that!"

Stede shook his head and let fly. The braided leather cracked in the air and snapped upon the massive pirate's bare flesh. Jules grunted satisfaction and rolled his shoulders backward. "Ah, that's real, now," said Jules.

Some taking a pair of lashes, others just one, the crew went to the rail. Anne stood by Jules and buried her head on his shoulder. For Cat, it was a misery to endure. Not only had Anne and the others been disciplined in his place, but there was something else. Cat watched the whip stream through the air over Stede's head, watched it curl like a snake behind him, and then suddenly reverse course, snapping violently forward. Cat's head began to throb. A muffled buzzing came to his ears. He blinked. He saw a flash of another place—definitely not the deck of the *Wallace*.

Cat turned and stumble-stepped through the crewmen. He disappeared around a bulkhead and leaned on the portside rail. *Take this, my son,* came a voice, feminine and deep. Tender like before, but with a trace of urgency or . . . alarm. An image flashed into Cat's mind—the leather satchel held out by a slender hand. Another hand receiving it. *Within this pouch, you will find help for your journey out of this life. It is everything that I can give you. Wait! One more thing.* The flash of a dagger, and she dropped a two-inch lock of her hair into the pouch. *Keep it safe, and when the time is right, get away and never look back.* Cat couldn't see her face, just a glimpse of a smile— loving and yet somehow full of sorrow. She turned suddenly. Her luxurious red hair swung round. A door opened. A scream. Then a loud crack of the whip. *Where is it, boy?* A different voice, harsh and angry, more like a feral growl. *I know she told you. Out with it!* Another crack of the whip, and Cat fell to his knees and wretched.

"Cat?" Anne came around the bulkhead. "Cat!" She ran to him, saw that he had been sick. "It's over," she said. "The whipping . . .

it's done." She put her arms around his shoulders and helped him stand. "Cat, I'm so sorry."

"It's not that," he whispered. His hand went to the leather pouch that hung from his belt. "I heard the voices again."

Anne took in a sharp breath. "Did you know them? Do you . . . remember?"

Cat shook his head. "I . . . I think one of them was my mother," he said. "She called me son."

"There were others?"

"One other," he said, his words barely audible. "I don't know . . . he frightens me."

Led by their captain and Stede, a number of crewmen came around the corner and found Cat and Anne. "Cat!" Ross exclaimed. "Are you all right?"

Nubby barged in. "No, he's not all right," he barked. "Can't you see?"

"Nubby, take Cat below," Ross ordered. "Give him fresh water. He looks pale."

"It's the whippin', isn't it, lad?" said Nubby, leading Cat away. "It brought something back."

Cat woke up with a start, rocking his hammock. *How long was I asleep?* he wondered. He remembered Nubby giving him three mugs of water, some fresh biscuits, and a plantain. But that had been in the broad afternoon sun. Now it was dark. An oil lantern hung near the door. Its flame was turned way down low.

Cat untied the leather pouch, reached in, and removed the lock of red hair. He smoothed it with his finger and wondered about his mother. He still could not picture her whole face. Just the sad smile and her hair. But somehow, he knew she had loved him. That brought Cat a mixture of comfort and pain. He wondered what had happened to her. He reached into the pouch and withdrew the cross. He'd managed to brush away most of the tarnish. The silver reflected back the orange lantern's light.

"Why did you give me this?" he thought aloud.

He reached once more into the pouch and removed the green jewel. He heard the echo of the other voice, hard and terrible. *Where is it, boy?* Cat held the cross in one hand, the jewel in the other. He wondered which one the hideous man from his memory was after.

28
THE ARTICLES OF AGREEMENT

The sun was bright overhead, but not as hot as the previous day. The crew of the *Wallace* enjoyed the stiff wind as they continued their voyage to the Caicos Islands. They gathered again near the mainmast. A black flag with the white silhouette of a prowling wolf above a Scottish claymore sword, the flag of the *Wallace*, flew high overhead. Jacques St. Pierre, Cat, and Anne stood in the midst of them. They listened as Drake continued the ceremonial reading of the Articles of Agreement. Drake held up the large parchment and read in a loud voice, "Article Seven. If any man shall not keep his arms clean and fit for engagement, or neglect his business, he shall be cut off from his share and suffer such additional punishment as the crew shall think fit."

Cat felt a little poke from behind. "I'll help you with that," said Red Eye.

"Article Eight. He that shall be found guilty of cowardly deeds in a time of engagement, that same man shall be marooned or hanged." At the mention of marooned, Drake made momentary eye contact with Cat. "And lastly, Article Nine. If any man shall lose a hand or foot in time of engagement, he shall have four hundred pieces of eight. If he shall lose an entire limb, that same man shall gain eight hundred pieces of eight."

"What'd ya do with all that money, Nubs?" cracked Midge to the general merriment of all. Nubby, on the other hand, wasn't very amused.

"I spent most of it on pots, pans, and knives," he said. "But I held back a wee bit of silver and bought a special poison that dissolves in food. You know, for a special occasion."

The crew roared at that, but Midge's laughter was nervous at best. All eyes then turned to the quarterdeck where their captain had just appeared. "Why is he wearing a dress?" Cat whispered.

"It's not a dress," Anne said, giggling even though she was trying to sound angry. "It's a kilt."

"It looks like a dress."

"Don't let him hear you say that," Anne warned. "You'll be scraping the whole deck by yourself. My family is very proud of its Scottish roots. The Clan Ross is very powerful in Scotland."

"Do they all wear dresses?"

Anne slapped him on the shoulder. "Just stop. Father only wears it for special occasions like this. I think it makes him look heroic."

She had a point there, Cat thought. In spite of his dress jokes, Cat actually liked the way it looked on the captain. The kilt was hunter green crisscrossed diagonally with bands of red and two lighter shades of green. It hung down to his knees and just above the top of his boots. He wore a belt with a dark leather satchel on one hip and a sword and sheath on the other. Ross's white shirt was open at the neck and billowed in the breeze.

The captain descended to the main deck and stood beside the quartermaster. "Mister Stede," he said, "it is time to add to our ranks."

"Aye, sir," said Stede. He took the articles from Drake and spread them across the tops of a couple of barrels. He dipped a quill pen into a dark bottle of ink and handed the pen to the Frenchman. "Do you, Jacques Saint Pierre, now swear an oath to—"

"Wait, Stede," said Ross. "Where's my Bible?"

"I don't know," replied Stede. "I figured since ya didn't bring it, ya didn't want it."

Ross frowned. "It doesn't seem right without it." With that, Ross went belowdecks. He emerged a few seconds later carrying a small Bible with a cracked and faded cover of brown leather. "Here we are," said Ross, handing the book to Stede.

"A Bible, Declan Ross?" said Padre Dominguez. "I did not know you were a believing man."

The captain felt suddenly as if the only beam of sunlight on the whole deck shone down directly on him alone. "Don't read too much into it," he replied, more bitterly than he meant to. "It's just custom." He nodded at Stede.

The quartermaster held out the Bible, and St. Pierre put his hand on top of it. "Do ya, Jacques Saint Pierre, swear an oath to obey and uphold the articles of the *William Wallace*? If that b' yer wish, so say ya, 'aye.'"

St. Pierre delighted in the whole ceremony. A successful business-man, he missed the adventure of life at sea. As he scanned the ship's articles, he lingered most longingly on Article Three: Of any prize by us taken, the captain is to have two full shares; the quartermaster one share and a half; the bosun, carpenter, first mate, doctor, and chief gunner will have one share and a quarter. Due to St. Pierre's obvi-ous skill with cannons and explosives, Captain Ross had offered to make Jacques the chief gunner of the *Wallace*. A share and a quarter of every prize sounded very good to Jacques St. Pierre.

"Aye!" Jacques declared. He took the quill from the bottle of ink and signed his name with a flourish at the bottom of the parchment. The crew cheered, "Hurrah!!"

Cat came forward next. He wore dark blue breeches and a loose-fitting white shirt. The leather pouch hung from a cord around his neck. He placed his hand over the Bible and swallowed. He'd spoken to Captain Ross earlier, and he had assured Cat that should he discover his identity and desire to go and resume his former life, Ross would release him from his duties aboard the *William Wallace*. Still, Cat felt reluctant. The crew had been so welcoming of him, had gone to great lengths more than once to rescue him, and he was grateful. But he couldn't get over the feeling that there was still something very wrong here. Pirates were notorious scoundrels, after all.

"Do ya, uh . . . Cat, swear an oath to obey and uphold the articles of the *William Wallace*? If that b' yer wish, so say ya, 'aye.'"

Cat looked around. Red Eye winked. Seeing that bloody eye wasn't the encouragement Cat was seeking. But then Captain Ross smiled at him approvingly. Anne's face was lit with joy, and she nodded at him as if to say, "What are you waiting for?"

Like St. Pierre before him, Cat studied the articles, and above all the others, one stood out. Article Two: "The crew of the *Wallace* in a time of engagement shall willingly offer just quarter to any who request it. We shall not needlessly murder or do bodily harm to our foe. Neither shall we impress men into service. We shall not torture prisoners. Nor shall we mistreat women or meddle with them without consent. Any man who does violate this article shall suffer swift death."

Pirates abiding by such a code seemed unbelievable to Cat. They were killers, weren't they? But perhaps Captain Ross was different. Cat found himself saying, "Aye!" He picked up the quill pen and found the feel of it vaguely familiar. He dipped the tip into the ink and began to sign his name to the articles. Only when he did, the first letter was not a "C." He stared at the parchment and the ornate letter "G" he had just written. It was as if his hand had done reflexively what it always had done, but try as he might, Cat could not remember what came next. He looked up from face to face. Stede's was a study of confusion. Captain Ross's eyes were thoughtful. But Anne wore a different expression. Her mouth dropped open in sudden discovery. And Cat remembered the initials they'd found in the cottage on Dominica. GLT.

Is that me? he wondered desperately. Feeling suddenly very tired, Cat wrote an "L" and a "T." And then, in much smaller letters, "Cat." Once again, the crew shouted out hurrahs. Even as Cat drifted slowly away from the articles, the crew cheered him and softly patted him on the shoulder.

When Anne came forward, however, some of the crew backed out of the circle near the mast. While Drake did not back away, he made his displeasure known by staring at the ground and shaking his head. But nothing could sour this moment for Anne. She had even worn her best womanly pirate garb. This consisted of a black wool skirt, a dark green tunic, and a lacy white blouse beneath. *Bad luck indeed*, she thought.

She put her hand over the Bible. When she did, the entire scene on the deck of the *Wallace* seemed to change. It was no longer the coarse wooden deck of an aging brigantine. It was a polished floor. The sea air became fragrant. The cry of the gulls, the slap of the waves against the hull, and the jostle of the rigging became like music. For Anne, this was the first day of her life's dream.

"Do ya, Anne Ross, swear an oath to obey and uphold the articles of the *William Wallace*? If that b' yer wish, so say ya, 'aye.'"

The words were barely out of his mouth when Anne shouted, "Aye!" She snatched up the quill pen and hastily signed her name. Half of the crew cheered, and Jules put Anne up on his shoulder.

But Drake walked away, fingering the handle of his dagger and muttering. "Trouble will come of this . . . make no mistake. A woman should ne'er be part of this crew or any. Bad luck, it is."

29

OF SLAVES AND CAPTAINS

Captain Ross sat with his feet up on his desk. Stede and Jacques St. Pierre sat near him. "A hull full of provisions and calm seas make life easy enough," Ross said. "But this journey is not likely to remain so peaceful. If we face half the perils the monk told us about, we're going to need more men."

Stede agreed. "The battle with Chevillard took more than a third of the crew, Cap'n."

"When we reach the Caicos," said St. Pierre, "I will talk to a man I know. He ventures in—what do you call it—black gold."

"Slaves?" Ross glowered. "I don't barter people's lives!"

St. Pierre was taken aback for a moment but returned fire. "Oh, you do not? Then tell me, mon capitaine, how did you get all these men that sail with you now? Surely these were taken from past conquests and pressed into your service."

Ross took his feet down from the desk and leaned forward. "You must not have read the articles very carefully," he said. "Article Two . . . we shall not impress men into service."

"Sadly, no," admitted Jacques. "I did not read that very carefully. I was slightly more absorbed by Article Three."

"That's what I thought," said Ross. The anger passed. He leaned back, folding his hands behind his back, and explained, "Not one of the crew was forced into service. Many served with me as privateers before all this. As for the others . . . each man chose to come aboard and sail with me. You'd be surprised, Jacques. These merchant ships, these Spanish galleons, even His Majesty's privateers—they are captained by tyrants. They break the backs of their crew and pay them next to nothing. We gain a dozen good sailors with each ship we raid."

"And, when we b' going to port," said Stede, "we find many a good mon wasting away with no wark to do. Men who know nothing but the sea, and can't find a job to feed their families."

Jacques nodded. "I understand these young men. They are much like the French sailors who King Louis trained to be warriors at sea. But when the fighting ended, the king abandoned them. With no money, no command, no other trade—they turned to the piracy."

"Have ya met any of them?" Stede asked.

"Met them? I am one of them. But I had a skill they did not possess. I could—how do you say—broker deals between rich men. Ha-ha!"

"It is the same in England," Ross said. "The same everywhere. Good men—honest men—turn to the sweet trade because they cannot earn a living any other way."

"The sweet trade? Ha!" St. Pierre laughed. "It is a funny name for stealing, no? We are thieves!"

"Yes," Ross replied quietly. "Yes, we are." His mind was turbulent, like the sea during a squall. *The Treasure of Constantine, if it is really on this Isle of Swords, and if we could really find it . . . that would be more than enough,* Ross thought. He and all the crew could at last leave the so-called sweet trade and live—settle, start a farm, raise a family. *I might finally get Anne away from the sea.* "Jacques," Ross said, "we'll find men on the Caicos to augment the crew, but they'll not be slaves."

St. Pierre snorted. "And just how will you get them to join you?"

"Weren't you listening, Jacques?" Ross replied. "I'll ask."

"I know," said the quartermaster as he stood. "I b' setting a course for the Caicos. Now, if we could just get some more wind to fill them sails, we might get there before winter!"

Edmund Scully's sloop was lighter and faster than most ships at sea. But it could not go fast enough for Scully—not with the news he'd just collected from the British. Thorne seemed desperate for information concerning Declan Ross. "Oh, do I have some," Scully muttered as his sails caught a stiff wind. The sloop raced across the sea toward Isla Mona.

Declan Ross sat in his quarters and pored over a sea chart under the light of a single candle. *Confound the monk!* he thought, jamming the point of his quill pen into a bottle of ink.

"Are you angry with me?"

"What?" Ross looked up. His daughter stood in the doorway. "Oh, Anne . . . I didn't know you were standing there." In the flickering light, he was amazed how grown-up his little girl had become . . . how much she now looked like her mother. He stared.

"Are you angry with me?" she asked again, biting her bottom lip.

"With you? No," he replied, motioning for her to enter. "It's the wind. We're making no speed at all."

Anne nodded. "The wind . . . are you sure that's all it is?"

"You're just like your mother." He laughed. "See right through me. Truth be told, it's the monk, Padre Dominguez. I'm trying to plot our course for the Isle of Swords. But he won't show me the map, and he's not telling me everything! All I know is the island's supposed to be west of Portugal. That helps! He says it's his insurance that I'll see to his safety. Pretty smart, actually. But it's maddening not to know."

"When he gets to know you better," said Anne, "he'll trust you more."

"Maybe." He looked back down to the chart.

Anne rocked back and forth on her heels. "So you're not mad?"

"Anne," Ross growled. "Mad about wha—oh—that."

"I can do this, Father," she said, tears already streaming. "I won't let you down . . . again."

"Come, sit," he said, pointing to the chair at the corner of his desk.

She sat and stared at the floor. Her crimson hair fell like curtains around her face. Declan reached through and lifted her chin. "All's forgiven," he said, locking her eyes onto his and taking her hands. "You made a mistake, and it could have cost us a lot. But you owned up to it, and in the end . . . you saved us from capture. And, you've no doubt earned the respect of the men." He laughed. "I've never seen a crew so willing to be whipped!"

The corners of her mouth curled into a slight smile. He could always make Anne smile. It was one of the few things he could do right for his child. "I had half a mind to jump in there and take a lash or two myself!"

"Father, stop!" But now Anne laughed through her tears. The laughs stopped eventually, and they stared at each other for a quiet moment. She kissed him on the cheek and said, "Thank you."

Declan Ross felt about as good as he'd felt in years. For once, he'd managed to build Anne up . . . to strike a chord in that complicated heart of hers. She got up to leave, walked a few steps toward the door, and turned back toward him. Still smiling, she flung back her hair and wiped the tear streaks with her hand. Declan smiled, plucked the pen out of the inkwell, and went back to the chart.

"You didn't want me to sign the articles, did you?" Anne asked.

Her father looked up, his smile disappearing. "The crew voted for you to join."

"That's not the same, Father," whispered Anne. "I want you to want me to be a pirate. Did you or didn't you want me to sign the articles?"

"Anne, you know how I feel about thi—"

"But why? I work hard. I have skills. I know the sea pretty well. I've learned all there is to learn about this ship—from you, mostly."

"It's not that," Ross replied. His reddening face felt hot. "You have very good sea legs. You're smarter than most of the lads."

"Then why, Father? Why do you spend so much time encouraging them and not your daughter? I've seen you. You find some skill in each of the men, some talent—no matter how small. You cheer them on. You celebrate whatever they accomplish."

"Anne, I'm the captain of this ship. I have to—"

"But you don't do that for me. . . . I bet you don't even know what my last coral carving was."

Ross stammered, guessing: "I, uh . . . it was a dolphin."

"A dolphin? I haven't carved a dolphin since I was a little girl."

She sighed. "I don't understand. The things I like, the things I want to do—either you don't care . . . or you just tell me no."

Ross rubbed his temples and shook his head. Once again, things had somehow spun out of control. His breathing became more rapid. He could hear his heartbeat pulsing in his head. To avoid breaking it, he put the quill back in the inkwell. "I do care, Anne," he said as evenly as he could.

"Let me show you that I can be a great pirate."

"But I promised your mother. I—"

"When did you promise her, Father?!" Her voice became shrill. "You were out to sea when she . . . when she killed herself."

"What did you say?" Ross stood. He could barely breathe.

Anne started to tremble. She knew she'd gone too far, but she kept going. "I know you and Aunt Isabel always told me Mother died of the pox, but when we were in port two years after, I heard you and old Mrs. Penniworth talking. I heard you say it."

"Abigail—your mother—did not kill herself!" Ross yelled.

"How do you know?" Anne asked. "You weren't even there."

The moment the words were gone from her lips, she wished she could get them back. She watched the anger in her father's face bleed away into a sad kind of exhaustion. He looked old. He sounded old when he said, "Go to your quarters."

"I'm sorry, Father, I shouldn't have—"

"I command you to go to your quarters, NOW!"

When Anne was gone, Declan Ross sank back into his chair and hunched over the sea charts. He remembered that day, so long ago. With the *Wallace* full of gold and other prizes, he'd made port in Edinburgh, ready for a kiss from his wife and a hero's welcome. He'd received neither.

He remembered the way everyone treated him so strangely. He

remembered when Isabel, his wife's sister, gave him the news. He hadn't believed it then. And he didn't believe it now. Abigail did not take her own life. One day, he'd prove it.

But none of that changed the fact that she was gone. And none of that changed the fact that Anne was right. When Abigail died, he hadn't been there to protect her. He was out to sea . . . just like now. Isabel had offered to let Anne stay with her, but he'd refused. It was one of a thousand decisions he'd probably wonder about for the rest of his life.

Declan Ross strode across the main deck just after sunrise. It had been a rough night. Little sleep. Too many unknowns—Anne being chief among them. He nodded to Stede and continued on. This time of the morning, he liked to go up on the forecastle deck at the front of the ship. With the deck all to himself, he could stare out at the endless horizon. And somehow, his thoughts would come together.

He climbed the ladder and went right to the rail and . . . and there was Cat.

"Cat," Ross said, "this isn't your watch."

"I know," Cat replied. "I couldn't sleep."

Ross nodded. They were quiet for some time, each busy with his own thoughts.

"It's nice up here," Cat said, and he smiled.

But Ross could tell that something troubled him. "You regret your decision?" he asked. "Joining the crew?"

Cat looked sharply at the captain and lowered his eyes. "I like the crew," he said. "I like being on the ship. I love being out on the water." Cat laughed. "It's so odd, though, knowing how to do things, learning so fast. Seems like I was born for the sea, but . . . I don't know."

"You're wondering if you should be a pirate?"

Cat nodded, embarrassed. "I think that's pretty much it." He looked out over the water to the clouds, gray-blue and strangely flat.

Ross fixed a shrewd eye on Cat and stroked his coppery beard a few times. "It's hard because so many pieces of your past are missing. But I'll tell you something that's as sure as Stede's hand at the wheel. You, my lad, were a pirate before you ever set foot on the *William Wallace*."

30

THREE FATEFUL DECISIONS

I don't understand," said Padre Dominguez. "We have provisions. Why do we need to stop again?"

Padre Dominguez pressed his hands onto the front of Ross's desk. Leaning forward and staring with those black eyes, he was an imposing man.

"Our crew is capable, but for this kind of journey we'll need more men," said Ross, his feet up, leaning back, and a knowing grin curling at his lips. "Besides, we don't have *all* the provisions, Padre. Let's not forget the monkey pee that you seem to think is essential for our success."

"Not essential," said the priest. "But it would be extremely helpful. Still . . . it may not prove worth the delay."

"Delay?" Ross waved a hand dismissively. "I'm as anxious to get to the treasure as any, but we're the only ones with a map. We're the only ones who know how to get to the Isle of Swords . . . right?"

The monk looked away. He said nothing.

Ross let his feet down with a thump. "No . . . no, you must be joking," said Ross. "You said Thorne was coming after you because you have the only map tattooed right there on your back."

"Those were not my words."

"Don't play games, Padre . . . what are you saying?"

"There may be . . . one other," the monk explained. "You see, the priests in charge of my order have utilized the talents of a small tribe native to the Marquesas Islands in the Pacific. These people are primitive and somewhat superstitious, but they have unequaled skill in the art of tattooing. They were ideal for our needs, but not just for their tattoos. The Marquesans believe that once youths have reached the age of fourteen—the age where innocence ends—evil is the only thing that will come out of their mouths when they speak. To prevent this, and as a rite of passage into adulthood, the Marquesans clip their tongues and cut their vocal cords."

Ross winced. "How horrendous."

"Yes," said Padre Dominguez. "But you see how this custom suits our need for secrecy?"

"Of course. The natives draw the tattoo, but will never be able to tell anyone where to find the Isle of Swords."

"That is what the priests of my order have counted on over the years. These obscure islands in the Pacific hide a more obscure tribe who, even if they should be found, are not able to speak. For more than three centuries this arrangement has served us well."

"But?"

"But someone found the Marquesans. A woman, a female pirate. We do not know how she discovered this secret or even how she knew where to begin to look. But she found the man who created my tattoo . . . and bribed him with rubies. From memory, he redrew the map for her."

"Who is this woman?"

"Katarina Thorne."

Ross banged a fist on the desk and stood up. "Hang me by the yardarm . . . Bartholomew Thorne's wife?! If she has it . . . it won't be long before she hands it over to him."

"Yes, but we are reasonably certain that Katarina Thorne was killed before she could have given the map to Bartholomew. There were terrible storms in the Pacific that season. She must have perished. Otherwise, he would not have needed to come looking for me."

Ross took a deep breath and nodded. "I suppose that makes sense, but then why are we in such a hurr—wait a minute! What if . . . what if she betrayed him? After his first wife died, Bartholomew wasn't exactly civil with women. How do you know Katarina didn't just go to the Isle of Swords herself and cut her husband out of the prize?"

"You are a shrewd man, Declan Ross," said Padre Dominguez as he turned to leave. "That is why we are in such a hurry to get to the Isle of Swords."

"Jacques Saint Pierre?" Thorne said, marveling at the name. "So he's thrown in with Declan Ross, has he?"

"It is certain to be so," said Scully. "My source claims that Ross's brigantine sailed from the eastern coast of Dominica less than three days ago. Jacques Saint Pierre has not returned to what's left of his mill in Misson."

"And the British?"

"As you know, the British have drawn the most potent measure of their fleet away from the Caribbean. They pursue Ross east of the

Spanish Main and into the Atlantic." Scully paused, fingering the little spider of whiskers under his lip. "Does this news meet your current needs?"

"Ever the profiteer, eh?" Thorne coughed out a hoarse, hacking laugh. "Go and see Skellick topside. Tell him to double your usual payment."

Scully stood and bowed. "Thank you, Captain Thorne. I will continue to monitor the British, and I will find you when I have something more to tell." He left immediately and shut the cabin door behind him.

As soon as Scully was gone, Thorne turned up the flame of the oil lantern on his desk and reached for one of several metal canisters from a rack behind his desk. He unscrewed its cap and let a long roll of parchment fall out onto his desk. He went to work, poring over the sea chart and thinking out loud. "So the British spoiled Ross's party in Dominica, eh? They forced him to flee east . . . but he will not cross the Atlantic and attempt the Isle of Swords without provisions. You've doubled back on the English, haven't you, Ross? But where would you go?"

His scarred finger traced a line south from Dominica. "Saint Vincent," Thorne muttered. "Barbados . . . Trinidad. No. I think not. The Isle of Swords is rumored to be in northern waters—some say as far north as Portugal. Ross is practical." Thorne reversed course with his finger and traced north of Dominica, past St. Kitts where Thorne was now, past Saba and Anguilla, and . . . out into the open ocean.

"Where?" His eyes scanned the chart. Then he saw it, and he knew. "The Caicos Islands. Saint Pierre had run a trading operation there, out of an old Dutch fort. Yes, they will go there to drop Saint Pierre off . . . or to get supplies for their journey." Suddenly,

Thorne's scarred right hand clenched involuntarily like a claw. Searing pain shot up his arm, and his head pounded.

All at once, it was gone. But his cabin was eerily silent once again. Thorne slowly opened the drawer and looked upon the silver locket. *You've done well, my husband.*

Thorne's heart hammered. But he reached into the drawer and removed the locket. He clicked open the locket and stared down at the painted portrait. "Heather?"

I told you Ross would not escape.

"How can . . . how can this be—"

Once you have the map, and then the Treasure of Constantine . . . the sea will be yours. Make them pay.

"I'll raise such a fleet," Thorne said. "A fleet to pay back the British for what they did."

"A little over twelve hours," Ross explained to Anne. "I want to get there under cover of darkness."

Anne nodded and was quiet. She needed to approach this subject carefully. "Will we linger in port long?"

"Not if I can help it," he replied. "I'll get new crewmen, if I can. Jacques will acquire the few remaining supplies we need. Then, with all speed, we'll get underway to the Isle of Swords."

"But why in such a hurry?" She could feel her opportunity slipping away.

"My reasons will remain my own until we have everything we need and get the *Wallace* far out into the Atlantic."

"I've never been to the Caicos," she said. "Will you take me ashore?"

Ross grimaced. He'd decided long before this moment, but he knew Anne wouldn't much like it. "This is not some pleasure excursion, my daughter. We have great need of haste. The British are no doubt scouring the Spanish Main and half of the Atlantic for us. Bartholomew Thorne wants us all dead—that's two fleets after us, Anne. But," he took a deep breath, "even if this were not the case . . . even if we had all the time in the world, I would leave you aboard the *Wallace*. And this time, you will obey your captain's orders."

He watched as the light in his daughter's eyes flickered and dimmed. But, to her credit, she did not try to argue. She didn't cry. She nodded thoughtfully before turning and walking away. Just before shutting the door, she wheeled about and asked, "What about Cat? Must he stay on the ship as well?"

Ross's eyes narrowed. "I grant you authority in this matter, Anne," he said.

Anne's jaw tensed, then relaxed. "I think Cat should be allowed to go." She turned and, without another word, left the captain's quarters.

Ross nodded repeatedly and smiled. Anne impressed him more and more each day.

31

HARBINGER OF DOOM

Blasted wind!" Ross exhaled loudly and paced across the quarter-deck. "Of all the times to lose speed. Maybe the monk was right."

Stede stood at the ship's wheel. His expression blank, he stared into the inky darkness of the sky. "This b' a bad omen . . . the winds changing like that."

"With all due respect, Quartermaster," said Jacques St. Pierre, "the winds in this part of the ocean are very fickle this time of year. But we are still at five, maybe six knots, no? Not exactly the doldrums. We'll make it by the middle watch?"

"Just so long as we can get in and out before sunup," said Ross. "I don't want our presence on the Caicos to be general knowledge."

"That is no problem," said St. Pierre. "We will have five hours of night left at least. You will see."

Smuggler's Bay was quiet as the *William Wallace* drifted slowly into port. It was well after the middle watch, and Declan Ross was as tense as a ratline. St. Pierre promised that he would have men at his fort to help carry supplies back to the *Wallace*, but to be sure, Ross planned to bring sixty of his strongest men.

Three longboats were lowered into the water. Ross, Stede, and St. Pierre led the group in the first. Red Eye, Midge, and Cat in the second. Jules and Cromwell in the third.

"I tell you," said St. Pierre as they rowed to shore, "when we get to my fortress, we will empty my arsenal and equip your old brigantine with the most potent cannons on the sea!"

His eyes scouring the dark palms that hung over the inlet, Ross did not look at St. Pierre. "What about the salted meats?"

"The best smoke-cured beef and pork," he replied. "I trade frequently with buccaneers from Hispaniola. There should be thrice a dozen casks of it in my cellar."

"That b' a lot of meat," said Stede. "Yer making me hungry, mon." St. Pierre smiled.

Their boats safely ashore, St. Pierre led them all up the steep incline through the palms. Ross looked back over his shoulder at the *William Wallace*. As ordered, Drake had doused all the lanterns. The ship was barely a shadow on the black water.

Around the bend just north of Smuggler's Bay, other large shadows moved silently across the water. Five of Thorne's warships had disgorged some thirty longboats and close to seven hundred pirates. As much as Thorne would have enjoyed opening up with his sixty cannons, sending the *Wallace* to the bottom in splinters, he could not risk killing or—worse—disfiguring his prize. He gave his men orders to bring the monk back to the *Raven* alive and completely un-scathed. The rest, including Ross, they could kill in whatever creative ways they desired.

On the gray deck of the *Wallace*, Anne tightened a cord of rope around a sail on the lowest spar on the foremast. As she tied it off, she turned and spotted Drake up near the forecastle. She couldn't see his eyes, but she could tell he was staring at her. Maybe he knew she was looking, for he shook his head disdainfully and disappeared behind the forecastle deck.

Anne shrugged, lifted a hatch, and climbed belowdecks. The dark didn't bother her. She had navigated belowdecks enough times to walk it with her eyes closed. Still, in many places it was very close quarters. She needed to squeeze between crates and barrels or duck under hammocks. Occasionally, her hand would brush against a frayed rope and give her a start. Then she found the narrow stairwell that switchbacked down to the gun deck and, eventually, her objective: the cargo hold. "There're a few honey cakes left," Nubby had told her. "Better get 'em before the rats do!"

Drake fumed. *Bad luck, but no one listens! If she wasn't the captain's daughter, they would. They'd have thrown her overboard as was right and proper.* He leaned over the starboard rail at the front of the ship and spat.

Drake turned and began to walk away from the rail when he heard an odd rushing sound like canvas being pulled off a spool. Before he could turn, he felt a prick in his lower back. His back, side, and chest began to burn. His knees buckled. He slumped face-first to the deck. Before his vision faded, Drake saw black boots moving across the deck, a never-ending stream of boots. Drake mouthed, "Bad luck. . . ." And then he lay still.

Anne stepped down into the cargo, ducked under a low beam, and straightened her back severely to get between two walls of barrels. When she slid open the door that led to the food stores in the deep bow of the ship, she was surprised by the soft glow of a light. Darting between casks and crates, she navigated the storage and saw Padre Dominguez. A lantern hung on a peg behind him. He sat on a small crate and had a barrel in front of him as if it were his private table at a pub. He held a small leather-bound book in one hand and a honey cake in the other.

"Padre Dominguez!" Anne said, trying to startle him. "Nubby said those cakes were for me."

Padre Dominguez didn't even flinch. "Odd," he said without looking up. "He told me not an hour ago that I could have them."

"What are you doing down here?" she asked. "Besides eating my cakes, that is."

"It was the only place I could risk a bit of light." He smiled and said, "And this isn't the last cake. There are two more. Pull up a crate and join me."

Anne did as he requested. He held out a brownish-gold rectangle, and Anne received it happily.

Munching, she leaned over the barrel table on her elbows. "What are you reading?" she asked.

"The Holy Scriptures," he said. "The Twenty-third Psalm. I turn to it whenever my heart is troubled. Would you like to . . . I mean, can you—"

"I can read," said Anne. "My father taught me."

"Here then." Padre Dominguez handed her the leather-bound volume. It fit comfortably in her open hands. He pointed to a very large and fancy gothic "T." Anne angled the book to get more light and began to read.

"The Lord is my shepherd, I shall not want. He maketh me to lie down in green pastures. He leadeth me beside the still waters. He restoreth my soul. He leadeth me in the paths of right . . . righ–tee—"

"Righteousness," he corrected gently. "It means to be on the path of truth and honor."

Anne nodded. "He leadeth me in the paths of righteousness for his name's sake. Yea, though I walk through the valley of the shadow of death—"

A muffled boom came from above. Her eyes big and white in the flickering lantern light, Anne looked up from the pages of Scripture. She said, "That was Stede's thunder gun."

Nubby had just wheeled a barrel into Captain Ross's cabin when full-out war erupted topside. He drew a long carving knife from inside his heavy coat and ran to the windows behind Ross's desk. He threw open a window and peered out just in time to see a dark mass hurtling down. He ducked back in as the body plummeted past the window and into the murky water below.

"We've been ambushed, and no mistake," he muttered, starting toward the cabin door. He stopped short, hearing voices on the stairs. He closed Ross's cabin door and locked it. "Buy me some time, maybe."

He looked frantically around the room. Remembering the pistol the captain left in the upper-right-hand drawer of his desk, he raced to the desk and opened the drawer. The gun was there. Nubby put the knife in his teeth and grabbed the pistol. The doorknob rattled behind him, followed by a sharp bang.

"You would do well to open this door," came a high, nasally voice from the other side. "My master, Captain Bartholomew Thorne, shows little mercy to those who delay his efforts!"

"You mean, no mercy whether they deserve it or not," muttered Nubby through his teeth gritted on the cold blade. He considered hiding behind the desk. *No good*, he thought. Another slam to the door. A loud crack in the wood. One more shot like that, and they would kick it in. Nubby rushed to the cabinets on the left side of the room. He barely had the cabinet door open, and all manner of clothes, books, and other assorted items began to topple out.

"Slob!" Nubby shouted, slamming the cabinet shut. Then he looked to the window. He ran over, gazed down, and saw several bodies floating in the water. But there were also ropes, ropes from the intruders' grappling hooks, dangling from the unseen rails above.

"You had your chance, Ross!" shrieked the voice. Nubby climbed up over the sill, tried to put the pistol in his coat, but missed. The gun fell and disappeared into the water. Keeping the knife in his teeth, Nubby clutched one of the ropes just as the cabin door crashed open.

"How in the world are we going to get the cannons down this hill?" Ross asked. They'd been climbing for over an hour.

"I have specially made carts, my friend," said St. Pierre. "Remember, these cannons are forged with a new process. The iron-bronze alloy is pumped full of air bubbles as it cools—it is lighter than you are used to. My men at the fort and your brawny crew should have little problem."

"Whatever they weigh," said Jules, "I can handle it."

Cat looked at him and didn't doubt him for a minute. Jules was massive, and his upper arms were bigger around than Cat's legs.

"Ah!" St. Pierre exclaimed. "It is just around this bend! Follow me."

They emerged from the tree line and navigated around a rocky outcropping, and there before them, high on a hill, was St. Pierre's fort. "Something is wrong," St. Pierre whispered. And they all saw it. Smoke poured from the windows of the square complex and its three turrets.

"No!" St. Pierre blurted out. "This cannot be!" He drew a pistol in each hand from his holsters and charged up the hill.

"Swords! Muskets!" Ross yelled. Stede pulled his two machetes; Red Eye and Cat drew their cutlasses. Together they raced after Jacques up the hill to the fortress.

But they were too late. They found Jacques St. Pierre on his knees, weeping, in the wide doorway of his main keep. And beyond him, strewn among still-smoldering fires, were dozens of bodies. Cat shut his eyes. "This b' Thorne's wark," Stede muttered.

Just then, Ross heard a muffled explosion. He sprinted out of the keep and looked all around. "Where?!"

"East," said Stede, pointing over the treetops from which they had just emerged.

Declan Ross could not see his ship from where he stood, but he could see the widest part of the dark bay. To his horror, three massive dark ships stretched almost the width of the inlet. Fire flashed from their sides. The booms sounded a second later. "The *Wallace*!" Ross yelled. "Anne!"

"Get away from the fort!" St. Pierre yelled. Then they all heard an odd kind of *whoosh*.

Ross turned and looked past St. Pierre into the keep. A harsh orange glow burned beneath the heavy door on the far side of the room. Ross's mouth dropped open, and he might have died there, but Stede grabbed him by the shoulder and rushed him down the stairs. The rest of the crew, some running, some leaping from the walls, got away from the fort just before a thunderous explosion. Fire, debris, and smoke sprayed into the dark sky. Chunks of wood and stone rained down among the crew as they ran. Several men were struck and fell. Others behind them grabbed up the fallen, unsure if they carried someone alive or dead. Ross stared hopelessly ahead and led his men recklessly down the hill. He knew that, somehow, Thorne had been in wait for him to arrive. And that meant he was too late to save his daughter.

32

THE FALL OF THE WILLIAM WALLACE

Keep reading," said Padre Dominguez.

"What?" Anne lowered the book and stared at the monk. "But the *Wallace* has been boarded. We're under attack!"

"They will be among us soon enough," he said. In his dark eyes dwelt a strange kind of melancholy—like one who is sad when a long journey has ended, but is at the same time still happily immersed in the memory of it all. "Please . . . read."

Heavy footfalls thumped from the stairwell on the other side of the cargo hold where the gunpowder kegs were kept. Then came muttered curses as men in the darkness bumped into sharp crate edges or bashed heads on low-hanging beams. "Have you lost your mind?" Anne asked, staring at the still-open door to their side of the hold. "We can't just—"

"READ!!"

She went back to the beginning of the Twenty-third Psalm, to the large "T," and began to read. "The Lord is my shepherd; I shall not want."

As she spoke the words, Padre Dominguez stepped from behind the barrel-table and looked back at her once more. His eyes smoldered with a cold fire so powerful it made Anne look away. Then, with his arms behind his back, Padre Dominguez faced the open door.

"He maketh me to lie down in green pastures," Anne continued. "He leadeth me beside the still waters. He restoreth my soul: he leadeth me in the paths of righteousness for his name's sake."

At that moment, the first enemy pirate squeezed through the barrel walls. Others appeared on either side. Some held swords or daggers. Some pistols or muskets. Anne saw Padre Dominguez's hands drop down to his sides. His fingers moved and twitched. "Louder!" said the priest.

"Yea, though I walk through the valley of the shadow of death, I will fear no evil: for thou art with me. . . ."

The pirate in the lead advanced slowly on the monk. He raised his pistol. At the same time, Padre Dominguez reached into his robe and drew out two pitch-black shafts of some kind.

Anne continued, trying to watch the monk and the enemy out of the corner of her eye. "Thy rod and thy staff they comfort me."

The pirate cocked back the hammer of his pistol. Padre Dominguez suddenly whirled around and cracked the pirate's wrist with one of the black weapons. The gun fell to the ground, and the pirate began to wail. The other pirates surged against Padre Dominguez. And he took them on.

Anne was so surprised she almost dropped the book.

"Read!" he called back to her.

"Thou preparest a table before me in the presence of mine enemies." Padre Dominguez ducked a nasty slash and drove his two weapons into an attacker's stomach. He blocked another sword swipe, caught the man's hand between his two sable rods, and flung him headfirst into the barrel-table. The man lay unconscious at Anne's feet.

"Thou anointest my head with oil," she said, a tremor in her voice, "my cup runneth over." Padre Dominguez stood, arms outstretched like a cross, as another pirate came on. This pirate had more skill than the others. He slashed and stabbed with a short sword. Padre Dominguez blocked and parried, moving backward. The thin blade clipped his robe, but caught no flesh. The monk was too fast. He slammed a rod into the middle of the short sword, and the blade broke in two. Then he kicked the pirate so hard in the jaw that he flew backward and crashed into a barrel. A crimson flood ensued, and the next two attackers slipped and fell from their own lack of balance.

"Surely goodness and mercy shall follow me all the days of my life: and I will dwell in the house of the Lord for ever." Suddenly from between two barrels, a pirate wearing a black bandanna lunged, driving his sword at the monk's gut. At the same time, another rogue leaped off a crate from behind, meaning to drive his two daggers into the priest's back. Padre Dominguez let his feet slide apart, dropped into a split, and held up his two black rods. He used the first pirate's momentum against him and threw him into the oncoming blades of the other man. They met with a tremendous wet crash. Then they both went down and lay still.

Anne closed the Bible and drew her cutlass.

"No, Anne!" the monk yelled, bashing one pirate across the cheek and jabbing another in the center of the chest.

Anne hesitated. She couldn't just let him fight alone. She stepped forward and brandished her cutlass, but someone called from behind the mass of pirates, "That's him! That's Dominguez! Capture him, but don't dare put a mark on him. Thorne's orders!"

That changed the battle. The pirates stopped charging at Padre Dominguez. They surrounded him, kept him turning. A tall pirate emerged from the door behind them. He had long greasy hair and a thin beard that sharpened to a point at his chin. His eyebrows were so arched, his eyes so large they looked like they might leap out of his head. Anne saw he had something in his hands.

"Padre Dominguez, watch out!" she cried.

The monk had been trying to turn around, for he sensed the danger behind. Anne's cry had confirmed it, but he was already occupied by the jabs of three pirates. Anne raced toward the bug-eyed man, but another pirate stepped in front and engaged her. Even as she blocked and countered, she saw the man with the pointed beard throw a huge weighted net over Padre Dominguez. His arms unable to swing freely, he could not defend himself. The other pirates grabbed the ends of the heavy rope net and began to twist it and pull. And that fast, Padre Dominguez was caught.

Breathless and exhausted, driven only by fear's pure adrenaline, Declan Ross crashed down the hill through the palms. In an effort to get quickly in and out of St. Pierre's fort with their needed supplies, Ross had taken the strongest and most experienced crewmen off the *Wallace*. With each thunderous *boom*, each flash of angry orange just visible through the trees, Ross knew that his decision had been a terrible mistake. He'd left the ship—left Anne—defenseless.

The silence suddenly hit him. The cannon fire had stopped. Ross knew what that meant. Screaming, "Anne! I'm coming . . . Anne!"

he at last broke through the last stretch of palms and crashed onto the shore. No sight had ever greeted Declan Ross that so wrenched his heart and his mind. Not even coming back to port in Scotland those many years ago to discover that his beloved Abigail had died—not even that—matched the horror of this vision.

It seemed half the inlet was ablaze. Hunks of debris, like islands of fire, floated around the gutted, sinking hulk of the *William Wallace*. Flames climbed the foremast and the bowsprit. The sails were long ago consumed, now just strips of char. Black smoke wreathed the inferno that raged still within the bow, even as it slipped slowly below the surface with a never-ending hiss. All around the debris, illuminated by the fires, drifted a multitude of bodies. And sharks had followed the scent of blood into the cove.

Ross cried out something guttural and barreled into the bay. He ran until he could not run and swam with wild, powerful strokes. "Anne!!" he screamed, coughing out gulps of bay water. "My sweet Anne . . . where are you?!"

He swam in circles, searching frantically among the bodies. He saw forms he recognized, but not Anne. Several times, he felt something under the water. Something nudged his leg or bumped his foot, but he went heedlessly on. The enormity of what had happened washed over him. He realized with dreadful culpability that once again, he had left someone he loved alone . . . alone to die. And then he stopped. A coldness gripped his mind and heart, and he stopped swimming and let himself sink.

At almost the same moment, the captain and his ship slipped below the surface of the dark water.

33

One Lash Too Many

"Get out of the wattah, thrice a Scottish—!" came a muffled voice from above. Ross felt an iron grip around his upper arm, and he was hauled upward. He broke the surface spluttering and coughing. "Yer coming with me, mon," said Stede as he hauled Ross onto his back and began to swim for both of them. "The sharks have had enough."

Stede drew Ross up onshore. Jules, Red Eye, and the others parted and watched numbly as their captain and quartermaster passed between them. But Cat stood apart from them, just a few feet from the tree line. His face was ghostly white, his eyes far away. Ross looked up and saw Cat, and something unspoken passed between them.

St. Pierre knelt just a few inches from where the water lapped at the shore. He grasped huge fistfuls of sand, stood, and squeezed so that ragged clumps bled out between his fingers. He stared at the burning debris and said, "I will break his neck."

Jules replied, "You'll have to get in line."

"Captain!" A voice came out of the darkness. They heard wet footfalls on the sand. Ross spun around—he knew that voice. "They took 'em, Captain!"

"Nubby!" Ross exclaimed and grabbed Nubby by the shoulders. "You said 'they took them,' Nubs. What did you mean? Took whom?"

"Why, Anne, of course. Anne and the monk. Thorne took 'em."

Ross swayed. His thoughts reeled. "Anne . . . she lives?"

"Aye!" He pointed out of the inlet, out into the dark sea beyond. "I was in your quarters when the attack began. Begging yer pardon, but you asked me to get a barrel in there to you. I just barely escaped through the window when Thorne's men broke in looking for you. Captain, while they were searching for the charts, I heard some of them talking—especially this one with a real pointy chin."

"Skellick," muttered Ross.

"You know 'im?" asked Nubby.

"He's Thorne's quartermaster, a wicked, skulking shell of a man."

"Sounds right," said Nubby. "He seemed to know quite a bit about Thorne's plans. Captain, he kept talking about Thorne seeking *black gold* for the mission. I think they're taking Anne and the monk to Spain, a place he called Cape Verde."

"Not Spain," said Jacques St. Pierre. "Cape Verde is a small chain of islands five hundred miles off Africa's western coast. Thorne has a huge stronghold on the biggest island, from which he deals sugarcane and . . . slaves."

"He will get word out to his other ships," Ross said, "and they will meet their captain at Cape Verde to bulk up their crews with slaves. Nubby, are you sure they took Anne off the ship?"

"They had Anne and the padre in shackles on a longboat. I'm sure of it."

Hope surged anew in Ross's thoughts. He'd let Anne down, but at least she was alive. And now there was a chance that he could get her back.

"Thorne has been building a shipyard in Cape Verde for years. On the backs of those slaves," Jacques said. "If he gets to Constantine's Treasure, do you know what he'll do?" Jacques spat in the sand. "He'll build a pirate fleet twice as big as any colonial power can put to sea. He'll own the North Atlantic and the Spanish Main."

"We can't let him do that," Ross said coldly. "And I will not let him take my Anne away."

"What do ya propose we do, mon?" Stede asked. "We have no ship. Barely a crew."

"We're going to need both," Ross said. "Jacques, can anyone on the island get us a ship?"

"I know a few men who might have something we can use," said Jacques. "But these will not be warships."

"Hmmm . . ." Ross muttered. "That's a problem. But I guess we'll just see what we can get."

"Captain?" It was Jules. He had a dark clump in his hands, and he handed the wet mass to Ross. At first, the captain did not recognize it. . . . It was badly burned and torn in places, but as he unrolled it a white wolf and a claymore sword appeared.

"The flag of the *William Wallace*!" Ross looked out to sea. "I'm coming, Anne," he whispered.

Belowdecks on the *Raven*, ship's mates Davis Lowther and Howell Ames decided to have a little fun with their prisoner and try to earn a little extra reward from their captain in the bargain.

"So . . . priest," said Lowther as he stood over the kneeling Padre Dominguez, whose hands were shackled behind his back. "Yer the one ol' Cap'n Thorne's been worried about findin', eh?"

But the monk said nothing.

Ames frowned. Perhaps the monk did not understand Lowther's gutter language, he thought. "Seems you have something valuable in your possession, old chap. Something Captain Thorne desires. You would do well to relinquish it into our possession."

Lowther frowned. "Re-what-quish?"

"Oh, do shut your mouth," said Ames. He turned back to the monk. "Padre, you would save us all quite a bit of duress if you would simply hand it over."

"Leave him alone!" Anne screamed from her cell a few yards away.

"Oh, you'll get yer turn, me pretty," said Lowther.

"Be quiet, idiot!" Ames said. "Thorne will have your head on a spit if he hears that kind of talk. This young woman is something special to Captain Thorne. Else why would she still be alive?"

Lowther swallowed and absently rubbed his neck.

"What do you say?" asked Ames, kneeling close to Padre Dominguez. "Will you give us what you have?"

He grabbed Padre Dominguez by the shackles and lifted him to his feet. He shoved him over to a single wooden beam that reached from floor to ceiling on the portside of the cell deck. Even in the dim flickering light of the lanterns, Anne could see that the beam was splotched with dark stains. "What are you doing?" cried Anne.

"Don't you worry yer pretty little head," said Lowther, reaching into a large leather satchel on his waist. "We're just goin' t' soften 'im up a bit. Make 'im more helpful." He removed a long whip and let its coils fall down at his feet.

Ames started to fumble with keys, but Lowther said, "I'd be

careful takin' off them cuffs, if I was you. I heard Skellick say this monk bested fifteen men 'fore they netted the blaggard."

"I have been duly warned." Ames unlocked Padre Dominguez's shackles and pulled his arms high up on the post. There, Ames quickly wound part of the chain around a peg and locked Padre Dominguez's shackles once more. "That should do it," he said. Now, my good sir, you may commence."

Lowther looked down at the whip in his hand and then up at Ames. "Com-what?"

"Just whip him, dolt!"

"No!" Anne yelled.

Lowther grinned at her and let fly with a terrible stroke. The whip crackled and hit Padre Dominguez's right shoulder blade. His robe split slightly, revealing a tiny patch of skin. Anne grimaced. She couldn't believe Padre Dominguez didn't yell out.

Lowther couldn't believe it either.

"That will never do," said Ames. "You barely hit him."

"I split 'is robe!" Lowther complained. "Maybe he passed out from the pain."

"Hardly," said Ames. "I can see his eyes. Try it again."

Lowther rolled up his sleeve and unleashed. This time the whip struck Padre Dominguez in the middle of his back. Again, he barely moved. Lowther struck again . . . and again. His last stroke split the robe even more and opened a gash on Padre Dominguez's shoulder. Anne could see the blood trickling over his welted flesh. And then she remembered. "No!" she screamed. "Stop! You'll tear up the m—"

"ANNE!" Padre Dominguez barked. "Be silent!"

"There now," said Ames. "At least the monk knows how to endure his due punishment."

"Yeah." Lowther laughed. "And he knows how to put a lass in 'er place!"

The whipping continued. Anne counted the strokes. Five, six, seven. Lowther must have been giving it all that he had because Padre Dominguez began to groan as the strokes fell.

"There, Lowther, I think that is enough punishment for one day."

"Aww, mate. Just one mo—"

"WHAT are you DOING?!!" The whip froze in Lowther's hand. Anne spun around and saw that both Lowther and Ames had gone sheet-white, their eyes fixed on the stairwell on the other side of the deck. From the shadows, a form advanced. He wore a long black frock coat with tails that hung down behind him like folded bat's wings. At either side there were sheaths as if he might carry two swords. And across his chest was a strap with no less than six pistols. He had a dark hat held in his hand and wore a black bandanna over long silver hair. Sideburns knifed down, meeting his frowning moustache and making it appear that his jaw was monstrously large. Anne could not see his eyes, for they were yet in the shadow of his imposing gray brow. But Anne could feel the intensity of his gaze just from the expression of abject terror worn by Lowther and Ames.

"I asked you, what are you doing?" This man's voice was raspy and choked, painful to hear. With several other men following him, he entered the deck a few paces and looked right at Anne, then into the next cell.

"Captain Thorne, I . . ." Words failed Ames as his captain turned and saw the priest slumping limply on the pole. Lowther dropped the whip.

"WHAT HAVE YOU DONE?!!" Thorne ran to Padre

Dominguez, tore wide the robe at his shoulders. The map was still intact . . . except for the area upon Padre Dominguez's right shoulder blade. There, a six-inch swath of flesh was shredded and bleeding bright red. "No, NO, NOOOO!!" Thorne bellowed. He drew something from the sheath on his left hip and swung it around so fast that Ames didn't have time to flinch. Whatever it was hit Ames in the upper cheek. Anne heard a sound like a dropped melon and looked away just as Ames fell limp to the ground.

Thorne bent down, took the key ring from Ames, and unlocked the shackles around Padre Dominguez's wrists. He caught the priest and carefully handed him to the men who had come in behind him. "Take him to the infirmary," Thorne rasped. "Tell Mister Flagg to do what he can to repair the skin here—stitch if he must, but not to cut. Is that clear?" The men nodded and disappeared. Thorne turned to Davis Lowther.

"Davis, Davis," said Thorne, sheathing the bleeding stick. "I know this wasn't your idea, now was it?"

"N-n-no, s-sir," said Lowther. "I could think a no such thing. Ames, it was. Not me."

"No, of course not," said Thorne. "You are not that much of an idea man. But what you did puts me in an awkward position. Before I decide, I must know a little more." Thorne bent down and picked up the whip. "Tell me, Davis, how many lashes did you give the priest?"

"N-nine, sir," said Lowther, not daring to lie. "No more'n nine. I'm sure of it."

"Ah, just nine," said Thorne. "Very well, that eases my conscience. Now, tell me, why were you whipping this man?"

"Well, Ames said the priest had somethin' ye wanted, somethin' important, and . . . well, we thought—"

"You thought you would get this item from Padre Dominguez and surprise me with it?" Thorne nodded as if he was satisfied. "Very well, here is what I have decided. You meant well. And really, you gave the priest a mere nine lashes." Lowther nodded repeatedly. He was relieved with the direction this was going. Even Anne turned around to see—though she avoided looking down at Ames.

"But since I cannot let you go unpunished," Thorne continued, "I will give you the very same number of lashes that you gave Padre Dominguez. There, does that sound fair?"

Lowther nodded—even smiled weakly as Thorne shackled him to the same whipping post they'd used for Padre Dominguez.

Bartholomew Thorne marched back several paces to give himself room to swing the whip. Anne shrank back in her cell. "Now, Mister Lowther," said Thorne, letting the whip slip from his fingers and fall to the floor. And he began to breathe audibly between his words . . . cracking, phlegmy, and harsh. "It is time for you to receive your due. I could understand if I asked you to give the priest seven lashes, and you lost count and gave him nine. But I did not ask you to whip the priest at all." Lowther pulled at the chains and twisted, trying to see what Thorne was doing.

Bartholomew Thorne slowly removed the bleeding stick from its holster. He lifted the cruel instrument to neck level and began to twist the top segment . . . the piece with the longest and most jagged spikes protruding from it. "I do not wish for my subordinates to take matters into their own hands. If I give the order that the priest should be taken to his cell, then that is exactly what should be done."

Thorne twisted the top segment around and around until, finally, it came free from the rest of the stave. He began to pull the segments away from one another, and a long, slender iron chain emerged.

When the last link of the chain came out, Thorne let the spiked segment fall. It swung like a pendulum near the floor.

"The priest, you see, does have something I want. Something I want very much. A map that will lead me to the greatest treasure the world has ever known." Anne flinched. He knew. He knew about the map.

"But unbeknownst to you and Mister Ames," Thorne continued, the spiked head hanging down like that of a medieval mace, "the priest does not carry the map. HE IS THE MAP!! And in your blank stupidity, you have ruined the most important corner of this map. Do you hear? RUINED!!"

Lowther struggled against the chains now with all his might, but it was useless. Bartholomew Thorne raised the flailing weapon. With a ferocious cry, he swung the spiked segment at Lowther. Anne turned away.

34

A Man about a Boat

What do you mean, no?" asked Jacques St. Pierre, standing at the door of Gerard Hossa, his longtime friend. "Mon ami, ever I have been your faithful trading partner!" Hossa's door, like the first six doors, slammed in his face.

"Apparently, your credit isn't as good as you thought," said Ross. He sighed.

"I am a shrewd negotiator, yes," said St. Pierre, "And yes, most of the time, I get the better of any deal I make, but still, how callous of these men to hold that against me."

Ross scanned the Caicos coastline hopelessly. "While we linger, Anne is slipping farther from my grasp. It goes against everything I stand for, but . . . we may have to steal a ship."

"There may not be a tall ship to steal on this whole island. You have seen. These are fishermen."

"I can't wait, Jacques," Ross said. "He has my daughter."

St. Pierre nodded. "He owes me for what he has done on this

island. Believe me, Declan, I want to get him also, but we cannot fight Thorne in a rowboat."

"If only we could get to Portugal," Ross said. "I know a man there who might have the kind of ship I need to face the *Raven*."

"Portugal?" Jacques exclaimed. "Why not Venezuela or even Jamaica?"

"I cannot afford to backtrack. Thorne will make haste to his shipyard on Cape Verde. Once he musters his fleet, he'll bolt for the Isle of Swords. If we don't get to him while he's in port, or cut him off, we'll never find him."

St. Pierre thoughtfully looked left, right, then up. "Ha-ha! I think I know someone who could get you to Portugal. But it will cost."

Near the shore of Smuggler's Bay, Ross looked over his remaining crew members. Slowly he held out a small bag. "Silver charms, doubloons, earrings, a dagger with a jeweled hilt—anything of value . . . put it in my satchel. It may be the only way to arrange passage across the Atlantic."

Most of the men immediately began removing necklaces and earrings. Some muttered quietly. "And whether we find the treasure or not," said Ross, "I promise you, I will pay you all back twice over."

One by one, the crewmen approached Ross and dropped something in the satchel. Midge shamed a few reluctant men by painfully plucking out one of his gold teeth. Even Red Eye, though it clearly strained him, gave up his marvelous dagger with a ruby in the hilt. Cat let his leather pouch hide under the folds in his shirt. More than anything he wanted to get Anne back, but . . . the green jewel . . . it could be the key to finding his mother, to finding out who he was.

"This is great, lads, really great," Ross said, his cheeks reddening. He held the contents of the bag to show Jacques, who clearly wasn't as impressed. "We'll take this and see if we can't be on a ship this afternoon! And, Nubby, why don't you see what you can do about feeding these men!"

"I'm on it already, Cap'n!" Nubby held up three lizards by the tail.

"Captain?" Cat came running and skidded to a stop beside Ross.

"Yes, lad?"

"I want to go with you," said Cat. "To see about the boat."

"I'm sure that Jacques and I can handle it—just rest up, stay out of the—"

"Please, sir, I've got to do something to help Anne."

Ross appraised the young man. "Right. Then follow me."

Vesa Turinen was an old Finnish sailor who operated a thriving trade business from his cliffside home two miles from Smuggler's Bay. Aside from St. Pierre's fortress, it was the highest elevation in the northern Caicos. When Jacques St. Pierre, Declan Ross, and Cat climbed the last step of the incline, they found that old Vesa was already quite busy. At least a dozen merchants surrounded the odd-looking man, who was seated at a desk and scribbling furiously in a ledger the size of a tabletop. His skin was tan and very wrinkled. His hair surrounded his balding head like a corona, and his moustache and beard fell like an avalanche of fresh snow.

Ignoring the others gathered round, St. Pierre pushed his way to the front of the line. "Vesa!"

"Yes, Miss Hillary, I know," the old man replied to one of his patrons. "I won't forget your inks."

"Vesa, it is Jacques Saint Pierre. I have a proposition for you."

"Get in line, like the rest," Vesa whined. "Can you not see the customers in front of you?" Some of the other customers scowled at St. Pierre.

Jacques was furious. "Vesa Turinen, you great imbecile! You look up at me this instant!"

· "Ohhhh," said Vesa, and he grinned. "It's you, Jacques! Why, you have come yourself, now haven't you? Usually you send Esteban or Rafael. I expect you want your usual side of bacon?"

"Bacon?" Ross stared hard at Jacques. "But you told me—"

St. Pierre held up a hand. "Never mind that," he said to Ross. He turned back to Vesa. "I need you to dismiss these others. I have a huge offer to make you!" This got Vesa's attention. In midsentence, Vesa closed up his massive ledger book and said, "Sorry, my good ladies and gentlemen. I need to attend to some personal business. I shall see you in one hour." The other customers moaned and scoffed at this. They waved bags of gold coins, but Vesa ignored them as he led Jacques, Ross, and Cat out on a wide balcony overlooking the Atlantic.

Vesa bade them to sit and poured them all a glass of something purplish and smelling of fruit. As they sat down, St. Pierre knew it was time to begin the game. "This is an exquisite view, Vesa," he said, his voice rich with awe.

"Yes," said Vesa. "Not quite as good as from your hilltop fort. Aw, where are my manners, Jacques. I am so sorry to hear about your fortress. Nasty pirate work, that?"

"It was," he replied carefully. "I lost all my wares to fire, but the structure is still sound."

"That is good, that is good. Now, tell me, what is this magnificent offer you mentioned?"

"Vesa, this is Captain Declan Ross and his ship's mate, Cat."

"Declan Ross? The pirate? The Sea Wolf?"

Ross inclined his head slightly.

"I am honored to meet you," said Vesa. "You are not here to rob me, are you?" He laughed and then took a deep sip from his glass.

"No, Vesa, we need you to take us to Portugal."

Vesa spluttered and sprayed juice off the side of the balcony. "Portugal?! Good heavens, Jacques, why don't you take one of your own ships?"

"Oh, that I could. None of mine are due back from England or Spain any time soon, and we are . . . in need of haste."

"But I am to leave for Venezuela in the morning. I have patrons to shop for and a pretty profit to make." Ross cringed. "Nonetheless," Vesa went on, "I might be persuaded if the price is right."

"I thought you might say something like that," said St. Pierre. "I came with a sampling of what we are prepared to pay if you'll make this journey." He nodded at Ross, who opened the satchel and showed its contents to Vesa.

"It is a long trip, especially coming home," he said, squinting into the bag. "And the weather this time of year is not so—you cannot be serious, Jacques! You want me to hire a crew and take you all the way to Portugal for this?"

"No, actually, I have a crew. There are sixty of us that we want you to take to Portugal."

"Sixty?! For this pittance of gold and silver? You must be joking—what is that, a tooth?"

"Vesa, Vesa!" Jacques implored. "This is just a sample of—"

"A sample of nothing!" Vesa crossed his arms. "Jacques, you insult me. First you chase my customers away. Then you ask me to abandon their monies for this little bag? You may swim to Portugal."

Jacques felt his throat constrict. "I will put my fortress in the trade."

Vesa stopped his tirade in midsentence. "Your fortress . . . and the land?"

"And the land."

"That is . . . more substantial. But no, forgive me for saying this, but there is not much left of your fortress. I would need to put in so much work, and I am old."

"But think of the view—a fine place to retire."

"Ahhh, yes, that is true. . . . No, I cannot! Jacques, my friend, . . . I . . . I just cannot. Now, I must go and open my ledger." Vesa finished his glass in one swallow, stood, and started to walk away.

"Wait," Cat said. "Wait, Mister Turinen, I have something . . . something to sweeten the deal." Ross and Jacques looked at him with a mixture of confusion and curiosity. Vesa turned slowly toward Cat.

Reaching into his shirt, Cat fished out the pouch and opened it. He reached inside and removed the green jewel. The sun exposed every brilliant facet. It flashed and sparkled like no jewel anyone on that balcony had ever seen before. Vesa nearly tripped getting back to the table.

"I have never seen an emerald that size before," said Jacques.

"Emerald?" Vesa scoffed. "You are losing your eye!" He reached into one pocket of his trousers after another until, at last, he brought out a small eyeglass. "This, this is a green diamond. I have never seen one before, but I would stake my life upon it." He turned to Cat. "Where did you find this, my lad?"

"I, uh . . . my mother gave it to me."

"And you would part with this for you and your friends to go to Portugal?"

Cat caught an odd glance from Captain Ross. It seemed he was willing Cat to say no. But Cat thought of Anne. "I will give this to you, Mister Turinen, if you would bear us to Portugal."

Vesa eyed Cat's pouch. "You, uh, have any more of these in there?"

Cat's shoulders hunched. "No, it's the only one."

"And one of a kind, I'll wager," said Vesa. "Very well. For this, the fortress, and the land . . . I accept your offer. When do you wish to leave?"

Ross looked at Cat, and pride swelled within him. He turned to Vesa. "By sundown today."

"Let me think. Portugal is a three-week journey—two and a half if we have prevailing winds the entire voyage. You don't just up and go. You need provisions for your crew?"

Ross nodded.

"Ah, I see." Vesa held the jewel up to admire it in the sunlight. "A green diamond! I must have it. Get your men, Jacques. Meet me at the sloop at sundown. I will make all the arrangements. I have not been to Portugal in a long time. I will bring many wares to sell. Tapestries, cane sugar, spices—this may well be more profitable than Venezuela, after all."

35

A Vast Ocean

Flagg, the *Raven*'s ship surgeon, lifted the bandages off Padre Dominguez's wounded shoulder. "The bullwhip those idiots used shredded the skin. Even so, I have done my best stitchwork. There just was not enough flesh left."

"That is the best you could do?" rasped Thorne. He looked down upon the purplish flesh and the crisscrossing stitches.

"It will look better when it heals. You may be able to make out more of the map's details at that time."

"It has been three days," Thorne complained. "How much longer will that take?"

"The color will fade and return to normal in another week, maybe two."

Thorne scanned the map, following the sea lanes he'd need to travel from the coast of Africa, slightly east of the Azores Islands, and north . . . but how far and through what peril, he could not tell. "I need this information, or we could be hunting in the open ocean for years!"

"There are other ways to get the information," suggested Flagg.

He reached for a long rectangular wooden case and delicately caressed its top. "When he has recovered, I feel certain I can . . . persuade this monk to describe the rest of the map."

Thorne smiled. "Very well. In the meantime, Skellick has a man good with a sketch. Marley, I think is his name. I will have him come and draw up a sea chart based on the monk's unspoiled flesh."

Flagg nodded and put his wooden case back on the shelf.

The hundred-gun HMS *Oxford* led a flotilla of five warships east across the Atlantic. Sir Nigel paced in front of his friend's desk in the captain's quarters. "We must turn back, Commodore," he said. "Or at least get word to a goodly portion of our fleet to turn back. Declan Ross is one pirate—a particularly irritating pirate, yes—but just one of many, nonetheless. We have left many of our settlements undermanned and our shipping lanes unguarded."

Commodore Blake did not respond. He held his head in his hands and leaned forward over the sea charts he'd scoured day after day. In truth, he wanted to return to New Providence, where his beloved wife, Dolphin, waited impatiently.

"Commodore? Do you intend to sail all the way to England?"

"Nigel, I am caught between the devil and the deep blue sea. To return to New Providence or sail on to England—without Thorne or Ross to show for the effort? That is no way to maintain a new commission."

"True, sir, but should something happen to one of our settlements in our absence . . ."

"Aw, this is madness!" Blake slammed his fist on the chart. "How do the pirates continually outwit us, Nigel?"

"It is a vast ocean, my lord," he replied. "His Majesty's Navy is yet too small to cover it all."

"Very well." Blake motioned for Nigel to look at the sea chart. "We will return, but what route do you suggest?"

"I do not think we should simply retrace our steps. Let us chart a more northerly route. If by chance we are ahead of Ross and he is making for his homeland, we may yet catch him in our snare."

"What a miracle that would be," said the commodore. "Send word to Mister Jordan, plot us a course back to the Caribbean. Keep a bit north of the usual trade route."

Bartholomew Thorne checked his compass. "Excellent, Mister Skellick," he said to his quartermaster at the wheel of the *Raven*. "Let's stay south of the trade route. We do not want to run into the British . . . not yet."

"Aye, sir."

Vesa Turinen was as good as his word. When Ross's remaining crew arrived at his dock at sundown, they found his ship, a sixty-five-foot sloop, loaded to the gills with supplies for the long voyage. Nubby found himself in heaven. There were casks of spices, crates of salted meats and fresh vegetables, and barrels of fresh water. There was even a small pen built into the hold for lambs. Vesa was very partial to freshly cooked lamb. Nubby had never cooked lamb before, but it couldn't be much different from iguanas, could it?

Unsure of Ross's men, Vesa brought a dozen of his own usual

crew. One of them, a Spaniard, went by the name Caiman because he was beastly strong, had a thick, muscular neck, and had skin so toughened by the sun and harsh weather that it appeared hard and scaly. And, to Cromwell's dismay, Caiman kept a pet crocodile in a crate belowdecks.

Three days into their journey to Portugal, the crew had fallen into a routine. Vesa, Stede, and Ross alternated at the ship's wheel. Cat and Midge led teams to handle the rigging and repair small tears in the ship's sails. St. Pierre and Red Eye oversaw the upkeep of the ships eight cannons—not that they would be much use in a fight. Sloops were good for one thing—running. Even with the weight of sixty men, ten lambs, and holds bulging with supplies, a sloop kept a very shallow draft and could make tremendous speed, especially in the kind of favorable wind they had now.

"Keeps blowing like this, mon," said Stede, "and we'll make it to Portugal in two weeks!"

"Never made a journey in such time!" said Vesa.

"With all respect to your men, Vesa, you've never had a crew like this one," said Ross proudly. He looked across the deck at his men. Every one of them had lost dear friends. Yet, overall, they seemed to be holding up well and finding ways to keep busy. Vesa played the fiddle better than any of the crew had heard before. Jules often sang in his deep bass while the old man played, and the men would dance. Cat and Red Eye loved to spar, and, Ross noted, Cat had improved with each session.

They'd had other entertainment as well. Ross laughed, remembering his encounter the previous day. Ross had been up on the bow when he'd heard bursts of raucous laughter from the stern. Ross decided to investigate. He walked past the mast and ducked under a spar when, suddenly, Caiman appeared. He wasn't looking and bumped hard into Ross. After dozens of heartfelt apologies, Caiman continued on toward the front of the ship. Ross scratched his head and noticed Red Eye, Jules, and St. Pierre leaning up against the poop deck. St. Pierre wore a grin that spoke of turbulent laughter simmering just below the surface. Cat couldn't control himself. He covered his mouth, but laughing snorts escaped. Only Red Eye was able to keep a straight face. "Say, Cap'n," he said. "What time do you have?"

Ross reached into his coat pocket . . . but came up empty. Then, with more urgency, he patted his other pockets, checked the satchel at his side, and began searching the deck—all to the roaring laughter of the others. "Are you looking for this?" Caiman called from behind. Ross turned and, to his astonishment, his old pocket watch dangled from its chain in Caiman's hand.

"How did . . . but . . . I know it was in my pocket," Ross stammered.

"And so it was," said Caiman. "But, with my fleet fingers, I picked your pocket."

Ross had been amazed completely. He hadn't felt the watch being removed when Caiman had run into him. For the entertainment alone, Ross was glad Caiman was aboard. Of course, no one felt too comfortable around his pet, or, as Caiman called it, his "little gatita."

Three shrill whistles shook Commodore Blake out of his narrow bed. Without his boots or his saber, he raced out of his quarters and up onto the main deck.

"Commodore Blake!" called his bosun, Ezekiel Jordan, a long spyglass in his hand. "Sir, there's a ship ahead!"

Blake's heart raced, but he scanned the horizon and saw nothing. "Are you sure?"

"Aye, sir."

"Give me the glass." Blake slowly traced the spyglass across the rolling seas. On his second pass he saw it. Just as a distant swell subsided, a dark shape was there. Miles off yet, but definitely there. "You are quite right, Mister Jordan!" he said. "Sir Nigel, see to it that we double Mister Jordan's rations at supper this evening."

"Aye, Commodore."

Blake continued to stare through the spyglass. "One mast," he said, and his shoulders sagged. "A galley, maybe a sloop. Alas, I suppose it was too much to hope for."

"What, sir?" asked Mr. Jordan.

"Declan Ross," he replied. "But Ross's ship is a two-masted brig. Nonetheless, let's pursue. There may be something of interest."

"That's a British ship of the line, first rate," said Jacques St. Pierre as he looked through the telescope.

"First rate?" Ross exclaimed.

"Three gun decks," Jacques went on. "Ninety cannons, at least. First rate is what they call such a vessel."

"That under a commodore's command?"

"Commodore Brandon Blake, to be exact," said Jacques gravely.

"How can ya possibly b' seeing that from here?" asked Stede.

"I cannot see Commodore Blake himself . . . obviously," admonished St. Pierre. "But I saw his ship, the HMS *Oxford*, off the coast of Dominica one time. That is him. Absolument!"

"So what?" Vesa asked. "I run into the British all the time. I might have to part with a case of this or a barrel of that now and then, but the British rarely give me any trouble. You'll just look like the crew of a merchant mission overseas."

"We left a rather . . . lasting impression on Commodore Blake," Ross explained. "He will recognize Jacques, Red Eye, Midge, Cat, Jules, and me. He'd hang us all here at sea, I'm sure."

"Ah . . . that bad, eh?" Vesa asked.

"I am afraid so." Ross took the telescope from Jacques.

"Do we run?" asked Caiman.

Ross shook his head. "We can't afford the time. Maybe we outrun Blake, but that lets Thorne get farther ahead . . . too far, and then Anne's gone."

"But, sir," said Midge. "If we get cau—"

"It will do us no good to run," Ross said. "I doubt we could lose him anyway. There are four frigates with him. If we run, they will fan out. We'd be swept up eventually."

Vesa looked around. "I will hide you."

"Where?" Red Eye asked. "Are you going to roll the six of us up in a tapestry?"

"Maybe just you," Vesa shot back. "Now, shut your mouth and let me think."

Anne had not seen another person since two deck hands came down to remove the bodies. They'd teased her before they left, and with the dead men's blood still wet on their hands, they'd thrown a long crust of bread into her cell. She'd left the bread where it fell. It wasn't long before the rats scurried away with it. And then it was quiet . . . until now. She could hear someone on the stairs.

"Annnnnne," rasped a voice from the shadows. The flicker of the lantern caught his cold blue eyes.

Involuntarily, she backed into the farthest corner of her cell.

"What ever is the matter, my dear?" Thorne asked as he stepped near to the cell's bars. A large key ring jangled at his waist. "Ah, yes, I know. It is a bit lonely down here. I rarely have a need for prisoners."

Anne fought to keep herself from trembling, but lost. His very presence seemed to bleed cruelty and death. "Please . . . please leave me alone," she said.

He ignored her and pushed his face into the gap between the bars. "Little Anne," he said. "Now all grown up." Anne felt a prick of cold, like a corpse's fingernail, run up her back.

"Yes," he went on. "So much like your mother. I knew her—for a time—before she died. Edinburgh is a marvelous port. I raised my first crew there. Pity your father wouldn't join me then. If he had, we wouldn't be in this . . . situation now."

"I don't ever remember seeing you," Anne said, emerging a little from the corner.

"Thirteen years ago," Thorne said with a sheepish smile. "I imagine you've forgotten much that you once knew."

"What do you mean?"

"Another time, perhaps," said Thorne, and instantly his demeanor intensified. "Anne, I have no desire to harm you." He stepped away from the bars, reached the lantern, and turned up its flame. "So long as you tell me what I wish to know." He removed a long parchment from his coat, unrolled the scroll, and showed her.

Anne recognized it instantly. It was the map to the Isle of Swords. "What have you done to Padre Dominguez?" she demanded.

"Nothing," he replied, studying her. "Nothing but heal his wounds after those two idiots flogged him. He is resting . . . for now. And he may fully recover. You have seen the map before. Tell me, what is missing from this section here?" He pointed to the upper right quadrant, where Padre Dominguez's shoulder had been ruined.

She stared and tried to remember. But the only time she'd seen it was fleeting. Padre Dominguez had been showing it to Stede and her father, but he'd quickly covered his shoulders with the remnants of his robe when Anne entered the captain's quarters. There had been some sort of triangles or sharp stones, she thought, and something about a serpent, but she couldn't remember.

"You don't know, do you?" It was not a question. "I can read it on your face and in your eyes. You have seen the map, but you have not studied it. Pity." He rolled up the parchment and slid it inside his coat. He turned and strode back toward the stairs, but stopped before disappearing into the shadows. "Your father killed my apprentice and tried to steal from me," he said. "He has made his life forfeit."

"No!" Anne flew to the bars. "No, please don't hurt him!"

"A noble request," said Thorne without turning. He waited a few moments as if weighing the consequences of his next thought. "When the monk is well, he will be placed in the cell next to yours. If you can discover from him the rest of the journey, the way to the Isle of Swords, I promise I will spare your father's life. In fact, I will leave you safely in Edinburgh with a portion of Constantine's Treasure. Enough that your father will never have to go to sea as a pirate again. Isn't that what he's always wanted?"

Thorne left the deck. The sound of his heavy boots on the stairs was gone. All that remained were the creaks of the ship and the hypnotic feel of the ocean rolling. Anne knew she could not trust Bartholomew Thorne. But in her putrid cell, she could think of few options.

36
VESA'S ARK

Have they changed course?" Blake asked.

"No, sir," replied Mr. Jordan.

"Done anything evasive?"

"No, sir. I've been watching." The sloop was close enough now that they could observe its movements without a spyglass.

Sir Nigel was at the commodore's side. "Perhaps we can get a barrel of salted beef for our troubles."

"We'll see," Blake replied. "Or maybe this sloop is captained by some lesser pirate . . . one we can catch."

"In the sheep pen?!" Midge exclaimed. "Are you mad? That's quite possibly the worst-smellin' place on the whole ship!"

"Except for yer mouth, mon," said Stede. He slapped Midge on the back so hard he nearly fell over.

"Look," said Vesa. "If they board us—which they will—they'll search the barrels, the crates, any normal place where items they might be interested in could be kept. You just stay low in the pens, and we'll cover you with hay."

"Stay low?" said Midge. "But that means we'll be in the—"

"That's enough!" barked Ross. "So be it. We have no more time to waste. In a few minutes Blake will be able to see us on deck. We need to get below now. Vesa, if you've an empty crate, have the men put their cutlasses and daggers in it. It will go well if you are a merchant selling weapons abroad, but not if your crew is armed to the teeth."

"Never in this life has Jacques Saint Pierre been forced into such a demeaning position," said the Frenchman, now buried in straw with a fresh pile of sheep scat three inches from his nose.

"Aw, Jacques," said Red Eye. "It could be worse."

"How?"

"Caiman's little croc friend could be in here with us."

"He's not, is he?" Midge lifted his head up through the straw.

"Get your head down!" Ross hissed. "And Jules, can't you get any lower? You look like a mountain of straw."

"I'll try," came Jules's deep voice from a massive pile of straw in the back of the pen. Two of the five remaining sheep stood in front of him, but still, Ross thought it looked strange.

"Quiet!" Ross whispered. "I hear something."

"Sloop captain," called a ship's mate from the prow of the *Oxford*, "state your business!"

"I am Vesa Turinen from the Caicos. I carry a variety of goods for trade in Portugal."

"Portugal? A bit late in the year for such a journey."

"Yes, well, it is my last trip for the season."

"We are looking for pirates who were rumored to be traveling in these sea lanes."

"Pirates?" Vesa feigned shock. "Good heavens."

A little farther back on deck and out of Vesa's field of vision, Commodore Blake and Sir Nigel listened intently. "What do you think?" asked Blake.

"Sounds dreadfully old," replied Sir Nigel. "Not likely to be a pirate."

"Yes, the scoundrels do tend to be short-lived, don't they? Despite that, we will board and search the decks."

"Aye, sir." Sir Nigel nodded to the ship's mate.

"Vesa Turinen," he called, "prepare to be boarded."

Declan Ross lay very still under the straw. He'd heard the ship's mate and knew that any moment Commodore Blake and his men would board the sloop. He also knew that if he was to be captured, Anne would most likely die, and Bartholomew Thorne would gain hold of the greatest treasure since the discovery of the New World.

Caiman came down through a forward hatch and shuffled through the crates and barrels until he came to a small crate that was covered with a piece of tarp. "Ah, mi gatita," he said. He pulled a piece of salted pork out of his pocket and reached under the tarp.

"There you go," he said. "You must be so lonely locked up in this crate. Sorry, but Vesa made me." Caiman turned and looked into the sheep pen. "Are we comfortable?" Caiman laughed. He turned and walked away, headed back to the hatch.

Suddenly, every one of Ross's muscles tensed. An idea took hold of him so powerfully that he could not will it away from his mind. It was brazen . . . and, he thought, probably stupid. He leaped up, sending straw in all directions amd startling the sheep. Caiman was so surprised by Ross's appearance, he neglected to secure the crate. Ross leaped out of the pen, took Caiman by the arm, and explained what he had in mind. Caiman nodded and said, "I can do it, but you better hurry." They heard a thud from above and then wood scraping against wood.

A gangplank, Ross thought. He looked around anxiously. "My kingdom for pen and paper," he muttered. He charged up the narrow aisle between crates and ducked through dozens of hammocks slung up in the rafters. Then, in Vesa's quarters, he found what he was looking for. Ross jammed the quill pen into the half-full ink bottle and scribbled furiously on a small piece of paper.

"Captain, they are on board!" Caiman called from the hold. Ross dipped one more time, knocked over the bottle of ink, and growled. The ink pooled around a little Bible and rolled down the desk. Ross finished the message, folded the paper, and glanced to the now ink-stained Bible. "Please," Ross said aloud—but to whom he was not at that moment sure. "He must find this at the right time and while he is in the right place."

"Captain!"

Ross raced out of Vesa's quarters and jammed the folded message into Caiman's hand. They heard voices overhead. Caiman immediately climbed the ladder to the top deck. Ross sprinted across the hold. He banged into a stack of crates. One teetered and fell with a crash just as Ross dove into the sheep pen. He landed in the straw and muck and apparently also on Cat's hand. "Oww, get off," Cat said. A sheep bleated at Ross, but there was nothing he could do. Two British sailors stepped off the ladder into the hold.

"Place is packed tight, now isn't it?" one of them asked. "Ought to be able to find somethin' of worth, eh, Johann?"

"Ahg, what is that terrible odor?" Johann scowled. "It smells like me mum's chicken coop back in Bristol."

"Don't know, mate, but it's not much worse than the bilge water in the *Oxford*. I'll look down this end. You take the other."

"Thanks, Patrick, you're a bit of all right."

Johann lifted a lantern off one of the posts and made his way quickly toward Vesa's quarters. But Patrick took his time examining crates, casks, and barrels. Soon, he discovered the sheep pen.

Several days after her encounter with Bartholomew Thorne, Anne awoke in her cell to the jangle of keys. Several of Thorne's men moved slowly away from the cell next to Anne's. She turned and saw that the other cell was no longer empty. The weak lantern's light revealed the still form of a man who lay on an uneven cot in the cell. He wore a dirty white tunic and brown breeches that were too short for his legs. Anne recognized him, even without his brown robe. "Padre Dominguez?" she whispered. "Padre Dominguez?"

"Anne," he said, and as he turned, she saw that his cheeks were tear-stained. Fresh tears rolled as he spoke. "I am so sorry, Anne. Sorry that I have gotten you into all this. I was foolish to put you and your father into harm's way."

"No, no," Anne said, reaching through the bars to touch his hand. "Thorne would have come for us anyway . . . after what happened with Chevillard."

The monk nodded ever so slightly. "Nonetheless, I am sorry."

Anne didn't know if she could bring herself to do it, or if she could, how? *If you can discover from him the rest of the journey, the way to the Isle of Swords, I promise I will spare your father's life.* A series of phrases came into her mind, a means to an end. And as she spoke the first, it felt like she had just sold her soul. "Padre, there's something that I don't understand."

He stared at her curiously. "What is it, child?"

"The treasure, on the Isle of Swords," she went on, carefully choosing her words. "It must be very great for Thorne to go to such lengths to get it."

Never taking his dark eyes off her, he said, "It is. More gold and silver than ten galleons could carry and vaults of jewels. The Emperor Constantine had amassed wealth from every corner of the known world."

Anne nodded. "But what I don't understand is, well . . . it's treasure. Greedy men like Thorne want it. My father even. But why . . . why you? Why the monks of your order? What do you care about such riches?"

The monk's eyes narrowed. "For hundreds of years, we have used the gold to buy freedom for thousands of slaves, to build monasteries like the one on Saint Celestine across the globe, and to spread the faith." He was silent for a moment. "To let a devil like Thorne gain such riches . . . this we could not bear. But . . . the Isle of Swords holds something more important to us."

"Padre, I need to—"

"Tell me, Anne," he interrupted. "What price did he offer you?"

Anne felt the prick of ten thousand icy needles all over her body. Her mouth fell open, but she did not speak.

"Your life?" the monk asked. "Your father's life?"

Anne's head fell against the bars, and she wept. "Yes . . . yes," she cried.

"You are forgiven, child," he said as he reached through the bars and laid a hand upon her head. "But it is better for you not to know. I alone must bear the burden of the Isle of Swords."

"Welcome aboard my little sloop," said Vesa with a slight bow to Commodore Blake and Sir Nigel. "I am Captain Vesa Turinen, and this is my quartermaster, Stede."

"That's a fine boat ya b' gotten there," Stede said.

"Thank you, Mister Stede," Blake replied. "His Majesty's finest."

"How many cannon, ninety, a hundred?"

"One hundred ten, to be precise," said Sir Nigel. Stede whistled.

"May I show you my ship?" Vesa asked.

"Certainly, Captain," said Commodore Blake. "Sir Nigel?"

"Actually, sir, if you do not mind," said Nigel, "I think I'll go check on the lads in the hold." The commodore nodded, and Sir Nigel went below.

Vesa led Commodore Blake fore and aft, boring him with details about the cleverly arranged rigging and sails. Just as they turned at the mainmast, another sailor ducked under the main spar and ran straight into Commodore Blake.

"Caiman!" Vesa exclaimed, aghast at his foolish deck hand.

"I am so sorry," Caiman said. "I was distracted. I did not see you."

"What's all this?" asked Sir Nigel as he came up behind Patrick.

"Sheep pen, sir," he replied. "First time I've seen anything like this in the bottom of a ship. Like Noah and the ark, eh?" He laughed, but Nigel was not amused.

"Except Noah's ship had two of every kind of animal, not just these putrid-smelling sheep." Sir Nigel stepped closer to the pen and stared. "An awful lot of straw for just these five creatures."

Ross felt like Sir Nigel was staring right at him. He hadn't had time to throw extra hay on top. He wondered if—

"Patrick, what do you make of that?" Sir Nigel asked, pointing into the pen. "See, in the straw there?" Ross's heart caught in his throat.

"I don't know, sir," Patrick said, staring.

Something hissed. They both jumped. "What the devil is that?" said Nigel, staring at the dark space between two fallen crates to the left of the sheep pen. The hissing continued. Patrick stepped slowly backward, drawing a short sword as he moved.

A tapered, curving snout appeared, and then pale greenish eyes with vertical reptilian pupils. The creature's jaws opened, revealing dozens of irregular sharp teeth. Patrick dropped his sword. "It's a croc!" he exclaimed. He and Sir Nigel tripped all over each other trying to get away. They ran all the way across the hold until they slammed into Johann.

"Patrick? Sir Nigel?" he stammered. "What's going on?"

"See, I told you it's like Noah's ark in 'ere!" Patrick yelled. "That was a blooming croc, it was!"

"What?" Johann laughed nervously.

"In the back of the hold," Sir Nigel said, regaining his composure. "There's a sheep pen and, apparently, a loose crocodile!"

"I've had a bit more luck up this end," said Johann, stifling a laugh. "Ten barrels of salted meat, maybe more."

"Lead the way," said Sir Nigel.

The HMS *Oxford* had left Vesa Turinen's sloop without any further incident. The ship was now a few barrels lighter, and while that frustrated Vesa to no end, Declan Ross and his crew were just glad to be rid of the British.

As the sun set that evening, Cat found Captain Ross at the stern rather than the bow. "We'll get her back," Cat said.

Ross nodded. But at that moment, he wasn't thinking of Anne, at least not directly. Instead, he wondered about a small piece of paper in Commodore Blake's pocket.

37

DESTINATIONS AND DETOURS

As far as Anne could tell, she had been a prisoner of Bartholomew Thorne for two weeks and four days. The ship had stopped moving, the temperature had risen, and the air was thick with humidity. Some of Thorne's men had come and taken Padre Dominguez away. She was not surprised when, minutes later, they returned for her. They led her to the main deck, and she shielded her eyes in the brightness. What she saw took her breath away. The *Raven* was docked among dozens of other tall ships, and each had its own pier that spread out from the island like a many-fingered hand. Every pier teemed with sailors. Some carried crates or casks, others led dark-skinned men in chains to a large plantation-style house just up from the docks. And high above it all, watching like a gargoyle from its perch on the rocky mountainside, was a dark fortress.

"Your new home," rasped a voice from behind. "For a time." Thorne's face appeared over her shoulder, and he leered as he strode around to face her. He reached into his coat and pulled out a rolled parchment. "I trust you can now complete this map," he said, his lip quivering with expectation.

Anne looked away. "I . . . I tried," she said, bracing for the sharp blow that would surely follow. "Padre Dominguez guessed your intentions. He refused to tell me the way."

Thorne did not strike her. He did not seem angry. His face was expressionless, which was somehow worse. "Clever man," he said. "So be it. There is due cause for the three of us to have a little party. A private affair, really. A select gathering. As soon as more of my fleet arrives and we make ready for the journey to the Isle of Swords, I will send out invitations. The three of us will attend, of course—oh, my ship's doctor, Mister Flagg, will be joining us as well."

"Two weeks and two days!" Vesa exclaimed. They had just tied off his sloop to a pier in Sines, a coastal city fifty miles south of Lisbon. "Never have I made such speed!"

"We had outstanding wind behind us," said Declan Ross. "But, as I said before, my crew may have had something to do with your speed."

Each with overstuffed satchels of provisions, Ross's crew stepped from the ship to the pier and waited for their captain. Ross lingered and shook Vesa's hand. "You have been a gracious host," he said. "Many lives may be saved because of this trip."

"Taking you to Portugal will save lives?" Vesa snorted. "Probably your own. I am glad to have been of service."

Ross saw Caiman over Vesa's shoulder. "Your man, Caiman, there," Ross said, wishing he had asked St. Pierre to attempt this deal.

Vesa looked back and nodded. Suspicion gleamed in his eye. "Yesss?"

"He has expressed to me an interest in pirating," said Ross. "And I could use a man like him. So I thought—"

"Can you get me another green diamond?" Vesa asked, his voice thick and lusty.

"Possibly, but I cannot guarantee."

"Caiman!" Vesa hollered. "Fetch your bag and get on with your new employer!"

Just a few days from New Providence, the HMS *Oxford* carved through the Atlantic with some decent speed. The winds had been less than favorable, making the journey much longer than Commodore Blake had hoped. The delay had given him too much time to think about his mistakes. He stood now in front of a long looking glass in his quarters belowdecks. The lanterns cast a warm glow on the golden lapels of his blue commodore's frock coat—a coat he felt sure he'd lose when he arrived at the British fort on New Providence and had to explain to Lord Admiral Konrath that he had failed to capture Bartholomew Thorne or Declan Ross. "Or any other pirate, for that matter," Blake grumbled aloud. He removed his coat and tossed it with disgust over a nearby armchair.

He went to undo a button on his waistcoat when he noticed a small square of paper on the floor beneath his coat. Being an orderly man, he knew very well the contents of his pockets. And this paper, he thought as he picked it up, certainly did not belong to him. Looking over his shoulder as if someone might be playing some prank upon him, and convinced that no one could be watching, he unfolded the paper and began to read.

Commodore Blake's eyes widened as he read. In disbelief, he looked up at last. *Can this be real?* he wondered. *Can I trust him?* Blake left his commodore's coat behind and ran to the main deck. "Mister Jordan!" he cried. "Call all hands; we are turning this ship around!"

As Ross, Cat, and Jacques St. Pierre hiked rapidly along the Portuguese coast, Ross noticed the rest of the crew had fallen behind. While Ross waited for them, he looked at the city. Aside from his beloved Edinburgh, Sines was Ross's favorite city in the world. Gabled roofs, tall steeples, and lots of cobbled stone—it all seemed so welcoming. And Ross had always wanted to explore the verdant foothills nestled in the distance behind the city. At last the others caught up, most of them huffing or gasping for air. "Ramiro's marina isn't far," Ross said to encourage them. "The path will level out somewhat."

The path wound around at the base of a large stony hill. Ross stopped short just after turning the corner. "I see Ramiro has not been idle these many years." Cat and St. Pierre joined him and saw a busy marina. There were three tall ships moored there, and onshore there was the skeleton of a fourth surrounded by men whose dark skin glistened.

As Ross and his crew entered the shipyard, men stopped working. Some leaned out between the ribs of the ship. Others reached instinctively toward a weapon. Suddenly, a man ran out from behind the construction. He was barefoot and wore olive green pants that stretched only to his knees. The large white shirt he wore billowed as he ran. As he grew near, he did not reduce speed. He slammed into the captain and embraced him in a crushing hug. "Declan Ross! So good to see you!"

Turning three shades of red—both from embarrassment and from being squeezed within an inch of death—Ross replied, "It's good to see you too, Ramiro." Ross coughed, and Ramiro finally released him. Stede, Red Eye, Jules, and the others raced in behind them. Thinking something was amiss, Red Eye had his sword drawn.

"Put away the blade," Ross said. "And allow me to introduce you to Ramiro de Ferro Goncalo." Ramiro shook hands with everyone nearby, and each one of them flexed the hand that had been shaken. Ramiro's grip was so strong that even Jules winced after their handshake.

"Sorry," Ramiro said. "All these years working with my hands, you see." They looked with wonder at Ramiro. He was two hands shorter than Ross and looked much older. He had gray hair tied back in a curly tail. His forehead was furrowed by deep wrinkles, and crow's feet sprouted from the corners of his eyes. His moustache was gray and curled wildly. Only his eyebrows were still dark. These arched devilishly above his restless brown eyes. Ramiro lowered his spectacles and looked over all his new guests. "So, Declan, what brings you all the way to Portugal?"

Ross noticed all the workers still staring. "Shall we walk and talk?"

"Absolutely," he said. "Come, bring your lads. I will show you my ships." He turned back to his own men. "Get back to work, ya sluggards!" Once again, hammers and chisels flew.

No sooner had they begun walking along the marina than Ross said, "Ramiro, my friend, I am in great need."

"Then I am glad you came to me," Ramiro said amiably.

"I need a ship."

If Ramiro was shocked he did not show it. He looked thoughtfully at Ross. "What about the *Wallace*?"

"Bartholomew Thorne burned it and half my crew, sent it to the bottom of Smuggler's Bay in the Caicos."

"That scoundrel," muttered Ramiro.

"And . . . he took Anne."

Ramiro's face became anguished. "Not little Anne! Why?"

"Not so little anymore. Sixteen now. And as to why, I can only guess he wants to draw me out, use Anne as the bait. I need a ship to go and get her."

Ramiro did not respond. He simply began walking. Ross and his men followed. They approached an impressive-looking two-masted brigantine. "I am not sure what I can do for you," said Ramiro, shaking his head sadly. "I cannot give you this brig. It is promised to a very powerful prince named Alphonzo who lives in Lisbon. He has already paid for it, and, as you know, I never go back on a deal."

Ramiro picked up the pace, and they closed in on the next ship. It had three narrow masts, and its body was longer, more sleek than the brig. Ramiro explained, "I cannot give you this frigate either. The East India Trading Company purchased it outright. They plan to make it an escort for their runs through the Spanish Main. And again, I will not break this deal."

Ross groaned. "Are you going to help me or—"

Ramiro raised a hand. "Follow me," he said. Ross and his still-murmuring crew did as they were told. Some looked back over their shoulders at the frigate. They stopped immediately when they came into the presence of the last ship docked at the marina. They had seen it from the hilltop and recognized its size, but so close now, it was breathtaking.

"Now, this," the shipbuilder said, "this is my masterpiece. I have combined features of the British ship of the line and the French corvette. I call it a man-of-war!"

"Great biscuits and gravy!" Nubby exclaimed. Cat, Jules, and the others began to file past Ramiro as he told of his ship.

"She is the ultimate blend of speed, gunnery, and maneuverability. Two hundred twenty feet long, and just a twenty-foot draft."

"Twenty feet!" Ross exclaimed. "How did you—?"

"No," Ramiro said. "It is my secret. Sixty guns, twenty-four eighteen-pounders, twenty-six twelve-pounders on the middle deck, and ten more six-pounders on top. She is fast, turns like a sloop, and, with those guns, she'll punch you straight in the mouth!"

Ross was speechless.

Ramiro was pleased by the crew's reaction to his finest ship. "I haven't sold her yet. Don't know if I ever will. I might be persuaded to let you borrow her, but—"

"But?"

"Stay. I'll be right back!" Ramiro scampered off down the marina. He flew up the gangplank and disappeared onto the man-of-war. He returned in like manner moments later, carrying something in his crossed arms. When he drew near, Ross saw that Ramiro had two rapier swords and a bundle of pads.

"Declan Ross," Ramiro said, "if you want the services of my ship, you must duel me for it."

38

THE ROBERT BRUCE

No, Ramiro," Ross implored.

Ramiro threw him the pads. Ross reluctantly slung the pad harness over his head. Ramiro handed him one of the rapiers, and Ross slid his hand inside the basket hilt. It had been a long time since he'd fenced. The two combatants slashed their blades and walked several paces away from the edge of the marina. Ross's crew looked on, wondering how all their hopes could come down to a single sword fight. Red Eye had half a mind to pull out a pistol and shoot the silly old shipbuilder. But he knew Ross would not approve.

The duel began with tentative moves. A slash from Ramiro, a poke from Ross. Suddenly, Ross lunged forward, and his rapier's point came within an inch of the middle of Ramiro's pads. But Ramiro denied the easy victory. He sidestepped like a matador and watched as Ross's momentum took him well past. Ramiro's rapier stabbed toward Ross's back, but Ross parried with a backhanded stroke. Back and forth it went, until Ross seemed to stumble. He backpedaled off balance and tried to ward off Ramiro's mad rush. But his block was weak. Ramiro knocked it down and jabbed his rapier into the center of Ross's pads. Ross fell backward and sprawled to the ground.

"I win again!" Ramiro exulted.

His disgusted face near burgundy, Ross stood, flung down his pads, and rubbed the center of his chest. "Yes, Ramiro, you win again."

"What was that?" Stede demanded. "The Declan Ross I know would have batted that sword away like it b' a mosquito!"

"Relax, Stede," Ross said.

"Don' tell me anything, Declan, ya—"

"He let me win!" Ramiro cried out. "And a fine job of pretending he did too. I almost felt like I'd really beaten you. Thank you, Declan, for again humoring an old man. The ship is yours . . . to borrow. If you like her, you can buy her outright."

Ross grinned. He looked up at the ship thoughtfully, then turned back to Ramiro. "You said if I like *her*, but, Ramiro, this ship is a *him*, not a *her*."

Ramiro cocked an eyebrow.

"For this ship," Ross explained, "shall henceforth be called the *Robert Bruce*!"

Ramiro clapped. "Planning to liberate Scotland from English tyranny?"

"Not exactly," Ross replied. "I need to free Anne and, if I can, Padre Dominguez. If, in the process, I can put down Bartholomew Thorne, then I'll do that too."

"I like the sound of that!" Ramiro said. "When do we leave?"

Ross looked at the old shipbuilder. "What do you mean, *we*?"

Ramiro patted Ross on the shoulder. "I trust you, Declan," he said. "But if you think I'm going to let this ship out of my sight without gold in hand, you're crazier than I am."

"You remember my ship's surgeon, don't you?" said Thorne to the priest who was strapped facedown on a stone table in the dungeon of Thorne's Cape Verde fortress. "Flagg is the one who restored your health."

His face pressed hard to the stone, Padre Dominguez could not see Thorne. But he felt a cold finger tracing its way up his bare back. "My good Mister Flagg patched your flesh back together with impressive skill. But he was unable to complete the task. The Isle of Swords remains beyond our grasp."

Anne watched from her cell. She saw Flagg open a long brown case. Whatever was inside glinted silver. "You know the rest of the map, Padre Dominguez." Thorne's raspy voice thickened, his breaths audible. "You hold all the cards . . . all but two. What do you say, priest; how will you play your hand?"

Padre Dominguez clenched his fists. Inwardly, he prayed not for deliverance, but for strength to endure the trial to come. He said nothing to Thorne.

"Very well," said Thorne. He nodded to Flagg. "You force me to play my first card." Flagg reached into the long wooden case. He removed a silver tool that looked something like a fork with long, sharp tines bent ninety degrees. A ghastly grin growing on his pasty white face, Flagg walked toward his helpless patient.

"Aw, Cap'n," Midge complained, "why do I always get stuck with the nasty jobs?"

"You're as tough a seaman as I've ever known, Midge. I know you won't let me down," Ross said.

Midge eyed his captain suspiciously. Then his crooked teeth appeared in a pride-filled smile. "All right, Cap'n," he said. "Where are the little buggers?"

"Ramiro put the monkeys in the hold," Ross said. "Nubby put a shallow pan under each cage, and that'll do for most of them. But watch the one with the white stripe between his ears. He tends to, uh . . . spray out rather than down."

"Oh, that's just smashin'," Midge replied. "So 'ow much do we need?"

"One barrelful ought to do it."

"Smashin', indeed." Midge turned and trudged down the stairs to the hold.

"You can stop this, Anne," said Thorne. "He told you the way, didn't he?"

"No, nooo," Anne cried. "He didn't tell me the way! Please stop. Please." She could barely look upon Padre Dominguez. His back glistened with fresh blood, and the ship's surgeon continued his work.

"I believe you, Anne," Thorne said. "Your face tells me the truth." Thorne knelt to be close to the monk's face. "Just tell me, Padre, and all the pain will stop." Padre Dominguez closed his eyes.

"I have used five of my favorite tools already," said Flagg. "He is a stubborn man."

"Yes, remarkable strength," Thorne hissed. "The vows of your order—you would rather die than violate them. I know all about the vows, Dominguez . . . and your beloved order. How noble and pious. But in the end, priest, you all are pirates just like me!"

Padre Dominguez opened his eyes. "Yes," said Thorne. "You know I speak the truth, don't you. The treasure on the island was never yours to begin with. You stole it from those who stole it from Constantine. How do you reconcile that with your God?"

"You are wrong," said Padre Dominguez weakly. "The Brethren are protectors, safekeepers . . ."

"Thieves!" Thorne barked. "You stole the treasure from Constantine!"

"We took the treasure," Padre Dominguez said with a knowing smile, "but we did not steal it. My order uses it as Emperor Constantine would have wished."

"And how do you know that?"

"Constantine was the founder of my order."

Thorne stood and reached for the bleeding stick, but Flagg said, "No, Captain, you will ruin my work. Let me finish." Flagg reached into his wooden case and produced a pair of shears.

"It is no use," Thorne said. "The monk cares nothing for his own life." The moment he spoke the words, his eyes drifted to Anne. "It is time to play my final card."

Cat had never seen a bow quite like the *Bruce*'s. The other ships, the brig and the sloop—even though Cat had no specific memory of ever sailing upon them before, the rigging, the sails, the masts and spars—all seemed familiar.

Not the *Bruce*. For one thing, most ships had a long shaft that pointed out of the bow like a unicorn's horn. This bowsprit was used to tie off one corner of a large triangular sail used to help the ship maneuver. The *Bruce* had no bowsprit, at least not in the traditional sense. Instead, the foremast was located much closer to the bow, and it had a long spar attached to it with a strange iron collar.

"Fantastic, isn't it?" Ramiro de Ferro Goncalo asked as he approached.

"Yes," Cat replied. "I mean, I guess it is. This spar, is it like a bowsprit?"

"Exactly like a bowsprit," said Ramiro. "With one major improvement. A normal bowsprit is fixed. It doesn't turn." Cat looked at the collar and noticed there were holes all the way around the collar and long iron pins in two of the holes—one on either side of the spar.

"Oh!" Cat exclaimed.

"Ah, you see?" Ramiro said. "This collar, which I call a gooseneck, allows us to turn the spar. The pins you see lock the spar in whatever position we want."

Cat imagined the ship needing to make a quick turn—or even a complete turn—with an enemy behind. To be able to adjust the bowsprit, to quickly change the angle of the sail—that would give them a huge advantage. "That's brilliant," Cat muttered.

"Thank you," said Ramiro. "The *Bruce* is really one of a kind. Should we come up against the infamous *Raven*, I suspect we will not find ourselves outgunned or outmaneuvered."

"Where shall I begin?" asked Flagg, holding up the shears so that Anne could see them. She lay on her back, strapped down to stone. They had positioned her so that Padre Dominguez could watch.

"Her pretty face," said Thorne.

"Excellent choice," said Flagg ghoulishly. "You will need to hold her head. I wouldn't want to cut . . . in the wrong place."

Anne thrashed about. "No! Nooo!" But Thorne held her head still. Tears streaked her face. Flagg pinched the skin at her jawbone and placed the scissor blades there. Anne cried out. Her legs and arms convulsed in the straps.

Padre Dominguez, weak from the ordeal, looked on and began to shake. He watched helplessly as Flagg closed the shears. Anne shrieked, and dark blood appeared on her jaw. "No! Thorne, you demon from hell!" Padre Dominguez screamed.

"Such language, Padre," Thorne mocked.

"I speak of the place," Padre Dominguez said. "The place where you will spend eternity. You will not go unpunished!"

"Shall we continue?" Thorne asked. He motioned to Flagg. The ship's surgeon wiped the blood away from Anne's chin with a cloth and moved in with the shears.

"NO!!" Padre Dominguez said, and he began to weep. "Stop. I will tell you what you want to know."

39

GHOSTS AT SEA AND ON LAND

Anne." Padre Dominguez's voice drifted through the cell bars.

Anne's eyes snapped open, and she flew to the bars. "Padre, are you . . . will you live?" she asked, trying to see his back. He turned so that she could not see the blood. "I'm sorry, you shouldn't have told him . . . not for my sake."

"Child," said Padre Dominguez, "bear no guilt for my weakness. But take this and find courage." He reached through the bars and handed Anne his small Bible.

"How?" Anne stared. "They took that from me on the *Wallace*. How did you get it back?"

"Thorne's men are superstitious about such things." Padre Dominguez laughed quietly, but stopped short and winced in pain. "They searched it to see if I had written any secrets . . . to lead them to the Isle of Swords. When they were convinced that it was just a Bible, they threw it into my cell."

Anne took the worn leather volume from Padre Dominguez. It

looked like it had been kicked around, and the cover was gouged. "Read the book of Romans," said Padre Dominguez. "There, you will find the knowledge you need to save your life . . . and perhaps much more."

Anne hurriedly flipped through the Bible. She had no idea where Romans was within the text, but she stopped when she saw something handwritten on several of the pages. She gasped when she realized the message had been written in blood.

"I'm sorry," said the monk. "But it was the only ink that I had."

Suddenly, a door slammed. Anne had no place to hide the Bible, so she shoved it down into her breeches just under the belt and let her shirt hang down over it. Four burly pirates and one older, graybearded man came to her cell. They hurriedly unlocked it, and the graybeard said, "Up you go, lass. The fleet has gathered, and Captain Thorne says you're comin' along for the ride."

"No, wait!" Anne said. "He promised to let us go."

"That's between you and Captain Thorne," he said with a snort. The burly men grabbed Anne and dragged her out of the cell. Even as she was taken from the room, she called back, "Padre Dominguez . . ."

The graybeard kneeled outside Padre Dominguez's cell. "Don't know what ya did to make Thorne hate you so much," he said. "He'd run ya through or cut yer throat most times. But not you. He's leavin' ya to bleed . . . leavin' ya fer the rats."

Padre Dominguez groaned and turned onto his side. He looked up at the graybeard drowsily but did not speak. "I'd hate t' see a man a' the cloth die like that, so . . . here." He placed a pistol and a small sack inside Padre Dominguez's cell. "There's powder and one shot in that bag. Don't miss."

The old pirate left Padre Dominguez alone in the cell room. The door shut, and it became unearthly quiet. The monk closed his eyes and began to pray. Then he heard small scratching sounds from some shadowy corner. He opened his eyes and stared at the pistol.

Anne was ushered out into the night air. She looked out from a wall, and from this place, high on Thorne's fortress, she had a panoramic view of the entire shipyard. The vision left her frightened and breathless. Moored along the many piers and anchored farther out, there were more tall ships than Anne had ever seen in one place. Not even the busy port at Edinburgh could boast such traffic. And farther out to sea, like a ghostly curtain on the horizon, there billowed an indistinct wall of gray.

"Fog," said one of the men who held her wrists. "As thick a bank as I've ever seen."

The bells sounded for the second watch of the night. Men came down from the *Bruce*'s crow's-nests. Others climbed up to take their place. The view hadn't changed much. The fog had not relented. Ross used only two small square sails to keep the speed low. He figured they weren't too far from Cape Verde. They'd have to swing out wide to starboard very soon, for there were several smaller islands to avoid before they came to the main island where Thorne had built his shipyard.

Shrouds of mist passed around and over the ship. An eerie quiet fell over the men on deck. But the quiet was far from relaxing. Sailors, better than anyone, knew the dangers of limited visibility. So they sharpened blades, carved pieces of driftwood, or just tapped their feet—anything to release a little nervous energy and help pass the time. Caiman felt the oppressive fear of the fog worse than the others. He paced constantly, at times switching to walking laps around the entire ship. On one of these circuits, he stopped on the port bow near the stern. He thought he had heard something out in the sea. A bell, or at least that's what it sounded like to him.

Caiman turned and looked up to the crow's-nest on the rear mast. Jacques St. Pierre was up there, but he didn't seem to have heard the sound. Caiman looked up on the quarterdeck. Stede standing over him, Cat had the wheel. Neither seemed interested in anything but steering the ship. *Probably a good thing*, Caiman thought. Clutching the port rail, he stared out into the fog. Wisps of white and tendrils of gray slipped by, and at times he could see a little farther into the murk than others. And just as he was about to resume his nervous lap around the ship, something appeared out in the fog.

"Aieee!" he cried out. "Ghost ships! Ghost ships in the fog!"

Men from all parts of the ship instantly surrounded Caiman, including Stede. "What did you see?" demanded Ramiro.

Caiman's eyes were huge as he explained. "I thought I heard something, so I stopped to look. At first there was nothing, but . . . gray shadows emerged—maybe a hundred yards away. Ships . . . they were huge, shadowy ships. Ships full of ghosts!"

"Ghosts?" echoed Stede. "Mon, ya been out in the sun too much!"

"No, listen," said Ramiro. "I've sailed this area before. We can't be far from the Widowmaker, a reef just outside the Cape Verde islands. That reef has taken down more than its share of ships. The locals claim that ghostly ships sail here in search of a port they will never find."

"That's just nonsense," said Stede, and he walked back to the quarterdeck to join Cat.

"Nonsense?" Ramiro looked at the still-terrified Caiman and then out into the fog. "If it wasn't ghosts, then what did Caiman see?"

"It was there, Captain," Jacob Briscoe said, pointing into the fog. Their ship—a Spanish carrack called *Mar de Brujas,* or *Sea Witch*—was the fourteenth ship in Bartholomew Thorne's caravan.

The ship's captain, Vittorio Maligno, had joined Jacob at the port rail. "What sort of ship was it?"

"I am not sure," he replied. "It came out of the fog, and then it was gone. Large, definitely large. A frigate . . . maybe even a ship of the line. Do you think we should tell Thorne?"

Captain Maligno shook his head. "No, not unless you see the entire British fleet would I trouble Thorne."

Hours later, the *Bruce* at last escaped the writhing mists. The ship emerged several miles off the coast of the main island of Cape Verde. As they drew near to the docks, Ross's heart fell. Aside from a few fishing boats and one small frigate, the marina was empty.

"We're too late," Ross muttered.

"Ya don't know that, mon," Stede said. "There still be lights on in that outrageous building up there." Stede pointed up the hillside at the dark fortress.

Ross nodded. At the deepest level of his soul, he felt that they were too late to save Anne, but he also knew he had to make sure.

Ross rallied his crew, as well as the forty sailors Ramiro had brought with him from his shipyard. When Stede brought the ship alongside the longest pier, Ross cast all subtlety aside. His men raced down the gangplank and streamed up the hillside.

Stede was one of the last men to leave. He noticed Cat standing at the rail and staring up at the fortress. "Come, lad," he said. Then he noticed tears forming in Cat's eyes. "Don't despair." Stede patted Cat on the shoulder. "We'll find her." Stede raced down the gangplank, jumped onto the marina, and disappeared into the trees on the hillside.

At last, Cat hurried to catch up. His mind swirled like a hurricane. Stede had been wrong. Cat's tears had nothing to do with Anne. Cat drew his cutlass and charged up the wooded incline. As he sprinted along the familiar path to Thorne's fortress, Cat wondered how he could ever explain what he feared—especially to Captain Ross.

Red Eye and Caiman spearheaded two rows of crewmen, and they came upon the hapless sentries at the fortress's gate like an avalanche. Inside Thorne's fortress, they found a skeleton detail of guards, many of them slaves impressed into service. Some fought and were overwhelmed by Ross's frenzied men. Others dropped their weapons and ran away. By Ross's command, they were not pursued.

Ross began to second-guess this command, for the initial search of the fortress had turned up no sign of Anne or Padre Dominguez. Red Eye and Caiman returned via the spiral staircase. Their expressions told their tale. They had found no one either. Ross kicked over a table. "There's got to be something!" he yelled.

"Wait." Cat emerged from the other crewmen. Unruly shocks of blond hair hid his eyes. He brushed his hair aside and said, "If they are still held in this keep, I think I know where."

"You remembered something?" Ross asked.

"Not exactly." Cat looked around nervously, feeling like a thousand pairs of eyes were on him, studying, guessing his thoughts. "I have no specific memory of this place—no faces or events. But, like the path in Dominica, it all feels familiar. I . . . I can't explain—"

"And you don't have to," said Ross, putting a hand on Cat's shoulder. He handed Cat his torch. "Just lead the way."

Cat led his captain and much of the crew on a winding journey with a general downward trend. He crossed an open courtyard where the moon cast eerie light on them until they disappeared through a door on the other side. Then down a ramp to a long chamber. There were three doors on the left and a pair of double doors on the right. Cat paused there, thinking, and then led them through the double doors and down a long set of stairs. "I went this way already, Cat," said St. Pierre. "Jules and I searched it well. Are you sure?"

"I'm not sure of anything," Cat replied, but he kept going. Cat picked up the pace, but stopped abruptly after passing a hall on the left. He turned and retraced his steps to the opening and then plunged down the hallway. The crew followed. The hall ended in a capital "T," and Cat looked to the right, holding up his torch. He shook his head. Then he looked to his left. It appeared the hall dead-ended. A tall bureau stood at the end.

"I thought for sure this was the—wait!" Cat held up his torch and advanced. The shadows moved as he approached the end of the hall. And there, barely visible until he was upon it, a narrow passage cut sharply away, left of the bureau. "This way!" he called over his shoulder.

"I didn't see that," murmured Jules.

"Neither did I, mon ami!" said St. Pierre. "How did he know?"

No one answered, and they choked down to single file to travel the narrow hall. It led to one last stairway. Cat turned and said, "I think there is a sort of dungeon at the bottom of these stairs. But be careful. The stairs are uneven. You don't want to skewer the man in front of you. So give each other some—"

Cat and the others froze. There'd been a gunshot from somewhere down below. Ross leaped ahead of Cat and led the way down the stairs. They burst into a subterranean prison and a horrendous smell hit them like a hammer. It was a mixture of decay and sewage, but the crew endured it and began to search. There were ten cells on either side of the room. They found long-rotted human remains in some, and some were empty.

"Declan, over here!" Stede called out. Ross sprinted to him. Cat and the others followed. There, slumped in the corner of a cell, was Padre Dominguez, and a pistol lay in his limp hand.

40

Ripples

"Why? Why would he . . ." Cat could not finish the question. The answer eluded him, pushed away by the persistent thought that if they'd only found the cells a few moments earlier, Padre Dominguez might still be alive.

"Open the cell," Ross said quietly. Jules looked around for something to pry open the door, but seeing nothing, reared back and kicked it in.

And, to everyone's astonishment, Padre Dominguez opened his eyes. "Declan," he said weakly, "I prayed that you might come."

"We heard the shot," Ross said. "We feared the worst."

"I shot a rat." Padre Dominguez pointed at the headless remains of an enormous rat.

"Midge!" Ross called. "Top speed. Get back to the ship and get Nubby!"

"No," Padre Dominguez said, his voice thinning to a whisper. "Too late. I am just a few beats of the heart from my Lord."

In spite of the monk's grave words, Ross waved Midge to go on. "Padre," Ross said, almost afraid to ask, "where's Anne?"

"He took her, Declan. He took her. His fleet departed for the Isle of Swords . . . I don't know. It seems like hours, but down here, I don't know."

"The ships," St. Pierre thought aloud. "Caiman, those were the ships you saw in the fog."

Suddenly, Padre Dominguez's eyes went very wide. He sat up and raised both trembling hands, reaching for Ross. "Declan, he has the map. He knows the way. He knows everything. My Lord, forgive me. I told him everything!"

Ross knelt at his side. "We'll follow him," Ross said. "We'll make sure—"

"No!" Padre Dominguez gasped and grabbed Ross's shoulders. "The true treasure, you must make sure he does not get it!"

"You said something like that before, Padre. What do you mean? Gold, silver, jewels—what?"

"Thorne can have all that." Padre Dominguez coughed violently. His eyes fixed for a moment, and he fell backward. Then he blinked and looked again at Ross. "Declan, come closer." His voice now was so weak and soft that none of the crew could hear it. Ross put his ear to the monk's mouth. Padre Dominguez whispered, and Ross's face went ashen white.

Ross pulled free of the monk's grasp. "How can that be?" Ross asked.

"Promise me," said the monk. His last breath escaped, and this time, his eyes remained fixed. Ross felt for a pulse and found none.

Ross stood and faced his crew. He wondered how much they had heard.

"Is he . . . ?" Cat asked.

Ross shook his head. Padre Dominguez was gone. "Thorne and his fleet are underway to the Isle of Swords. If Anne is to live . . . and if we will ever see that treasure, we must stop him."

"But Captain," said Jules, "what did he mean when he said Thorne has the map? The map is . . ."

Ross turned back to the dead priest. He motioned for Jules to help, and they carefully laid the monk on his stomach. Ross and Jules recoiled when they saw the amount of blood on his back. Then, hating to have to do so, but needing to be certain, Ross gently brushed away the blood and looked at his back. One glance, and Ross shut his eyes and looked away. "Thorne took the map."

"Brandon, be reasonable," Sir Nigel said in the commodore's quarters. "How can you possibly trust the word of a pirate?"

Blake paced quietly for a few moments. "I do not think Ross is typical of most pirates."

"You are right in that," Sir Nigel scoffed. "Most pirates do not blow up the islands they visit!"

"That is not what I mean. Declan Ross is a scoundrel, there can be no doubt. He has not earned the moniker of the *Sea Wolf* for nothing. But he has some honorable qualities."

"Ha! Name one."

"He is loyal to his crew."

Sir Nigel nodded. "Name another."

"He is merciful. After all, he spared my life in Misson."

"True, I suppose. Name one more."

"Sir Nigel, I'm not recommending that Ross be recognized as a saint! I just feel like we must trust this letter."

"But to sail all the way to Cape Verde?"

"Yes!" Commodore Blake pounded a fist into his open hand. "Tell me, why would Declan Ross risk his own capture with the note, if he was not attempting to eliminate his competition?"

"I can think of a hundred other reasons."

"No, Sir Nigel. Thorne's stronghold is on Cape Verde. We will endeavor to make top speed, and, if providence allows, we will catch Bartholomew Thorne or kill him."

Sir Nigel stood at the rail on the *Oxford's* stern. Disgusted, he spat over the side. This far out in the Atlantic, he knew there was no way to contact Scully. Thorne was a potent force at sea, but would he be able to defend his fortress against the might of the British Royal Navy?

Bartholomew Thorne had placed Anne in the same cell she had occupied before on the *Raven*. He'd made sure that she had better food—salted meat and fresh bread—but it was the same disgusting cell. It was dark outside, and the lanterns only gave off a little light. Still, she could not risk opening the Bible because several pirates lingered on the cell deck. She waited for what seemed an eternity until the men at last ascended the stairs.

She scooted to the most-well-lit corner of the cell and slowly drew the Bible out of her clothes. She flipped through, searching for the book of Romans and the message written in blood. Finding it, she paused. Chills shot up her arms. His message went on for page after page. Knowing that Padre Dominguez had written to her with his own blood was more than a little disturbing. But what had been so important? Anne could no longer delay. Glancing up for a moment to the shadowy stairwell, she began to read.

Anne,

I told Thorne how to get to the Isle of Swords, but I did not tell him everything. I tell you now in the hopes that you might yet be able to bargain for your life—and because you must help me. There are two keys. One of them, the key to the cliff-top castle itself. Thorne knows it is hidden at the bottom of the shallows of the bay near the island. I told him he must dive for it. But what he does not know is that something lives in that water. The Watcher, we call it, a creature that will not suffer an impure soul to enter its domain. The other key is to a chest on the altar where the candles are. You will find a silver cross alone on a wall. The cross is the key. Take the contents from that chest. If you can escape, deliver them to the abbey of San Ravelle in Venezuela. If you cannot escape, do anything you can to keep the true treasure from Thorne.

Now, read Romans.

Anne sat lost in thought for some time, rereading the blood letter again and again. When at last she looked up from the Scriptures, her body jolted and she caught her breath. Bartholomew Thorne stood at the door of her cell. "Anne," he said, his eyebrows not quite low enough to hide the cold fire in his eyes, "I do not recall providing you with anything to read, especially a book for weak-minded fools like Dominguez."

Anne snatched several pages out of the Bible, but before she could do anything with them, Thorne's bleeding stick slammed her wrist to the ground. One of the spikes pierced her hand just above the wrist. She dropped the pages and screamed in agony.

"What were you going to do with those pages?" Thorne asked. "Eat them? But if you had done that, you would have forced me to fetch Mister Flagg. I'm certain he could have found a way to get them out of you. But that would have been very . . . unpleasant."

He lifted his stick, and Anne clutched her bleeding hand to her chest. Then Thorne unlocked the door of her cell, took the Bible from Anne, and picked up the ripped-out pages. He said to her, "Do you have any other tricks, my dear?" She shook her head no.

He locked her cell door. "Good girl," he said. "Now, if you excuse me, I feel the need upon my soul to do a little reading in the Good Book."

The deck of the *Robert Bruce* unexpectedly felt very alien to Cat. The ship sailed northwest at the highest speed the prevailing winds would allow. Ross, with the help of Ramiro de Ferro Goncalo, had the crew working feverishly to adjust and repair sails for optimum performance. And everywhere Cat turned, there was tension. Crewmen spoke in whispers or argued. Once, when Cat walked past a group of men eating, he heard someone mention his name. Cat slid around a corner and listened.

". . . Cat knew," said one man. "Saint Pierre and Jules searched the place out, and they missed it."

"He couldn't have just seen it?" said another. "He had to *know* it was there."

"So what if he knew?" This voice Cat recognized. It was Red Eye. "Maybe he was held a prisoner there. Did ya ever think of that?"

"Since when did Thorne ever keep prisoners?"

"Yeah, I say he's one of them."

"Them who?" said Red Eye, growing irritated. "One of Thorne's men?"

"Why not? Maybe Thorne's plantin' his men on other pirate ships to spy on us or . . . to pull some treacherous act."

"Obviously yer not capable of thinking," said Red Eye. "But try to see what yer suggestin'. So Thorne is sendin' out spies, and the way he does it is by beatin' 'em near to death and then leavin' 'em on islands in the hopes that rival pirates will pick 'em up? Fool. Use yer head. And what about Cat's memory . . . you think he's faking that?"

"Maybe not," said one of the men quietly. "But isn't it odd the things he seems to remember?" Red Eye had no answer for that.

Shaking his head, Cat walked away. He needed to get off the deck, to find a quiet place to think. But on his way, Declan Ross and Stede crossed in front of him. "Captain Ross," Cat called. "Captain Ross, may I talk with you?"

Ross and Stede were talking animatedly. Looking annoyed, Ross turned and said, "Not right now, Cat."

"But, sir, it's important." Ross did not reply. He and Stede thundered away and climbed up to the quarterdeck where Stede took the wheel from Ramiro. Cat followed but did not join them on the quarterdeck. He didn't have to. Anyone within twenty feet could hear their conversation.

"We'll make for the Azores," Ross said, sounding like he must have already said it before but was being questioned. "The monk said the Isle of Swords was a hundred miles due west of the Azores."

"I've been there," Stede replied. "A dozen times, mayb' more. I haven't seen a thing. The monk said the currents will b' throwing us off. So, mon, how will we b' finding it?"

"We'll use our compass and the stars, like he said."

"But what stars, mon?! Do you remember the map?"

"NO!" Ross yelled. "No, I don't remember, Stede! But Thorne has my daughter. I've got to try! What else can I do?"

"We can wait," Stede answered. "We're not far from the Azores, mon. Let's wait for Thorne to make his return trip. Then we have him."

Ross thought for a moment. He wondered if Commodore Blake had found his note. He wondered if the British would do what he asked. "Every time I wait, someone dies. I will not wait this time. If you prefer, I can drop you off on the Azores, but I'm sailing for the Isle of Swords."

"Aw, don't b' a fool, mon. Ya won't b' dropping me off, not without the gold from that island."

Cat climbed down the nearest hatch. He went to the third deck and found his hammock and lay down. Then he took the leather pouch out of his coat and began to put the clues together.

41

CROSSCURRENTS

Shouts came from down the hall. Blake and Sir Nigel ran to investigate. "Commodore Blake," said Mr. Jordan between gulps of air. He had a dark-skinned man by the arm. "Sir, we found this man hiding near the back of the estate. He's a bit hard to understand, some sort of mixture of local dialects, Portuguese, and English. But I think he knows something about Thorne."

Commodore Blake towered over the wiry, dark-skinned man. "Do you know what happened to Bartholomew Thorne and his fleet?"

He nodded his head emphatically. "Si, Thorne, 'es my master. Pero, if I tell you, you give me freedom. No more cativo, no slave?"

"Freedom." Sir Nigel clucked. "Look here, you'll get the gallows if you do not speak."

"Silence, Nigel!" Blake looked at his second-in-command hard before turning his attention back to the man. "Yes, tell me what you know about Bartholomew Thorne, and I will purchase your freedom. I'll even give you a plot of land for your very own."

"Land, para me?" That was all it took. He told what he knew. "Thorne and el navio, his ship and his fleet, they leave here four nights ago tras por do sol."

"That is after sunset," said Mr. Jordan. Blake nodded.

"Then, much later, another pirata navio, grande ship, came."

"Ross," Blake whispered.

"Piratas search everywhere. They dig a grave in the garden. Then they leave."

"We found the grave, sir," said Mr. Jordan. "There's an open-air courtyard on the west side of the estate. There's no name on the grave, but it is marked with a cross."

"The place is deserted, Commodore," said Sir Nigel. "If Thorne was ever here, we've missed him."

Commodore Blake wondered if, perhaps, Ross had just sent them on an epic wild-goose chase. Finally, he said, "Take this man aboard. Give him a hot meal." He turned to Sir Nigel. "Thorne was here. We missed him."

"Where do we go now?" Sir Nigel asked.

"North by northwest," said Commodore Blake. "Just as Declan Ross suggests."

Anne woke up in the dark. She tried to sit up only to be greeted with a surge of fresh pain. She remembered almost falling asleep when the sea had started to roll. She had heard frantic shouts from above as men ran about on deck. Ten pirates each with coils of ropes draped on their shoulders appeared on the cell deck. They scurried back and forth, tying down anything that hadn't already been secured. "What's happening?!" she'd shouted at them, managing to stand.

None of the men answered her directly, but as they left, one of them threw her a coil of rope and said, "Tie yourself t' the bars, lassie!"

She remembered doubling the rope, tying off both ends, and slipping into the loop she'd made. That was when the world seemed to turn upside down. Anne remembered nothing more until she awakened with her head throbbing and her body aching as if she'd been beaten with a staff. She felt fresh bruises on her knees, elbows, back, and even on her head.

"You did survive," came a rough voice from the stairwell.

"No thanks to you." Anne looked at the wound on her hand. It had scabbed over, but still looked raw.

Thorne approached her cell. "Yes, well, a captain must maintain the discipline of his crew."

She ignored his comment. "Last night, was that a storm?"

"No," Thorne replied. He stared blankly in her direction. "I am not altogether sure what we experienced. Padre Dominguez warned me of a place where the ocean currents collide. He said that the sea would erupt in mountainous waves . . . that we must ride the wind down the backside of the wave before it crested. This we did, but it was not easy. I have never seen an angrier sea."

Thunder rumbled in the distance. Anne felt its vibration in the wood of the deck. "Where are we now?" she asked.

"By my reckoning," he said, sorting through the keys on an enormous ring, "we are but five miles from the Isle of Swords." He opened the cell door and said, "You will come up on deck. I have something to show you. A sight unlike any you have ever seen in your life."

Cat awoke with a start. He was breathing hard, sweating, and swaying rapidly in his hammock. The images were still fresh, swirling in his mind. He blinked and drifted back into them. *Where is it, boy?! The harsh voice. I know she gave it to you. Out with it!*

Stop! Leave me alone! Another voice. Cat recognized it as his own. *I don't know what you're talking about!*

Don't you lie to me. Whelp! Cat felt the blow to his back. The sting. *She must have told you. She gave you the map, didn't she?*

Cat saw cold blue eyes glaring at him from a dark shadowy figure. Unexpectedly, someone burst into the room. A woman, a beautiful woman with red hair. She grabbed the man by the shoulders. *Don't you dare lay a hand on him! You coward!*

The man slammed the back of his fist into her jaw, and she fell to the floor.

The man drew back and began to kick her. Cat saw himself rise to his feet and run to the woman's aid, but the man shoved him so hard he fell to the ground and rolled. He saw the man kick her too many times to count. Then the man walked toward Cat.

"Nooooo!" Cat choked out a cough and rolled out of his hammock. He fell to the floor on deck three. He was back on the *Bruce*. He looked to his right and saw that his leather pouch had also fallen to the ground. He picked up the pouch. *She gave you the map, didn't she?*

Cat untied the leather lace and tipped the bag. The silver cross slid out into his hand. A few shakes, and the lock of red hair came. The jewel was gone, no doubt lining Vesa Turinen's pockets with gold.

Cat stared at the pouch. Slowly, he removed the leather lace from the guide loops around the mouth of the bag. Grasping the edges, he spread open the material and pressed it flat on the deck. The golden lantern light revealed an intricately detailed map . . . a map to the Isle of Swords.

The bells for the middle watch on the *Bruce* had sounded long ago. Ross, Stede, Ramiro, and Jules stood on the quarterdeck.

"Ramiro, give me the logbook again," said Ross, holding up a hand. The captain stood next to the wheel. He stared through a sextant, measuring the angle of the horizon based on a prominent star. Ramiro handed Ross a weather-beaten book as thick as a man's fist. Ross found what he was looking for and announced, "It's got to be here! Dominguez said we'd hit the crosscurrents a hundred miles west of the Azores. We are precisely one hundred miles due west of the Azores."

Stede was at the wheel. "Plenty of stars," said Stede. "But without the map, we b' not knowing which ones to use!"

Ross growled and turned to Jules. "Has anything odd happened with the compass?"

"No, sir," he replied. "I've been closely watching it. We've stayed due west, just like you ordered."

"Captain Ross," a quiet voice drifted up the ladder. Declan leaned over the edge of the deck and gave Cat a hand up.

"Cat, it's not your watch for another couple of hours," Ross said.

"I know, sir, but I thought you might be able to use this." Cat showed the captain the wrinkled piece of leather that had once been a pouch.

Ross couldn't believe his eyes. "Is this real?" he asked. Cat nodded. "A map. You have a map to the Isle of Swords?!"

"How b' that possible?" Stede gawked.

"My mother gave it to me. It was on the inside of my pouch." Cat bunched the leather together to show them. "I carried it around all along . . . I just didn't know."

Astonished and speechless, they stared until they heard bells from the rear of the ship. Two bells. Pause. Two bells. Pause. Two bells. Pause. And two more bells.

"That b' morning watch, Declan. You got mayb' an hour left to use the stars!"

"May I?" Ross asked, and Cat handed him the map. They both knew they had much more to discuss on this matter, but Ross couldn't spare the time now. He scanned the map, noted the constellations and their positions. Then back to the sextant and then the logbook.

"I can't believe it!" he shouted. "We've drifted too far to the south."

"That cannot be," grumbled Jules. "As I said before, I've been watching the compass."

"No blame to you, Jules," said Ross. "Padre Dominguez told us that's what the strange current would do." He went to the sea chart, scribbled a few figures from the logbook, and then drew a line. "Mister Stede, follow this course!"

"Aye, Cap'n!"

"You had better wake your men, Ramiro," said Ross. "If what the monk told us is true, that swinging bowsprit will be needed like never before!"

Ramiro said, "We'll be ready!"

But before the Portuguese shipwright could get down the ladder, Cat yelled, "May I go with you?" Ramiro looked at Ross, who nodded.

"Follow me," he said. "I understand you are a quick study." Cat grinned and leaped down the ladder.

"Jules, wake the crew—the whole crew!" Ross said, putting a hand on Jules's massive shoulder. "The ship's already locked up pretty tight, but make sure everything that can be tied down is— especially the barrel of monkey pee! This could be the roughest ride any of us have ever had."

"There it is, sir," said Jules. "We just changed direction. It's slight, but it's there."

"Stede?"

"I'm correcting now, mon," said the quartermaster.

"Again," said Jules.

"I'm starting to feel what it's doing," said Stede.

Ross looked up at Midge in the crow's-nest. "You see anything?"

"Nothing unusual, sir," Midge called back.

Ross looked out on the dark sea. Nothing unusual. He scanned the skies, saw a faint glow in the east. Not much time before sunup. Without the stars, how would they—then he felt it. Ever so gently, the ship rose. "Midge!"

"Swells comin', Cap'n!" he cried. "Swells like mountains!"

"Tie yourself in, Midge!" The winds intensified as Ross yelled to the front of the ship. "Ramiro, be ready!" Ross heard no reply, but leaned over the rail of the quarterdeck and saw Ramiro nod and salute.

The *Bruce* rose up on a massive wall of black water, and from their perch, the entire crew witnessed what lay in wait for them. The ocean as far as they could see was a roiling, undulating cauldron. And among the swells there appeared ominous patches of darkness and sudden eruptions of sea spray and foam.

Trying always to keep the ship firmly in the grasp of the steady wind, Stede guided them carefully among the swells. Just as they crested the top of a towering wave, Midge yelled, "Starboard!!"

Ross turned and saw the monster wave that was headed right for them. The *Bruce* was riding one wave right into another. "It's coming across, Stede!"

Stede spun the wheel hard as they braced for impact.

It never came. The *Bruce* seemed to grab the wind and spin forty-five degrees to the left. It coasted down the back of the first wave and slid out of harm's way before the two waves collided. The sound of that collision, like sudden thunder, jolted the crew. Spray rained down and blew horizontally across the deck.

"How did we . . . ?" Ross realized how. He looked across the deck, and there were Ramiro, Cat, and the others—all sopping wet, but grinning like mischievous kids.

On the bow, Ramiro's head went back and forth, watching for rogue waves and looking to see which direction Stede was steering. Cat, holding on to the rail—and the ropes—for dear life, felt his stomach drop. The *Bruce* abruptly rose up. They were cresting a gigantic wave as if it had grown up beneath them.

Ramiro barked out orders with zeal. "Claudio, pull the fore halyard, now!" And Claudio, a man with forearms like tree boughs, yanked a line, and the sail on the bowsprit fell limp.

"Enrique, pull both pins!" With two men keeping the bowsprit from swinging wildly, Enrique pulled the pins out of the gooseneck and waited.

Ramiro looked back to see what Stede would do. He watched until he saw the wheel spin rapidly to starboard. "Starboard!!" Ramiro yelled, and Enrique dropped the pins into two different holes.

"Now, Claudio—" Ramiro started to say. His mouth remained wide open, but his voice failed. He heard a sound like the echo of a thousand cannons. And off the starboard rail, the ocean fell away. Down it went as if sucked into the depths by some gigantic beast. A hundred-foot chasm opened up, and Ramiro could not see the bottom. A monstrous shadow fell over the ship. And dead ahead, another wave had gathered strength and height. It towered thirty feet above the *Bruce*'s highest mast and threatened to slam them into the chasm that yawned open beside them. Ramiro didn't need to see what Stede was doing.

"Port! Port! Port!" he screamed. Enrique pulled the pins out of the gooseneck. But as he jammed one into its appropriate spot, the other pin slipped out of his hand. It flew backward and rolled along the deck. The ship started to turn. Stede was doing his job, but it was not enough. The *Bruce* was sliding over the edge. It began to lean toward the roaring gulf.

The pin bounced around on the deck until Cat dove on it. He snatched it up and clawed against the slippery deck. Finally, he slammed the pin into the gooseneck in exactly the right hole.

"Now, Claudio!!" Ramiro screeched. Claudio pulled a different halyard, and the huge triangular sail rose from the bowsprit to the mast and snapped full of wind. The *Bruce* hugged the edge of the wave upon which it rode. The wind held it up and began to push the ship to port. But the oncoming wave curled and came smashing down. It clipped the highest spar on the foremast, but that was all.

The *Bruce* sailed safely behind the monster wave, which crashed over the chasm like a gigantic lid.

The sun rose over the *Bruce* and found the ship's deck teeming with activity. They'd survived seven miles of the most unimaginable peril. Sails had been torn, spars cracked, and a few barrels had broken loose and gone overboard. But no lives had been lost. The crew took turns working on repairs and running to the rails to be sick.

Even Ross, who had spent most of his life at sea, felt a little queasy. "We're through," he said to Stede. "That's another lifetime of friendship I owe you."

"Six now, and countin'!" Stede replied.

"What are the shards?" Cat asked, looking at the map.

"In about sixty miles you'll see them for yourself," said the captain. "But Padre Dominguez described them as hundreds and hundreds of sharp rocks and coral thrust up through the surface like blades—hence the name, Isle of Swords. This waits for us at the bay and is the only access to the island."

"It's a good thing we have the map," Cat said.

"Yes, my lad, it is."

42
THE ISLE OF SWORDS

Thorne pointed over the bow. "What do you think of that?" he asked.

Anne squinted, still adjusting to the morning sun after long captivity in darkness. Then she gasped. In the distance, not more than a few miles away, a massive plume of cloud shimmered in an otherwise cloudless sky. Like a fountain, this mist ascended from some unseen central point and arced down toward the water below. Like a curtain, it undulated and made brief, curving shadows from the sunlight. And like a mountain it loomed before them, dwarfing all other sights that could be beheld.

"A curtain of mist and ash that surrounds the island," Thorne explained just as a deep rumble emanated from the scene before them.

"Thunder?"

"Yes," said Thorne. "But thunder churning in the molten belly of a volcano. Arrojar del Fuego, he called it. We will soon walk at its feet."

A cool wind blew from behind, and the *Raven*'s sails filled. Anne shuddered. As the ship moved ahead, she looked in its wake. "What happened to your fleet?" She had no idea how many ships there had been, but whatever the number, there were far less now.

"During the first watch of the night, we entered a calamitous rolling sea. I warned all my ships' captains how to navigate those treacherous waves. Some clearly did not listen and so were over-whelmed. But others—their ships—simply could not handle the strain. Eighteen ships survived. The loss is grievous, but expected. I still have what I need."

Wavering shadows fell on the *Raven* as it passed under the canopy of mist. And then, all was gray and wet. Tiny droplets of water clung to Anne's skin. She put her fingers to her face. When she drew them away and looked at her fingertips, they were smudged a murky white. She looked at Thorne, and upon his dark coat there were innumerable flecks, like snowflakes—only these were gray and left ugly trails as they ran.

The shadow lifted, and some sunlight returned. The gray curtain parted, and they looked upon the Isle of Swords for the first time. The island looked as if it had once been a huge mountainous mass of earth and stone, but all of its gentle slopes had been cut away by a great and terrible blade, leaving a high sheer wall of unassailable rock.

Anne searched the contours of the crescent-shaped island from right to left, beginning with its inhospitable rocky tail. These twisting slate-gray clumps formed a series of high coves and rested on a scarce bed of sand, the only shore Anne could see. Beyond the sand and rocks rose a massive cathedral of dark stone, pitted and crevassed, reminding Anne of a certain type of coral she'd once carved. A thin tree line gradually thickened into dense forest as it curled left, almost to the base of a pyramidlike mountain. *No* . . . Anne realized.

A volcano, not a mountain. Gray vaporous smoke puffed out from its mouth and rose high in the sky. There, sheered by wind, the ashen mist spread outward like the spokes of a wheel, feeding the curtain that enveloped the island.

The volcano sloped into an unseen valley. And a menacing cliff rose up on the left side of the island. "There is our destination," said Thorne lustily. He pointed with the bleeding stick, and Anne saw a stone castle at the cliff's edge. It was spare in its design. Three towers, a gabled roof over a square keep, and only one window that looked out over the sea from its blank wall.

But before it all, guarding the mouth of the island's bay, jagged blades of glistening stone thrust up out of the water. How many there were, Anne could not tell, but it was as perilous a gauntlet as any ship-killing reef in the world.

"The shards," Thorne muttered. "The stone blades that you see are only a tenth of the danger. Beneath the surface, sharp ridges of hull-splitting coral wait for careless captains and their crews. We shall be anything but careless." He turned and called, "Mister Skellick, raise the death's-head!"

Anne watched the dark flag rise high on the *Raven*'s mainmast. Following the signal of their commander, the captains of the rest of Thorne's fleet began to sail into the shards. The first ship, a schooner with one tall mast and one short, slipped between the rocky blades with little difficulty. A larger galleon went slowly next. Both navigated with no incident.

"Padre Dominguez charted this peril for us well," said Thorne. "Honest fool. He could have misled us. It might have cost me half my fleet to figure out the safe passage through." He laughed.

"I'd have sent your ships into the teeth of that coral," Anne whispered.

"Would you?" Thorne asked. He smiled. "So would have I." His smile faded as, within the shards, one of his ships drew too close to another. This large brigantine could not stop—not without plowing into the galleon in front of it or turning. Its captain chose to turn. The ship went left when, according to the map, it should have remained straight.

"Idiot, what is he doing?" Thorne croaked. But to everyone's astonishment, nothing happened to the brigantine. The captain had seemingly found another route through. Several of the other ships' captains, tired of waiting in line on the approved paths, veered off in the direction the brigantine had taken. Some even turned to strike new ways themselves.

Thorne was beside himself with wrath. He slammed his bleeding stick against the rail and tore out a chunk of wood. Then they heard a tremendous *crack!* The brigantine had struck something. Anne watched in horror as the waves and current drove the impaled ship into the unseen fang below. Its bow began to crumble, and the fore-mast toppled into the water. Men began to dive overboard. Some of these never returned to the surface. Others were smashed against the rocks.

"Leave them!" Thorne ordered.

Within moments, the brigantine had split apart and sunk. The other ships that had gone off course met the same fate. Any sign of the men or the ships having existed now rested deep below the surface.

"Fools," Thorne muttered.

"You heartless beast!" Anne yelled.

"Save your energy for the swim," he said.

At the same time, still fifty miles from the island, the *Bruce*, with Stede and Ramiro at the helm, gathered speed and sailed north. Declan Ross was at a desk in his quarters. He held a large magnifying glass over the map.

Cat rapped softly on the already open door.

"Ah, I wondered if you'd come."

"There was a bit of repair work to do," Cat said, "after the ride we had last night."

Ross nodded. They stared at each other in silence for a moment. "Sit," said the captain.

Cat did as he was told and looked down at his hands in his lap. "I wish I'd realized sooner," he said. "Might have saved us all a lot of trouble . . . and time."

"Has it all come back?" Ross asked.

Cat shook his head. "No. Just bits and pieces. And it's still not my own. It's still like I'm watching scenes from someone else's life."

Ross leaned forward, his hands clasped on the desk. "Padre Dominguez told us there might be another map. He told us who might have it."

"Captain Ross, I can explain—"

Ross held up his hand. "You don't have to say another thing. You are a member of my crew. I trust you."

Cat stood to leave, but Ross urged him to wait. "I've been thinking a lot about how we came to have you with us."

Cat nodded. "I guess . . . I'm just lucky."

"Are you?" Ross asked. "I wonder about that. I'm beginning to wonder about a lot of things. See, I used to hold to luck. We pirates are a superstitious lot." He laughed. "Never set sail on Friday, don't bring a woman aboard—why, I bet old Ramiro has a gold coin in the keel and a silver coin under the mainmast."

Cat smiled but didn't know what the captain was trying to tell him.

Ross went on. "But luck doesn't weave together the kind of intricate strands I'm beginning to see. I'm beginning to feel like maybe we were meant to find you . . . that we were meant to be mixed up in the search for Constantine's Treasure."

Ross got up, walked quickly behind Cat, and closed and locked his cabin door.

"Before he died, Padre Dominguez told me something," said Ross quietly as he sat back behind his desk. "I've shared this with no man, not even Stede, whom I'd trust with my life a hundred times and one. You see, along with the gold, silver, and jewels, there is one other treasure. It is the treasure that Padre Dominguez feared losing the most." Cat leaned forward, and Ross explained. "Somewhere in the castle on the Isle of Swords, there is a small wooden chest. And in that chest, there are three long nails."

Ross waited a long moment for that to sink in. Cat squinted. "Nails?"

"Not just any nails, lad," said Ross gravely. "These are the nails— the very three nails—used to crucify Christ."

The *Raven* dropped anchor in the main cove. The water there was deep blue and fairly shallow but not transparent like the waters of the Caribbean. "If the priest's message to you is to be believed," said Thorne, "then something lives in these waters. Sharks, more than likely. He claims that only one of pure intentions can make this dive and return with the key. We'll just see if he told us the truth."

Thorne gestured, and a man with long, straight black hair, deeply browned skin, and dark paint beneath his eyes came forward.

"Arturo here," said Thorne, "was once a champion cliff diver on his little island. He can hold his breath for a very long time. He will make the first attempt to retrieve the key."

Arturo smiled, climbed up on the rail, and speared into the water. Thorne, Anne, and many of the crew went to the rail. They saw Arturo's brown legs kicking away for a moment, and then he was gone. Several seconds passed. Then they all felt something. A small jolt to the bottom of the ship. Thorne scanned the water. A strange ripple spread out from the hull. Everyone at the rail jumped back. They'd seen something moving in the depths. It was just a fleeting glimpse—something long and dark. If it had indeed been a shark, it would have to have been one of the largest ever seen.

Thorne waited longer than any man could possibly hold his breath. His eyebrows lowered. He turned from the water and looked at the crew. "Five hundred pieces of eight for the man who brings me the key!" Thorne looked first at Skellick.

"What?" said Skellick, clinging to the ship's wheel. "I can barely swim."

Thorne started to growl, but turned when he heard three splashes. "It's Oliver!" cried one of the crewmen. "Christopher and Douglass too!"

The men crowded the rail and watched bubbles form three foamy rings on the water's surface. Seconds ticked by, feeling like hours, and still they watched the water for any sign. "Look!" someone yelled. They all turned. Forty yards from the bow, a large irregularly shaped blotch of foam appeared on the surface. And swirling beneath the foam like a gigantic submerged rose was a massive plume of blood.

"Apparently," Thorne said, "the priest knew what he was talking about. Your turn, Anne."

Anne crossed her arms defiantly. "I won't do it. You kill me, and you'll never get your key."

Thorne looked amused. "I predicted you'd say as much. Stupid girl. Mister Flagg is very imaginative. If I must turn you over to him to be persuaded, I think you might find there are some agonies worse than death." He watched Anne shrivel as she thought about the possibilities. "And I promise you, Anne, if you fail me here, I will hunt your father down, him and the rest of his crew, and string their entrails across the entire Caribbean."

Anne knew she could not win. One way or the other, she knew Thorne would kill her. But if she could get the key, at least she had a chance. Slowly, she climbed up on the rail. Anne took several breaths, inhaling and exhaling longer each time. She wanted slower, more even breaths. Anne had done a fair amount of diving in the islands, mostly to retrieve hunks of coral that she could carve. She hoped her previous experiences would keep her alive here.

She held her next breath and dove into the water. Her momentum carried her far beneath the surface, and as she slowed, she opened her eyes and began to kick. The dark shadow of the *Raven's* hull loomed on her right, and a faint pale glow beneath her must have been the sandy floor. She swam rhythmically, not rushing, not panicking. She needed to pace herself if the breath would la—

The heel of her right foot had struck something. She spat out half of her air, turned, and looked frantically behind her. She saw nothing, just the deep blue of the sea and the shadow of the ship. She regained her composure. *It could have been a fish, a piece of seaweed . . . anything at all.* She swam deeper, pinching her nose a couple of times and blowing to depressurize her ears. The stale air in her lungs began to burn, and she had to suppress the panic. Thorne had said the key was encased in wax and held within a stone chest.

As she neared the soft sandy bottom, she found large sea rocks, a few massive patches of brain coral, and old timber from a long-submerged wreck. She was about to give up and return to the surface when she spotted something on the seafloor to her far right. She swam toward it, and it grew darker.

Her lungs were fairly screaming at this point, but she pushed herself on. The vision was still cloudy, but as she grew near, she realized there were large stone rings on the seafloor. The gigantic rings coiled one on top of the other, and there in the center was the stone chest. *Thorne didn't say anything about stone rings.* Feeling confused and somewhat disoriented, Anne swam toward the chest. She found the lid was on tight, but once lifted, slid easily off. She saw a square glob of white. When she touched it, she realized it was the wax case. It dangled upward, anchored by a hook embedded in its side.

Anne yanked out the hook, grabbed the wax case, planted her feet on the ocean floor, and pushed off with all her might. Her mind felt muddled, and she began to see little flickers of light. Some corner of her awareness recognized that as she lunged away from the chest, the dark rings slowly uncoiled.

Anne found herself being hauled carefully onto the deck of the *Raven*. "Well done, Anne!" Bartholomew Thorne cried, holding up the wax case. Anne blinked. Mr. Flagg put something with a sharp smell under her nose, and her eyes opened wide.

Thorne took out a dagger and stabbed it into the wax. A few moments later, he had a dark iron key in his hand. "This, gentlemen," he said to the crew, "is the beginning of a new life for us all!"

The crew whooped and cheered. Someone helped Anne to her feet and put a blanket around her shoulders.

Thorne laughed aloud as he slid the key into the pocket of his coat. "Fetch me my Viking horn, Mister Skellick!" he said. "We'll launch the longboats. Once we're ashore, I want you to take the ship. Lead the others into hiding among those coves. I am not expecting any company, but I don't want our unmanned ships lying in the open."

"Aye, Captain Thorne," said Skellick. He disappeared below and returned a moment later with a long, curved white horn. It had gold bands at the narrow blowing end, as well as at the wide opening.

"Ah! I feel like a Viking!" Thorne reveled. "After all, they were the first pirates!" He grinned at Anne and gave a long blast on the horn. It made Anne's ears ring and echoed off the cliff walls.

"I will wait for your signal and come quickly," said Skellick.

Thorne grabbed Anne's wrist, sending a bolt of pain shooting up her arm. "Now, Anne," he said, "it is time to plunder the Treasure of Constantine!"

43

THE WATCHER

When the *Bruce* arrived at the shards, the wreckage of Thorne's destroyed ships had burned itself out and slid beneath the water. "I can't believe it!" Declan Ross exclaimed from the quarterdeck. "Where is he?"

"There are only two possibilities," said Ramiro. "Either we beat him here or . . ."

"Or?"

"Or, he's already come and gone."

Ross's shoulders fell.

"If the ships Caiman saw off Cape Verde b' Thorne's fleet, the mon has not had time to b' here, load the treasure, and scoot back off," Stede said.

Ross shook his head. "He had a good five hours on us at least. I don't see how we could have beat him here."

"Unless the monk deceived that outrageous pirate!" said Stede hopefully. "Mayb' Thorne b' still sailin' around the North Atlantic looking for the island!"

It was possible that Padre Dominguez had misled Thorne. Ross couldn't be sure. One other thought had occurred to him as well, but it grieved him to consider it. The waves in the deadly cross-current could have claimed Thorne's life. But that would most likely mean that Anne was gone as well.

"Too many possibilities," said Ross. "And they're all out of our control. We will sail through the shards and dive for the key. Then we'll know."

Stede had guided the *Bruce* through the shards without mishap. They dropped anchor as far inland as they dared to go. "I've got pure intentions!" Ramiro said indignantly. "I should be the one to dive."

"Aw, yer too old," said Red Eye. "I'll go."

"Right," said Midge with a cough. "'Ave you ever had noble intentions?"

There was general laughter. But Captain Ross said, "I am the captain of this ship. I have led you into peril. But I will not ask any of you to do this task. Padre Dominguez said that the key is encased in a stone like any other, that he alone knew what to look for. I will dive and see if my knowledge of the sea is as vast as it should be!"

"But," said Cat, standing rapidly on the rail, "this ship needs its captain!" And before anyone could stop him, Cat dove into the water.

"I'll go after him," said Red Eye.

"No," Ross ordered. "No. We will wait."

As soon as he hit the water, Cat knew something was wrong. He'd dived close to the ship and begun kicking too soon. He felt a pinch on his ankle and knew he'd slashed it pretty deeply on a barnacle. Still, he kicked and swam down, down, almost to the ocean floor. His breath already beginning to thin in his lungs, Cat searched among the sea rocks and debris but found nothing.

From his perch in the crow's-nest, Midge cried out, "Captain, off the port rail!"

Ross and the others ran across the deck. There, not fifty yards away, three dark fins closed in on the ship. "Sharks," Ross whispered.

"The devils," said Red Eye, and he drew pistols from his bandolier and opened fire. Others did as well. But Ross yelled, "Stop! You might hit Cat!"

They immediately stopped firing. Midge suddenly let out a high-pitched screech. "What was that, Midge?" Ross said. He'd never heard such a sound come from a man.

Midge jumped up and down in the crow's-nest, pointing at the surface. "The water!" he cried. "A shadow . . . a shadow in the depths!"

Cat saw it, just yards away in a great wide-open area of seafloor. It wasn't a sea rock at all, but a huge stone chest. A bloody cloud trailing behind him, he swam for the chest. As he closed in, he choked out a mouthful of air. The lid to the chest had been thrown aside. He swam up to it, reached in, and felt frantically about. He found a hook. There was a small hunk of something soft on it, but no sign of a key. Cat felt a presence and looked up.

Three large sharks—dark on top, white beneath—raced toward Cat with alarming speed. Cat planted his feet on the chest and pushed off, dispelling most of his remaining air. He expected to feel the sharks' jaws clamp down on his ankle, but the water all around him surged rapidly as if an unseen current had just begun to stream through. Cat turned to look behind him, just as one of the sharks raced forward. Cat strained to see. Something huge was behind the shark. Jaws the size of a small ship's hull crashed shut upon the shark, and the shark was gone. Gigantic claws stretched out from the darkness. They grabbed the other two sharks, constricted, and released. The sharks floated slowly out from the claws but made no motion to swim.

Cat blasted out the rest of his air and clawed for the surface. Through the bubbles and the graying fringes of his vision, Cat saw an enormous webbed fin and luminous yellow eyes.

"Lad, open yer eyes." It was Nubby . . . and half the crew.

Cat sat up quickly. "Monster . . ." He coughed.

"What?" said Ross.

"Something down there," Cat said.

"Sharks," Red Eye whispered.

"No . . . something else."

Ross squinted. "What about the key? Did you find it?"

Cat shook his head. "It wasn't in a rock at all. There was a stone chest."

Ross thought of Padre Dominguez's story. "That son of a gun."

"The key, it was gone!"

"Thorne has been here already," said Jacques St. Pierre. "But how could he have done it so quickly?"

"I don't know," Ross said. "But I'm not leaving the Isle of Swords until I'm sure. If Thorne is here, perhaps Anne is too. Stede, get the men ready to go ashore. Red Eye, make sure every man is armed to the teeth. Swords, pistols, daggers, grenades—everything."

"Aye, sir!" Red Eye sped off with a spring in his step.

"Jacques, did you finish that special barrel I asked for?" Ross asked.

"Absolument!" he replied. "Light the fuse and let it fly. There will be enough smoke to see it for miles."

"Good." Ross turned to Ramiro. "You will have the helm. I will leave you with enough men to move the ship, but nothing more."

"As you wish," said the old shipwright. "I will take care of the ship as if it were mine—which, of course, it is."

Ross patted him on the back. "Once we are on land, sail the *Bruce* to the base of the cliff beneath the castle. I don't know how long it will be or what we will find when we get up there. But when you see the smoking barrel, be ready to receive cargo!"

"Midge, make sure we have the rope and the baskets."

"Aye, Cap'n."

"Oh, and get the barrel of monkey pee. We can't forget that!"

"Awww, Cap'n!"

44

THE RED TRAIL

Declan Ross watched the *Bruce* come about and sail beneath the cliff. *Smart*, he thought. Ramiro had let the ship coast behind an outcropping, a sort of root at the base of the rockface. Ross couldn't see the ship at all from the shore. They formed three teams of twenty men. Some carried rope. Some carried woven baskets. All of them carried weapons. And Jacques St. Pierre and Midge each carried a barrel.

"Declan, look," said Stede. "Footprints."

"And not very old," said Ross. "Let's go." They had about thirty yards of easy footing as they marched across the narrow shore. But after that the ground became rocky and uneven. As they clambered up, they found long-cooled lava deposits and marveled at their size. Every few moments, the volcano rumbled. Midge cringed looking up at the smoking mountain. "You don't think it's goin' to go off, do you?"

"Nah, mon," said Stede. "Those lil' rumbles b' just the mountain lettin' us know it's here."

Still, the crew marched on warily. After an hour's uphill journey, they came to an area where they could climb no farther. There was no place to go . . .

But in.

In the side of the rockface, a wide cavelike entrance beckoned. "Okay, men," announced Ross, "it's time." Midge came forward reluctantly and popped the top off his barrel.

"Oh, that is horrendous!" bellowed Jules, who stood near Midge.

"Yes, but that's what keeps the wee beasties away," said Ross. "Padre Dominguez said we need to rub it on every area of exposed skin."

"You're kidding," said Red Eye. "I'm not putting that on."

"It's an order!" said Ross, and, being the captain, he went to the barrel first, put his hand in, and brought out a dripping fistful of the rancid liquid. In all of his years of commanding a crew, Ross had never heard so many complaints. In truth, he would have complained too, but he was the captain. A distant part of him wondered if Padre Dominguez had made this part up . . . some sort of practical joke.

A reeking, griping lot, the crew of the *Bruce* entered the tunnel. And in the closed space of the tunnel, it was ripe indeed. Four crewmen in all—including Red Eye and Caiman—found a way to slip by without putting on the potent primate perfume. The sunlight ended almost immediately, and the men lit small lanterns. The walls became smooth, almost glassy, and the footing was fairly even. As they traveled on, they began to notice pockmarks and holes in the walls. Some of these were only an inch or two deep, but others went as far in as the men could see with the lantern light.

"What do you suppose these creatures are?" Cat asked.

"Mayb' some kind of bat," said Stede. "But I've never heard of a bat that's drawn to the heat of the body."

Jacques St. Pierre laughed. "And how in the world did the monk know that monkey pee would keep these—these things away?"

"It's keeping me away!" said Red Eye. "You gentlemen smell right horrible!"

"STOP!!" Ross shouted from the front of their line. He leaned over and held out his lantern to get a better look. The others gathered behind the captain, nearly pushing him over in their effort to see.

"What do you see?" whispered Jacques.

"Blood," he replied. "And lots of it." They looked on the stone floor and saw a wide splash of blood. Several spatters led up the tunnel.

"That is fresh blood," whispered Stede. "Footprints on the sand. Fresh blood. They still b' here."

The trail of blood spatters was inconsistent for the next forty feet. There were other large puddles, even splashes on the walls in some places. But in other spots, no blood at all. Farther still, and they found side tunnels shooting off from the main. These were smaller, perhaps large enough for a man, if he crawled. The concentration of blood was heaviest around these smaller side tunnels, and the crew gave them a wide berth whenever they found one.

"What's that sound?" Cat asked. Everyone froze.

"I don't hear anything," said Jules.

"Nor I," said Ross. "Wait." Then he heard it. A short, high-pitched whistle.

"Where's that coming from?" Cat asked. No one answered. They heard it again, many times more. Many at the same time. "It's all around. It's getting louder."

"Daggers, men," Ross ordered. "Give yourselves a little room." Metallic rings filled the tunnel, joining the strange whistling. All sixty men spread out. The men with lanterns held them high so all could see. The whistles grew even louder and more frenzied.

Suddenly, the tunnel filled with the sound of flapping, but there was nothing in the air near the roof of the tunnel. "Ah!" St. Pierre exclaimed. "Something just ran across my foot!"

"Ahhhh, get them off!" Caiman cried out. Cat ran toward the sound of his voice. He stepped on several things that squished. The lanterns were being swung about as the men stabbed their daggers into the darkness. In the swaying light, Cat saw things darting across the floor and leaping out of the holes on the wall. They were stark white and fast, whatever they were. "Ahh, they are eating me!" Caiman was in agony. "Help! I didn't use the monkey—ahhhghh! Where's that barrel?!"

Cat grabbed a lantern out of another man's hand and ran on. He found Caiman near the end of the line. White creatures the size of rats were all over him. Cat flashed his dagger and cut at the creatures. Pieces of them fell away, but their heads remained somehow attached to Caiman's skin. "Midge!" Cat screamed. "Midge, where are you?"

"Ahhhh!!!" Caiman thrashed about. One after the other, he tore them from his body, but their teeth and jaws stayed clamped to his skin. Screams echoed from up ahead.

Cat continued to cut. "Midge!!"

"Right here!" Midge ran up, and Cat grabbed the barrel from him and began to pour it all over Caiman. The high-pitched whistles filled the tunnel, so loud that Cat could barely handle it without covering his ears. The white creatures fell off Caiman's body in clumps. They crawled away and soon were gone. But there were other screams wailing at the other end of the tunnel.

"Midge, help Caiman!" Cat yelled. "If there are others, I've got to get to them."

Cat raced up the tunnel. He found one man covered in the white creatures. They were actually dragging the man into one of the smaller side tunnels. Cat splashed the fluid on him, and again the creatures screeched and fell away. But it was too late. Blood oozed from a hundred wounds, and he was not breathing.

"Die!!" someone screamed up ahead. Cat heard a pistol shot. Then another. The clash of a sword on the stone wall. "Filthy little maggots, die!!"

That had to be Red Eye, Cat thought. He had only a small amount of the monkey pee left in the bottom of the barrel. He hoped it would be enough. Cat found Red Eye slamming himself backward into the wall of the cave, mashing dozens of the creatures. Cat splattered him with all the fluid that remained. As the creatures fell off, Red Eye began stomping them furiously. "Lousy little . . . take that! Yeahhhh, now you feel it! Arrrrr!"

"THIS WAYYY!" Captain Ross called from somewhere up ahead. Midge and Caiman sprinted past. Cat and Red Eye were right behind them. "THIIIIS WAYYY!!"

They emerged at last from the tunnel under the shade of wide tree boughs. All of them panted from the exertion; many of them were streaked in blood. Red Eye had cuts and wounds all over. Caiman was worse. "We lost two men," Ross said sadly.

"They should b' listening," Stede said. "Mon make their own choices. This b' true."

45

THE HOLY KEEP

Thorne and his men are still here," said Ross. "I'm sure of it."

"I hope yer right, Declan," said Stede. With the forest now behind them, they marched warily up the steep incline. The volcano rumbled even more ominously than before. The ashen darkness overhead had thickened. Cat looked over his shoulder at the smoky crater and wondered. Their view was spectacular. If not for the fear cast over them all, each would have stopped to marvel. They saw the treetops of the forest and the pitted rock formation with its tunnels hidden within. They could see the edge of the bay and, in the distance, the shards.

At last, Ross and his crew came within sight of the castle they had been seeking for so long. Made of black and gray stone, or just covered with a layer of ash, no one could tell. But the building maintained by the monks for so many long years looked solid and impregnable. It had three windowless turrets, the largest of which faced the hill that Ross and his crew were climbing. Behind this turret rose a high gabled roof over a magnificent square fortress.

Ross's mind churned. They had met no resistance, other than the creatures in the tunnel. If Thorne was still on the island, where was he? Each man's heart pounding in his chest, every sense on alert, they slowly drew near to the castle. They found a huge stone door ajar. Ross pushed the door open, and they gazed down a long corridor with small paintings on either side. The crew pressed in behind Ross, and they walked cautiously to the end of the hall where an engraving of the crucifixion of Christ gazed down on them.

Cat stared at the wounded Christ and found himself reaching for the silver cross in his coat pocket. Could they really be here, in this building? Cat wondered if the captain was thinking the same thing.

Ross had felt a strange gravity since he entered the holy keep. He had no reason now to doubt anything Padre Dominguez had told him. Still, he'd never really believed in God. He'd told his wife that on many occasions. Abigail had dragged him into church a few times, and he'd repeated after the vicar with the rest of the crowd. But he hadn't believed any of it. The volcano rumbled outside. Ross looked away from the engraving. Still, he felt like Christ's eyes were following him.

Short passages led right and left of the engraving, and an odd glow came from doors at either end. It was a golden glow. Ross looked back at his men. He motioned for Jules to lead his group to the right. Ross went left. From both doors they entered a vast sanctuary lit by hundreds of candles and one large window. The men gasped as they entered, for the light was reflected in a million different directions and hues by gleaming gold, polished silver, and many-faceted jewels. It was not at all the sort of treasure the crew had pictured—massive, hedonistic piles of gold coins, with fallen silver statues, and jeweled trinkets hanging from chandeliers or tossed hither and thither.

No, what Ross and his men found was that the monks of the Brethren had organized the treasure into dozens of magnificent open stone vaults. There were vaults heaped with gold and others with silver. Many vaults were filled with jewels: red rubies, white and green diamonds. Some others contained all manner of weapons— gilt staffs, swords and daggers with jeweled hilts, and ornate shields of silver and gold. The immaculate orderliness of the monks made the Treasure of Constantine all the more impressive.

Ross and his men walked down two aisles between twenty rows of wooden pews. All had their eyes forward on the treasure, so they did not notice the numerous doors on either side of the sanctuary. Stede ran his fingers over the green diamonds. Red Eye began sorting through the weapons. Jacques St. Pierre put down his barrel and lifted a pile of gold coins and finger bars up to his nose as if he could savor the smell of these riches.

Ross and Cat saw the altar at the same time and walked toward it. If they'd turned, they would have seen that everything in the sanctuary, the seats, the aisles, the vaults—even the candles—was angled to draw attention to the altar. Upon the altar were two items, a wooden chest and a large leather-bound book.

Stede turned and watched Captain Ross go to the wooden chest. The others began to turn as well. Ross and Cat gazed at this chest. It was more than large enough to hold the contents described by Padre Dominguez. There were carvings and designs engraved with gold and silver: a lion, a lamb, a tree, angels with flaming swords, and an intricate cross on the top. Declan Ross put his hands on the chest. He looked at Cat as if to ask, "Should I?"

Cat nodded. Captain Ross grasped both sides of the lid and began to lift. But the lid did not move. He tried harder, but it did not budge. The chest was locked, but look as he might, he could see no keyhole. And even had he found one, they had no key. Suddenly, Ross spun around, almost knocking a lit candle off its stand. Captain Declan Ross knew he had been beaten. He had led his men into this sanctuary. In a gilded trance, he had marched them up to dip their hands into the treasures. Then, ignoring all common sense, he went to the altar among the candles and let himself be captivated by the chest. He closed his eyes and drew his cutlass. Someone had to have lit all those candles.

"Men," Ross said quietly, "I may have doomed us all. Raise your weapons! Stand your ground and prepare to fight for your lives!"

A deep, thunderous blast came from the volcano. Harsh orange light flashed in the lone window, and pistol shots rang out from above. Men appeared at the balcony of an upper story Ross and his men had not even noticed. The doors on both sides of the sanctuary opened, and enemy pirates streamed out like a torrent.

The crew of the *Bruce* dropped their baskets and their massive coils of rope. They let the riches from their hands fall back into the vaults. Every man took up arms and ran to meet the enemy. Jacques St. Pierre lit two grenades from candles and tossed them into the oncoming pirates. Jacques had crafted these weapons, making them as potent as the ones he'd used in Dominica. They exploded, sending heaps of men flying into the pews. But even as he spent grenade after grenade, the enemy kept coming in increasing numbers. Red Eye fired all seven of his pistols, felling seven of Thorne's men, but more rushed forth to challenge Red Eye's cutlass. Stede hacked through men with his machetes as if cutting grain during the harvest. Jules and Caiman knocked enemies to the ground with their bare fists. Ross and Cat defended the altar with cutlass and dagger, and for a time held off any challenge.

But this enemy had far more skill than Chevillard's men. They used their far greater numbers and began to whittle away at Ross's crew. Having spent his last grenade, Jacques St. Pierre was left to fight with his cutlass and dagger. Pirates closed in from both sides, but Jacques was agile and very fast. He ducked under a high attack meant to take his head and leaped over a swipe at his knees. He jabbed one enemy in the gut with his dagger, ran a few paces, and slashed his cutlass at whoever pursued. But his stick-and-run method of combat only worked when there was room to run. Jacques leaped up on a pew near the back of the sanctuary and hacked an enemy across the shoulders. He slashed and stabbed, but the enemy hemmed him in. There was nowhere left to go.

From across the great room, Jules saw St. Pierre, and he realized with dreadful certainty that there was no one from his crew near enough to help the Frenchman. St. Pierre continued to fight, but in one moment he pointed down near Jules's side. Jules looked down, saw the barrel, and understood. He kicked an attacker into the vault of green diamonds and then grabbed the barrel. He held its fuse in a candle's flame and hurled the barrel across the room. A smile of gratitude on his lips, Jacques St. Pierre dove off the pew. He caught the barrel for a split second, flung it at his attackers, and fell into one of the vaults of gold. *FOOM!!* The barrel ignited, and though Jacques had designed it mainly to produce smoke, its explosion incinerated dozens of Thorne's men.

Smoke billowed and swirled from the explosion. Many of the

pirates still fighting could not see. Swords slashed from unseen places, daggers stabbed from the dark, and pistol fire laid many men low. In the chaos, Ross and Cat still held the altar. Jules, Stede, and Red Eye stood between the treasure vaults and fought valiantly.

Suddenly, there came a horn blast from within the sanctuary. The sound rang out near the window. For a moment, the fighting stopped. The smoke was beginning to clear, and pirates on both sides of the sanctuary turned to look. Bartholomew Thorne stood at the window. He had Anne in the crook of his elbow and quickly brought a pistol up to her head. "Stop!" he rasped, his eyes fixed on Ross. "You are wasting my men!"

"Father!" Anne cried out. Thorne tightened his grasp.

Behind Ross, Cat heard Thorne's voice and looked up. And at last, he knew the man with cruel blue eyes, the man who had mercilessly beaten Cat's mother to death.

"Tell what's left of your men to stand down!" Thorne commanded. "Or your poor daughter, Anne, will die today."

Ross moved fast. He kicked the sword from Cat's hand, swung round him, and held a pistol to his head. "Tell your men to drop their weapons, Thorne, or I'll kill your son!"

"Captain, what are you doing?" Red Eye whispered urgently.

The color drained from Bartholomew Thorne's face. He stared through the drifting smoke. "Griffin?" he said, with shock and recognition. "How . . . how can this be?"

My name, Cat thought. *Griffin Thorne.*

Thorne's brows lowered, and he leered at Ross. "Go ahead, Declan. Go ahead, Sea Wolf, kill the little blighter. You'll only be finishing my job for me."

Ross cocked his pistol. Cat pleaded, "Captain, no."

"I'm not bluffing!" Ross exclaimed.

"I expect not," said Thorne. "Not with your only daughter's life on the line. You had better not be bluffing. Kill him, Ross. Put him out of my misery."

Ross looked into Cat's eyes, then back at Thorne.

"Why do you now hesitate? Maybe you were bluffing after all." Thorne cocked the lever on his pistol and moved the barrel to Anne's temple. "You fail again, Ross. You wait too long to act. Just like when you lingered on the Caicos, allowing me to take your daughter. And just like that extra month at sea, away from your beautiful wife back in Edinburgh, eh, Ross?"

A ringing came to Ross's ears. His blood turned to ice.

Cat reached into his pocket, felt the lock of hair. He grasped the silver cross and closed his eyes.

"Surely you didn't think strong Abigail would take her own life—hang herself," Thorne said. "I killed her, Ross, strangled her with my—"

Ross swung the pistol away from Cat and fired at Thorne, but his aim was off. A second shot rang out a split second later. Ross recoiled, a spurt of dark blood erupting from his neck. He slammed into Cat, and they both fell hard. Blood flowed out from Declan Ross. It spread on the cold stone floor and pooled around Cat's silver cross. And the volcano outside rumbled louder.

46
THE FIRST MUTINY

Bartholomew Thorne shoved Anne against one of the stone pillars near the aisle. She sprawled onto her back, writhing in pain.

Thorne stepped up onto the dais where Ross and Cat lay stricken and picked up the silver cross. "I have been looking for this," he said, wiping the blood off on his coat. He cast his gaze on Jules, Red Eye, and Stede. "Your captain is dead. Do you wish to join the dead and dying, or will you enjoy the spoils of this vast treasure?"

Thorne's men had had time to reload. Dozens of pistols lifted and pointed at the last of Ross's crew. "And that goes for the rest of you!" Thorne looked into the crowd. The remnant of Ross's crew felt Thorne's icy stare fall upon each of them. "I do not easily grant quarter, but I need more hands to carry this treasure out of here!"

"I will not ask again," said Thorne. A low rumble shook the holy keep. Men glanced furtively at the window. It was nearly night, or so it seemed.

Anne looked up through a matted mess of her own hair. She saw

305

her father sprawled lifeless near the altar. When men came forward out of the pews, men who had served Ross, some for many years, Anne wept.

"Good . . . good," muttered Bartholomew.

Stede looked down at his captain and lifelong friend. He was prepared to die if need—wait! Stede turned his head subtly, stared for a moment at the area where Captain Ross's chest met the floor. Acting quickly, Stede dropped his machetes. They hit the floor with a dull clatter. "I'm sorry, Anne," he said, and he turned quickly away from her anguished sobs. As he looked up to Thorne, he said, "I b' wanting my fair share of that treasure. Especially them green diamonds."

Thorne's smile widened. He stepped down off the platform and grasped a fistful of sparkling jewels. He brought them to Stede, and let them fall one at a time into Stede's hands. "A man knows what he wants," said Thorne, his voice harsh and thick. "A man gets . . . what he wants."

Stede turned to Red Eye and Jules. They looked at him with rage and murderous contempt. "What's the matter with ya?!" Stede screamed. "Fool, mon! Don' b' throwing yer life away for nothing!" Stede snatched a pistol away from one of Thorne's men. Others nearby started to react, but Thorne held up a hand.

Stede took the gun and leveled the barrel right at Jules's chest. "Make the right choice," Stede said, glaring into the big man's eyes. Jules gritted his teeth and dropped his cutlass.

Stede brought the gun to bear on Red Eye. The man's scarred face twisted in confusion. He trembled with rage, but he bowed his head. His sword fell to the ground. His dagger followed. He reached into his coat and dropped two small axes onto the ground. He pulled a long thin knife out of one boot and a snub-nosed pistol out of the other. Last, he reached into a satchel at his side and removed a grenade. He handed that reluctantly to one of Thorne's men.

Stede nodded and handed Thorne the pistol he had taken. Thorne held Stede in his gaze and then said, "I can use a man like you."

Thorne stepped up on the altar and stood near the wooden chest. Another rumble reverberated through the building. "Now, lads," Thorne commanded, "load the sleds! And don't leave a bit of gold or a single jewel behind!" Thorne's men watchfully ushered Stede, Jules, Red Eye, and the others away. They joined squads of Thorne's pirates as they shot into the rooms on either side of the pews. Men in leather harnesses returned pulling large carts on skids. They formed lines and began emptying the vaults of Constantine's Treasure, one pailful at a time.

Cat groaned and started to push himself up from the floor. Thorne motioned to a bald pirate with a stringy beard. "Mister Grimly, take some rope, tie Griffin to one of the pillars. Anne too— but to a different pillar, mind you!"

Grimly nodded and pointed to Ross. "What about 'im?"

Thorne gazed at the wooden chest and did not turn around. "I hardly think it necessary," Thorne said. "But if he breathes, tie him up as well."

"Aye, sir!" The rope Ross and his men had brought lay strewn across the sanctuary floor. Grimly ran to it, pulled out a boarding axe, and cleaved the rope in two. The first section he drew out was far too long. He walked back to its middle and cut it there. Then he yanked Anne by her hair and slammed her up against the stone pillar. She groaned and started to slide away, but Grimly sat her up. He pulled her arms back behind her in a kind of reverse hug of the column and began to cinch her tight with the rope. Round and round he went, until Anne was so constricted she could barely breathe or move her arms. Finally, in an oft-practiced motion, Grimly tied a devious knot behind her.

Cat had risen to his knees when Grimly slammed the flat of his axe against the side of his head. Cat fell over unconscious, and, like a spider, Grimly bound up his prey with the rope.

Grimly reached down and put two fingers on one side of Ross's neck. To his surprise, he found a pulse. He thought about finishing him off with the axe. After all, being the pirate who killed Declan Ross would make for a nice reputation. Grimly glanced up at Thorne and thought better of it. He dragged Ross to another pillar, cut another piece of rope, and tied up his third captive. Suddenly, the whole building shook. Light flashed again through the window, and there came a roar like a roll of thunder.

"Captain Thorne!" a man yelled from the window. "Terrible black smoke is billowin' out of the volcano! The sky is growin' black!"

Thorne growled. He'd planned to have time to savor this victory, but he didn't like the signals the mountain was sending. "Did Skellick bring the *Raven* round? Have all the ships come back?"

The man answered, "They have, sir! Moored offshore, ready and waitin'!"

Thorne turned and faced the sanctuary. "You men!" he yelled to a group milling by the right-hand door. "Light torches, all of you! Get down there and make ready the longboats!" The men by the door scattered.

Thorne continued barking orders. "Get those full sleds out of here!" He looked at the massive vaults that weren't quite empty. "And the rest of you, faster! Get all of it, ALL, do you hear?!"

Thorne turned back to the wooden chest. He felt around the sides for a place to insert the cross. There seemed to be no indentation or slot. He held up Cat's cross to the design on the wooden case's lid. They were an exact match. He pressed the cross lightly onto the lid. There was a clicking sound, and the cross dropped down below the surface of the wood. Another sound, this time metal sliding against metal, and the chest's lid began to rise.

Thorne's mind had conjured all sorts of images of what might be inside the chest. The true treasure, the monk had called it. What would it be? A scepter held by the emperor Constantine himself? A gigantic jewel?

But as the lid continued to rise, revealing the contents of the chest, Thorne's eyes narrowed. What was this? Within the chest was a kind of three-tiered rack of gold. Three identical holes were cut into each level of the rack, and three dark gray nails pierced through all three tiers. *Nails?*

Thorne lifted the golden case out of the chest and held it at eye level. His face twisted in a sickening scowl. Enraged, he slammed the case against the floor. The case snapped in pieces, and two nails scattered across the ground. One came to rest in a pool of Ross's blood, and all at once, every man in the sanctuary felt his heart skip a beat. Men gasped as if to catch a breath that had been stolen. Thorne stood stock-still, knowing with eerie certainty that something had gone horribly wrong.

47

TRIAL BY FIRE

A blinding flash lit the entire sanctuary, and a sound that was not so much of a boom as a wave of pressure slammed into the holy keep. Beams in the rafters cracked, one of the balconies collapsed, and all manner of dust and debris rained down.

The pirates who had been busy loading the last of the treasure onto the sleds all fell to the ground and covered their heads. Even Bartholomew Thorne found himself on the floor. A horrible wind began to howl down upon the keep. Everyone in the sanctuary listened as things began to creak and crackle above. The rafters groaned. All turned to the window as something red and orange careened by. Suddenly, a piece of the roof collapsed, and a flaming piece of rock slammed into the pews. Two of Thorne's men were crushed beneath it. The fire spread quickly.

Still stunned, Thorne's crews looked to their captain. Thorne had pulled himself to his feet and yelled to them, "To the ship! Take what you can carry!"

But his pirates—so entranced by the shining riches—paid no heed and continued to fill satchels with the remaining jewels, gold, and silver. More flaming projectiles struck the roof, and patches of the ceiling burned.

Stede and several men ran out of one of the adjoining rooms. Thorne motioned for Stede to draw near. "Help me!" he commanded, trying to lift the wooden chest.

Stede took one side of the chest and Thorne the other. They pulled with all their might, but there was no give. The monks had somehow secured the chest so that it could not come free. Thorne growled and gave up. The entire building began to shake. Thorne shoved Stede down off the platform and rasped, "The lava! If it reaches the tunnel entrance, we'll be trapped."

"What was in there?" Stede asked as they stomped away.

Thorne stopped and pointed to the floor. "Nails, bah!"

Stede saw one nail that had slid half under a broken pew. Another was still stuck in the golden tiers from the case. A third lay in a puddle of blood near Ross's feet. The moment Thorne turned his back, Stede kicked the bloody nail. His aim was perfect. The nail slid and bounced as it struck the pillar where Cat was tied.

Stede raced out the entrance. Thorne shut the heavy door and locked it. "There will be no escape for the Sea Wolf this time," Thorne rasped.

Far below the clifftop castle, Thorne's men continued loading their longboats with treasure from the sleds. Much had been lost as they raced through the forest and the tunnels, but less than might have been. The pale creatures that had assaulted Thorne's men when they traveled the tunnels the first time did not attack on the return trip. Grimly figured the eruption and the ensuing quake had a lot to do with it. He didn't really care why; he was just glad to get through without being bitten again. Another explosion from above. Grimly looked back over his shoulder as a great spray of fire and ash spewed into the sky.

"Shove off, ya louts!" he roared at them. "We don't have much time!"

"We've still more to load!" a sailor hollered back.

"We'll put the rest in a different boat, ya fool! Shove off, I say, or you'll capsize!"

Grimly looked back up at the black mouth of the tunnel. Where was Thorne? It was Grimly's job to hold one last longboat for his captain. But where was he? What if he never showed up? The thought made Grimly grin. *Captain Grimly*, he thought. *Has a nice ring to—*"

"Mister Grimly!"

He turned and saw his captain and the other man loping down the hill.

"Cat," a female voice yelled. "Cat!" Louder now, higher pitched. "Cat, grab the nail!"

Cat opened his eyes, blinked. And there was Anne. She was bound to a pillar, he realized, just as he was. Blood streaked down her left temple and her face was swollen with bruises, but her eyes were clear. Planks and bits of the roof lay burning all around. The air was half filled with choking smoke.

"What happened?" he asked pitifully.

"The volcano's erupting. Oh, Cat, listen to me!"

"What . . . ?" he asked, still disoriented.

"Grab that nail, Cat!"

He looked frantically, right and then left. And there on the stone was an eight-inch nail, half coated in crimson. Cat looked up to the altar, saw the open chest, and gasped. "Anne, this nail . . ." His voice trailed off.

"Can you reach it, Cat?"

"Ahgg." Cat dropped his shoulders as much as he could and stretched out his left hand. "Got it!" he yelled. The keep shook again.

"Can you pick apart the knot?" Anne asked. "From here it looks like a hitch. I—I'm not sure."

A tremendous crack sounded overhead. They both looked up. A huge portion of the roof had begun to cave. The fire continued to lick all over it, and the sky was an angry black. Then they heard a groan.

"Da!" Anne screamed. Cat turned his head and saw Declan Ross tied to the column nearest the altar. Ross opened his eyes, but his head swayed.

"Anne," he said. "You're alive."

"Yes, Da," she said, and tears spilled down her cheeks.

"You haven't called me that since Edinburgh, since . . ."

"I know," she said. "I know."

"You put a gun to my head," said Cat.

Ross swayed his head to look at him. "I was bluffing."

"Cat, the knot!" Anne yelled.

Cat went to work on the knot. He poked and prodded it with the nail, but nothing pulled loose. At last he found a place that the nail could pierce through. He slid the nail in and lifted. He felt the pressure of a strand of rope and angled his hand enough so that he could pull. It came free. Cat grabbed the strand with his right hand

and pulled like mad. The knot unraveled, and the ropes that bound his arms and shoulders loosened. In a moment, Cat was free.

He had Anne and her father untied a few moments later. He inspected Ross's wound. "This doesn't look good," Cat whispered. The sanctuary shook. Cat and Anne steadied themselves on a pillar.

"I'll live," said Ross, but his eyes looked weak.

"Okay, we'll carry you."

"Wait," said Anne. "I think Thorne locked the door to the keep. I heard it slam when he left."

"I'll check," Cat said, and, jumping over fires and broken pews, he raced out of the sanctuary. He returned quickly. "You were right. It's locked. There's no latch on this side, no way to open it."

"How do we get out?" Anne looked around.

"Lay your father down. We'll check all the rooms. There's got to be another passage or door or something."

Listening to the howling wind and intermittent rumbles from the mountain, Cat and Anne darted in and out of the small rooms on both sides of the sanctuary. They found the stairs leading to the second level and more rooms. But not one had an exterior door or a window.

They raced down to find Declan crawling across the floor. "Father, what are you doing?" Anne cried. "Lie still!"

"Rope," Ross said with a pained cough. "Like the treasure."

"What?" Cat asked. But as he looked at the rope, he began to understand.

"Ah, he's right!" Cat ran to the window. He saw the last of Thorne's ships exiting the shards, and, down below, he saw the *Robert Bruce*, waiting. "We'll lower your father down to the ship in one of the treasure baskets!" he yelled, and ran to the first basket. Next, he combed through the pews and found a massive coil of rope. Realizing he still had the nail in his left hand, he dropped it into his pocket.

"Here!" he cried, and tossed one end of the rope and the basket to Anne. "Tie this end to the basket hoops!" He took the other end and ran to the pillar closest to the window. Around and over, back and through—twice more—and then he put a foot up on the column and pulled the end of the rope with all his might.

"Okay," he said, "give me the basket!"

Cat ran to the window and tossed the basket out. He watched it plummet. Down it went, until, finally, the rope went taut. "NO!!" Cat yelled. "It's not long enough—not near long enough!"

"Oh no, Cat, what can . . . wait, what about these other pieces?" She pointed to the pieces that Thorne's men had used to tie them up. "Can we tie them to each other?"

"We could try," Cat said doubtfully. "But rope this thick . . . it could slip, and then we'd all be dead."

A large piece of rafter fell, crushing a pew beneath it. "We've got to do something!" Anne yelled.

Cat ran about the room looking for something, anything he could use to connect the strands of rope. He saw so many familiar faces among the fallen as he ran. Midge had been shot from behind by the look of it. And Caiman was half-buried in debris. Cat had to stay focused.

Anne fished up the basket. She untied the end from the basket loops and grabbed another section of the rope. It may not work, she thought, but she was surely going to try.

Cat looked into all the vaults. There were a few small daggers in one of them, but weapons were not what they needed. He charged up the altar and looked all around it. A tapestry on the wall might help. No, that would slip just like the rope. There was nothing he could use. He turned too quickly and slipped in the blood, almost falling. He looked down and saw one of the other nails, the one still stuck in the golden section of the rack. An image flooded into his mind. The *Bruce* that night in the crosscurrents. There was Ramiro barking orders. Enrique and Claudio shifting the bowsprit in the gooseneck. The gooseneck! As if in another life, Cat saw himself grabbing the tack pin off the deck and shoving it into the thread holes on the gooseneck. That's when he knew what to do.

"Anne, I've got it!" he yelled. "Get me all the pieces of rope! Tie off the last piece to the treasure basket."

Cat reached for the other nail, let it slide out into his pocket. Then he banged the broken three-tiered rack against the side of one of the treasure vaults. That left him with three rectangular pieces of gold, each with three holes in it.

"Where's the other nail?" he yelled.

"There," Ross said. He pointed. Cat saw it half-buried in the debris of a broken pew. He grabbed the third nail and put it in his pocket as well. He took the gold tiers to the edge of one of the vaults and held half on the edge as he pushed down on the other half. The gold bent easily against the pressure, giving Cat a U-shaped piece of metal with a hole on the top and the bottom.

"Please, let this work," he said. He found a piece of broken stone from one of the crushed treasure vaults. He grabbed one end of the rope, took out a nail, and aimed it in the center of the thick rope, far above its cut end. He slammed the stone down like a hammer and pierced the rope through. He yanked out the nail and did the same to one of the other pieces of rope. *One last step*, he thought.

He lined up the holes in the two pieces of rope with the guide holes in one of the bent pieces of gold, and hammered the nail through them all. Then he slammed the rock-hammer down on the end of the nail until it bent at a right angle. He gave a yank on the two rope ends, and it held.

With Anne's help, he repeated the process twice more. At last, they had the rope reattached and at its longest possible reach. Cat ran with the basket to the window and slowly lowered it down.

The roof partially caved in. Anne shrieked. The fire spread across the floor. "Help me, Cat!" she screamed. "My father!"

Cat let the basket fall the rest of the way, not sure if it reached the *Bruce* or not. He helped Anne move Declan closer to the window, but the fire threatened to hem them in. Cat ran to the window and looked down. There was someone on the deck waving what looked like a flag. Cat hoisted up the long rope and found the old banner of the *William Wallace*, Ross's beloved claymore and prowling wolf.

"It's long enough!" Cat yelled. "It reaches the ship!" Cat touched the flag and smiled.

They carefully eased Declan Ross into the basket, but before they lowered him down, Cat ran up onto the altar. He wasn't sure why he did it, but he grabbed the leather book that lay next to the wooden chest. Its cover was singed, but it looked mostly intact. He laid the volume on Declan's chest and crossed the captain's arms over the book.

Ever so slowly, they lowered Declan Ross back to his ship. "You're next," he said to Anne. She might have once argued, but not now. She knew that Cat could climb the ropes better than she could. She would ride in the basket.

Cat held the basket tight near the window so that Anne could get in. "Ready?" he asked.

"Not yet," she said. And shocking him completely, Anne leaned over and kissed him on the cheek. "Not bad for a pirate," she said with a wink. Cat almost let go of the rope, but caught it just in time. He winked back and lowered her down.

Once she was on the deck, Cat took a deep breath and began to slide over the side. "Wait!" came a voice from behind. From behind one of the columns walked a pale figure with wild, somewhat-singed hair.

"Jacques!" Cat yelled, and ran to the Frenchman.

"Oui," he said, falling into Cat's arms. "But I am not well."

Cat pulled up the rope one last time. His arms burned as he lowered Jacques down to the deck. Then, with the roof caving in behind him, Cat climbed over the side, grabbed the rope, and began his descent. Cat slid down the rope a few yards and ducked as small pieces of debris came hurtling down. He waited a few beats and continued down the rope. His arms ached, and each time the rope blew across the rockface, he had to brace himself to keep from slamming into the cliff. He passed the first nail joint, and then the second. He reached the third and stopped.

He looked at the nail joining the two pieces of rope. If it had not been for this nail and the other two, Cat knew he, Anne, and Captain Ross all would have died in the fires raging above. The rope, joined with these long nails, was a lifeline. But it was more than that. Cat thought about how the three nails had once been used for a completely different purpose.

Cat climbed back above the third nail-joint and wrapped his right arm in the rope. He began tugging on the nail-joint. He yanked at it with his left hand. Then he shoved it between his knees and tried to use his entire torso to separate the joint.

"What is he doing?" Nubby asked. "Is he stuck?"

"I don't know," said Anne. "Ramiro, keep the ship steady."

"I'm trying, young miss. I'm trying. But the wind might have something to say about it."

They watched Cat struggling on the rope. Then, to their horror, the entire rope fell. Cat plummeted toward the deck of the ship. Anne closed her eyes. They heard a splash. Ramiro, Nubby, and Anne flew to the rail.

"Is someone going to help me up?" Cat asked. He floated in the midst of what looked like a mile of swirling rope.

48

THE SECOND MUTINY

Stede was now aboard the *Raven*, and they had sailed with all speed away from the shards. Thorne had given Stede plenty of work to do on deck. "Fix the jib sail! Tack that rope down! Fix the rail on the quarterdeck!" But Thorne hadn't once let Stede out of his sight. Stede had heard the *Raven*'s quartermaster, Skellick, calling out distances. They were now just a dozen miles from the crosscurrents and the maelstrom of waves and sucking chasms. *When we b' getting to those outrageous waves*, Stede thought bitterly, *I b' fixing this ship, all right.*

Red Eye, who was on board one of Thorne's galleons, and Jules, who was on a two-masted sloop, had the same idea.

After carefully navigating back through the shards, Ramiro called out to his now-skeleton crew, "Ease back on the sails, lads! There's no rush!"

"Go after them!" a wheezing, throaty voice commanded from below. Declan Ross had somehow made it to the stairs. He leaned on the rail and knelt on the top step. Nubby came charging over to him with Anne at his heels.

"What are ya doin'?" Nubby chastised. "This isn't a wee scratch! You've got to stay in yer bed!"

"Da, listen to Nubby! You're not well."

Cat, Anne, and Nubby helped Declan to a bench by the helm.

"I said, go after them!" Ross exclaimed, his head rocking gently.

"Who?" Ramiro asked. "Bartholomew Thorne?"

Ross nodded.

"He's gone mad," Nubby said.

"Go after the *Raven*!" Ross muttered. "Treasure."

"Who cares about the treasure?" Ramiro bellowed. "We've got a skeleton crew. He's got a dozen ships or more!"

"It's still my ship," Ross said. "I'm ordering you to go after Thorne."

"Ah, now there's where you're mistaken," Ramiro said. "You let me win the duel, and I said you could use the ship, not keep it. You have to pay me if—"

Ross reached into his pocket and let a handful of green diamonds spill out onto the deck. "That ought to be enough."

"Biscuits and gravy!" exclaimed Nubby. "Is that part . . . is that . . . ?"

Ross nodded. "Now that the ship is mine, I command you to chase Thorne."

An ominous rumble came from the volcano a mile behind them.

The mantle of smoke and ash had spread far and wide, and they couldn't see the end of it.

Ramiro bent down to pick up the diamonds. "Look here, Ross," he said. "I accept your bid for the ship, but I'm a sailor and a shipbuilder. I can sail, and I can fish. But I can't fight a pirate like Thorne."

"I'll tell you what to do," Ross said, wincing and closing his eyes.

"But, Da!" Anne was at his side.

"NO!" Everyone turned and looked at Cat. "Declan Ross, you will do no such thing. You are injured, sir, and therefore unfit for command. As the senior member of your crew, I hereby relieve you of duty."

Declan's face became a mask of anger. "Cat, you . . ."

"You are relieved, sir," Cat said. "Now, with all due respect, please leave me to my command. Bartholomew Thorne is far ahead of us. I'll need to concentrate if we're going to catch him."

Ross struggled to understand for a moment. Then he grinned wildly. "That's a man, Cat. That's a man!"

Ross closed his eyes, muttering something about "a surprise for ol' Bart."

Anne looked at Cat. "What does he mean by—"

Suddenly, a flash lit the sky and the looming clouds above. A thunderous blast from behind made them all jump and then look off the stern. The entire top third of the volcano blasted into the air and disintegrated. A massive, angry red inferno rose up as the Isle of Swords was consumed. Pieces of debris began to fall all around the man-of-war. One burning hunk went right through the top deck.

"Nubby," Cat shouted. "See to it that doesn't start a fire in the powder kegs."

Nubby's eyes went as big as eggs, and he charged down the steps.

Cat squinted off the stern. The ocean behind them looked strange. The others looked too. It was as if the Isle of Swords was sinking. No, not sinking. The ocean was rising.

"Ramiro," Cat said nervously, "would you be so kind as to man the swinging bowsprit, on course due south. I think we are about to make up a little time."

"Aye, Captain!" Ramiro yelled as he sprinted from the helm.

"Full sails!" Cat bellowed. The rest of the crew, all eighteen of them, flew into action, climbing the ratlines, pulling halyards, and raising sails.

The massive swell rolled up behind the *Bruce* just as the southerly prevailing wind grabbed the sails. The ship sprang forward as if shot from a cannon. The *Bruce* sailed after the *Raven* at a speed few sailors had ever experienced on a ship that size.

"He's gaining on us, sir!" said Skellick.

"Who's gaining on us?!" Thorne rasped. He stared off the stern, but night had fallen and all he could see were tall square sails.

"It's Ross's ship," his quartermaster replied.

"Ross?" Thorne stared. "He's dead!"

"Well, someone's in his ship and right at our heels!"

"Crosscurrents ahead!" someone shouted as the ship rocked to its side.

Thorne looked out and saw the same wild phenomena he'd witnessed just the night before—the same perilous seas that had decimated his fleet. Of course, the men who survived were his best captains. If half of them survived, he'd have enough treasure to create his fleet. "Batten down the hatches, lads!" Thorne yelled.

"But, sir," said Skellick, "what about Ross?"

"It's not ROSS!!"

"Uh, sorry, Captain. What should we do concerning the ship behind us?"

"Let him come!" Thorne yelled lustily. "When we get to the other side of the crosscurrents, the fleet will turn and blow him out of the water!"

I don't think so, Stede thought. While Thorne was busy looking at the *Bruce*, Stede had slipped around the side of the quarterdeck. He ran to the port rail and grabbed an axe from a pirate climbing the ratline. "Aye!" the man said, but as he turned, Stede hit the man so hard in the jaw that the man flew off the ship and disappeared into the churning sea.

Staying low, Stede took the axe and ran across the deck to the mainmast. Then he waited.

The *Raven* was nearly out of the crosscurrents. Thorne checked the stern. No sign of the ship that had been following them. He stared out off the bow. They were pointed almost due south now. He lifted his spyglass and saw something white, but massive rolling swells kept getting in the way. *What is that?* he wondered.

"Sir, look!" Thorne turned to where his quartermaster was pointing. He watched in horror as the Spanish carrack carrying the most treasure was slammed by a wave, turned sideways, and pushed into one of the bottomless black gulfs. Another wave crashed on top of it, sealing its fate.

"Noooo!" Thorne screamed.

"Skellick," Thorne shouted. "We don't want to—" The mainsail on the aft mast fell from its spar. "Get the sail!" he bellowed. "Hoist the sail!" As the ship rose up on a huge wave, Thorne looked again to the south. This time, he thought he saw several white objects scattered east to west across the horizon.

Then the mainsail on the mizzenmast went down. "What is happening?!" Thorne cried out. "This is madness!"

The *Raven* was still able to maneuver enough to stay out of harm's way, but just barely. In vain, the crew raced around trying to get the sail back up just as the mainsail on the foremast came down.

Stede thought it dreadfully funny how Thorne's men scrambled to try to raise the sails. Every time they grabbed a rope, they found it had been severed and was of no use. Stede had been busy with his axe. It was too bad, Stede thought. Too bad he wouldn't be able to enjoy the victory over Thorne. By cutting down the mainsails, Stede had crippled the ship. Still in the crosscurrents, it would no doubt be smashed to pieces and take everyone, Stede included, to the bottom of the Atlantic.

Bartholomew Thorne pushed Skellick aside and took the helm himself. He saw a giant wave coming from far to starboard. Thorne spun the wheel frantically, but without the mainsails, the ship wouldn't respond. But just as the deadly curling wave approached the starboard side of the ship, another swell, this one mountainous and wide, drove under the *Raven* from behind. As this wave rolled through, the sea began to calm. It was like a great rolling pin on lumpy dough. Thorne could not believe his good fortune. He looked left and right and saw several of his ships, galleons, frigates, and a schooner. The great chasms had closed. The waves grew less and less. The crosscurrent was gone, and the *Raven* was safe.

"We've done it!" Thorne yelled with maniacal joy.

But before anyone else could speak, flashes lit the sea from the south. A cannonball whooshed overhead. When the last swell sank into the sea, tall masts rose up across the horizon. Each had full square sails. Thorne lifted his spyglass and saw the red cross of St. George on flags flying high above five different ships. *The British!*

"Come about!" Thorne screamed. "Fire the port cannons!"

The British warships fanned out, firing at will. A cannonball crashed into the center of the main deck. One of Thorne's men went cartwheeling into the air and overboard. Another shot blew apart a cannon bay belowdecks. Still another struck the stern.

Stede had hidden himself under a tarp when the shooting started. The last cannonball had gone right over his head. *I think it b' about time for me to leave*, Stede thought. He sprinted through the men scattering on the deck and found what he needed. He took his axe and cut the two lines that secured a small rowboat. As it fell, he dove in and rode it the rest of the way to the water.

"The British?" Nubby yelled. "Where did they come from?"

Declan Ross opened his eyes briefly and began to laugh.

Cat closed on the *Raven*'s stern and then gave the order, "Fire starboard cannons!" There were only ten men on the gun deck, so they could only fire a few of the cannons. But it was enough.

Thorne watched with horror as Ross's ship appeared behind the *Raven*. "Fire the chasers!" he yelled, referring to the two cannons he had on the stern just above the waterline. The command came too late. The *Bruce* fired, missing with two shots, but the third tore violently into the back of the *Raven*. The poop deck and the rear cabins exploded, and debris showered the quarterdeck and the helm.

With the explosion, Bartholomew Thorne had fallen to his knees. He stood now and looked at the back of his ship. The rear cabins, including his captain's quarters, had been ravaged by the cannonball and, in its aftermath, the fires. Nothing remained of his quarters. The fires once again had taken his Heather away.

When the HMS *Oxford* drifted alongside of the *Raven*, the British met little resistance. Thorne's crew had been thinned by their experiences at sea and on the Isle of Swords. And many had died during the battle. Commodore Blake found Bartholomew Thorne at the helm, his hands on the ship's wheel. He stood as if frozen, even as Blake's men surrounded him.

And discarded at Thorne's feet, the infamous bleeding stick lay soaking in a puddle of seawater. Blake lifted the stave from the deck and held it up as if it were a scorpion. Water droplets, tinged with crimson, ran off the ends of the spikes.

Blake looked at it, his face a mask of disgust.

When Thorne looked upon his bleeding stick, a chilling, dark smile curled at the corner of his mouth. Blake saw in the vanquished captain's glare a murderous cunning so black and ruthless that he stepped backward a pace. Then Blake turned and, with a mighty heave, hurled Thorne's weapon far out into the ocean.

"All secure?" Commodore Blake asked, referring to the other ships from Thorne's decimated fleet.

"We can't be sure, sir," said Mr. Jordan. "Some of Thorne's vessels may have come out of the crosscurrents far from where we intercepted the *Raven*. But of the ships we engaged, only one got away."

"What?" said Blake. "How?"

"The schooner, sir," said Mr. Jordan. "Its sails were down. We thought it dead in the water. But when we boarded the *Raven*, the sails on the schooner flew up. It caught the wind and fled. The *King Richard* and the *Triumph* opened fire, but . . . missed."

Blake nodded. Bartholomew Thorne had been captured, and that's all that mattered for now.

"What about Ross?" Sir Nigel asked. They turned and stared across the waves to the *Bruce*. "We can't just let him go."

"I don't see anyone else out there," said Commodore Blake. "Do you, Mister Jordan?"

"No, sir," he replied. "No one at all."

49

GHOSTS OF THE PAST

There weeks had passed since Commodore Blake's fleet sailed for the British fort at New Providence. Bartholomew Thorne and his remaining crew would there await trial and, eventually . . . the gallows. The *Robert Bruce* made sail for Scotland and Ross's beloved Edinburgh. There, Ross and Jacques St. Pierre convalesced under Nubby's care in a small manor home. To pass the time, Anne took Cat to see the sights all over the city. Ramiro had been itching to get back to his shipyard in Sines, but waited until he was convinced Ross was out of the woods to depart. He left the *Bruce* with its new owner and chartered a schooner to Portugal.

"I've got to go out," Ross said one day. He threw his legs over the side of the bed and began to stand.

"You just lay yourself back down!" Nubby commanded. "Or I'll fetch my spoon!"

"I'm well, Nubs," he said. "And a nice meat pie from O'Lordan's—that would do me right. Besides, you let Jacques go out a week back."

"But he wasn't hurt near as bad as you."

"Nubs, he was almost blown to bits." Ross put a hand on Nubby's shoulder. "Really . . . I'm fine. And I'll just be gone for a little while."

Nubby shrugged. He knew his captain would go with or without permission.

"Thanks," Ross said. He dressed warmly and left the manor home. A cool mist drifted over the cobblestone streets and between the crowded buildings. With some urgency in his step, Ross turned a corner and strode up a hill . . . right past O'Lordan's.

At last he found the gate he was looking for and passed under a wrought-iron arch into a vast cemetery. Trees flourished among the tombstones. *She always loved the trees*, Ross thought as he meandered among the plots.

Then he saw it. The sight of her gravestone constricted Ross's chest. He coughed, and tears trickled into the creases near his eyes. He knelt in a patch of ferns and laid his head against the stone. "I know what Thorne did, Abigail," Ross said, rubbing his fingers along the engraved contours of her name. "I'm so sorry I wasn't there to stop him . . . then. The British have him now. And he'll hang for sure."

He wept quietly for some time, and it seemed years of anguish flowed out of him. The tears eventually began to dry. He lifted his head a little and said, "Anne's well. She has your spirit . . . and your beauty. But she has far too much of my love of the sea in her. I tried, Abigail . . . and we were so close to treasure that would have freed us. But what little I salvaged won't be enough. And the British took the rest. Abigail, . . . ," he hesitated, "I must still remain a pirate."

"Now where'd ya get a fool idea like that, mon?" came a voice from behind.

"Stede?" Ross turned and leaped to his feet.

Three figures stood atop the hill above Ross. It was hard to see their faces, for the mist swirled among them. But one of the shadowy beings stood a foot or more taller than the other two. "We just made port," came a deep voice from the giant.

Ross ran to them. "Stede," he cried. "Jules, Red Eye! By the grace of the Almighty, you . . . you're alive!" He embraced them each in turn and then backed away. "How?"

"Thorne put me on a schooner," said Red Eye, a mischievous smile curling. "And see, me and the captain of the vessel had a bit of a quarrel. It seems after the crosscurrents, the crewmen began to disappear one by one. I found old Stede here in nothing but a rowboat."

"It b' a good thing ya picked me up!" said Stede. "Or the British would have put ya on the bottom!"

"Jules?" Ross cocked an eyebrow. "What happened to you?"

"Thanks to a few of Thorne's former slaves," Jules replied in his thunderous voice, "I managed to commandeer a ship. Near as I can tell, we came out of the crosscurrents miles from everyone else."

Stede laughed. "With the British firin' on us, we b' haulin' out of there as fast as the wind would take us. We b' not knowin' what happened with the *Bruce*. So, thinkin' ya might head back to Portugal with Ramiro, we sailed there. Jules and his crew b' havin' the same idea. We met there and figured b'fore we sail back to the

Spanish Main, we might take a look in Edinburgh. Glad we did! When we saw the *Bruce*, we came close to swimmin' to shore."

Declan Ross clasped his men in turn on the shoulder. "I can't tell you how much joy you've brought me."

"And more b'sides," said Stede. "There'll b' no need for any of us to remain pirates a day longer. The two ships we took from Thorne, they b' plenty heavy with treasure."

Ross eyed the three men. "How soon can you be ready to set sail?"

"What ya b' thinkin', ya outrageous mon?"

Ross nodded. "Saint Celestine, gentlemen. The treasure belongs to the monks, after all." Stede, Jules, and Red Eye exchanged worried glances.

Ross grinned. "Though I expect when Cat shows the monks what he brought back from the Isle of Swords, they'll happily part with enough to meet our needs."

50

THE EVE OF DESTRUCTION

A few months later, Commodore Blake ushered nine monks into the cavernous receiving room of his hilltop estate.

"Father Gregory," Blake said with a humble bow. "Welcome to New Providence."

"Thank you, Commodore," the monk replied, lowering his hood. The other eight kept their faces cloaked. "You are kind to provide our passage here."

"I must admit I was intrigued when I received your letter," said Blake. "But I suppose Ross and his crew decided against joining us in this meeting after all."

At that, seven of the monks let their hooded robes fall to the floor. And there before Commodore Blake stood Declan Ross in a new hunter-green kilt, his daughter, Anne, uncomfortable in an elegant evening dress, Jacques St. Pierre attired more or less like the King of France, and Stede, Red Eye, Jules, and Cat. "I stand corrected. I am pleased you were able to make it," Blake said, "and I am a man of my word. You and your crew are guests, not prisoners."

"Now, allow me to introduce you to my lovely bride, Dolphin," said Blake as a youthful beauty walked into the room. She had crimson hair, porcelain-white skin, and lips like rose petals.

While Blake introduced his guests to Dolphin, Jules and Stede picked up the robes from the floor, folded them, and placed them on a nearby bench.

Father Gregory gestured, and the other man at last revealed his face and head. "This is Father Brun. He is of a special clerical order sent recently to Saint Celestine to help, uh . . . resolve a few matters."

Pale skin and very light blond hair, intelligent blue eyes that darted side to side restlessly—a curious-looking man, for a monk, Blake thought. "Welcome to New Providence, Father Brun."

"You showed remarkable faith, Commodore," said Father Brun, "agreeing to this meeting. I believe God will do wondrous things through our efforts tonight."

"Yes . . . well, quite." Blake felt awkward for a moment, but recovered and said, "It is true we have much to discuss . . . and to plan—"

"And to eat?" asked St. Pierre.

"And to eat," said the commodore, laughing. "Let us retire to the dining hall. Sir Nigel and his radiant wife, Carinne, are waiting."

Once they were all seated at a long table laden with every imaginable delicacy, the conversation was jovial. "Look at the two of you," said Sir Nigel, gesturing to Anne and Dolphin, who sat together. "You could be sisters."

"Sisters? I could never be as pretty as Lady Dolphin," Anne said.

"You are beautiful," Dolphin replied. "Mister Thorne certainly thinks so." Anne had glanced more than a few times in Cat's direction also. She thought he looked rather dashing—though she would rather be boiled in pudding than admit it.

Commodore Blake turned to Cat. "Should we call you Mister Thorne? Or do you prefer Cat?"

"My name is Griffin Thorne," he said hesitantly. "But I am fond of Cat."

Ross put a hand on Cat's shoulder.

After dinner was heartily consumed, Dolphin and Carinne excused themselves and went to the parlor for tea. Anne was invited, but politely refused. She and her father had agreed earlier that she would be allowed to be present for the discussion.

The mood of the conversation changed considerably. "Your other crewmen?" Blake asked.

"Some returned, but the others . . ." Ross's voice trailed off. "I fear they perished aboard Thorne's vessels or in the perilous cross-currents."

"My heartfelt condolences, Captain Ross," said Blake, and he meant it. "My wife and I both have lost men at sea before. It . . . is never easy."

Ross nodded. "How many were lost on the *Oxford*?"

"I was not actually referring to the *Oxford*," Commodore Blake replied cautiously. He glanced at Cat. "With all due respect to Cat, I was serving as a mate on a frigate called the *Trafalgar* when Thorne attacked one stormy night. His cannon fire was precise, and one by one, he took out our masts. I was struck by debris and rendered unconscious. When I awoke, the ship was aflame and listing to port. Bodies were strewn from one end of the deck to the other. Still, I traversed it looking for survivors. I went below and searched the cabins. In one of them, I found Dolphin . . . weeping over her father. She was just a girl, and her father had hidden her in the wardrobe."

"How . . ." Cat cleared his throat. "How did you get off the ship?"

"That, my friend, I can answer only by saying it was divine providence. Thorne had, of course, cut all the rowboats adrift. And yet I found one hanging by the side of the ship—hanging by the fraying edge of a single piece of rope that had wedged between splintered planks of the hull."

"Still . . . the storm?" suggested Ross.

"Providence," Blake said. "I do not remember much about that night in the rowboat upon that rolling sea. I only remember the sunrise and the white sails of the Spanish ship that rescued us."

Cat had been thinking a lot about providence lately. The three nails that crucified Christ—without them, he, Ross, Anne, and St. Pierre would have perished in the flames of the burning clifftop castle on the Isle of Swords. He knew the nails were in good hands with Father Brun and the Brethren. But he wondered if, one day, he might look on them again.

As the others talked, Sir Nigel quietly squirmed. Finally, he abruptly interrupted the conversation. "What of the treasure?" he asked.

Ross shifted uncomfortably in his chair. Commodore Blake was first to reply. "In all, we captured three of Thorne's ships, including the *Raven*. The treasure that was on those three is immense."

Father Brun spoke quietly. "The Brethren would like one-third to go to the British and an equal portion to the Brothers of Saint Celestine for the rebuilding of their abbey and all that Thorne destroyed."

"And the rest?" Sir Nigel asked. "What about the final third of the treasure?"

Father Brun hesitated. "Various charitable endeavors. And of course, Ross and his crew must be compensated for . . . services rendered."

An awkward silence descended. Blake's eyes shifted from Fathers Brun and Gregory to Ross and back.

"And now for the matter at hand: Father Brun's proposition," Father Gregory said.

Father Brun nodded. "As we wrote in our initial correspondence, the increase in pirate attacks on settlements and ships at sea concerns us greatly."

"As you wrote, Father," said Blake. "But I'm not sure what more England can do, which is why I found your proposal intriguing. But how would it work?"

"You will need the right kind of help," Father Brun said. "Based on the advice of Captain Ross and his crew, we could create a fleet of pirate hunters manned by pirates themselves."

"I have connections in the sweet trade," Ross said. "If His Majesty of England would offer a full pardon to any pirates who want to turn and hunt down those who wreak havoc on the seas, I believe some former privateers would join the cause. We'd clean up half your problem that way, and it would only be the hardened, most destructive lot left to catch. And who better to hunt pirates than the pirates themselves?"

"Commodore, this is nonsense," said Sir Nigel. "Pirates . . . sailing for England? Whoever heard of such a thing? They are scoundrels—reprobates!"

"And so are we all," said Father Brun. "But for the grace of God. Many of those who now haunt the seas would still be honest sailors—if their governments had not cast them aside."

"Our plan," said Father Gregory, "will be an offer of redemption. For years, the monks of Saint Celestine have harbored pirates on our island. Always we hoped they would turn away from piracy, but rarely did they. If one of their own could lead them, then maybe . . ."

Ross waited for a moment and then said, "These pirate-hunter captains and their crews would be paid. And they'd need new ships, the best cannons, and other provisions."

Blake's eyebrows rose high, and he shook his head. "Ross, it's a good idea—in principle—but supposing I could get my government to support this, do you have any idea what this would cost?"

"Already, the Brethren has had the good fortune to recover more of its treasure, with the assistance of Captain Ross and his crew," Father Brun said. "So we have the ability to pay them. There need be no money spent from the king's coffers."

Blake raised an eyebrow.

"So, Commodore, will your government grant pardons and commit letters of marque to Ross, his crew, and other pirates who willingly turn?"

Commodore Blake smiled and nodded his head. "Considering it will cost England nothing and likely rid the seas of many of England's enemies . . . yes, I think so."

"I have been empowered by the Brethren to sign any documents the king might request," Father Brun said.

"I shall have the papers drawn up immediately," Blake said.

Sir Nigel excused himself. "If you'll pardon me, gentlemen, I think I will retire for the evening. But I want the ladies to have their fun. Do tell my Carinne that I have gone and will send a carriage for her later."

The conversation carried on for several minutes, and then the commodore led his guests out onto the balcony. "Quite an extraordinary view, wouldn't you say?"

"Magnifique!" exclaimed St. Pierre.

"Breathtaking," said Ross. The commodore's residence was very high on a hill overlooking the port of New Providence and the British fort. A full moon shed glorious white light on the ocean, the furled sails of the tall ships, and the tops of the palms.

Commodore Blake noticed Cat looking down at the fort. "I suspect you know," Blake said. "His sentence will be carried out at sunset tomorrow. Are you sure you want to see this?"

"I'm not sure," Cat replied. He stared at the dark building, the sharp stonework . . . the gallows platform. His father, Bartholomew Thorne, was down there in one of the cells. Cat wasn't sure at all that he wanted to see. "If somehow, even if it's the last moment before . . . If he should show some remorse—I need to see that."

A frantically ringing bell snapped them all out of their thoughtful trance.

"That is the warning bell from the fort."

Cat pointed. "The sea—"

As they watched, the tide drew back from the fort's sea wall, exposing the seafloor, first leaving small boats leaning on the ground and then landlocking tall ships. As the bell continued to ring furiously, men on the decks of the leaning ships jumped overboard and tried to run toward shore, only to be bogged down in silt. Those onshore rushed en masse toward the highest point they could reach.

"Follow me," Blake yelled as he sprinted through his estate. Ross, Cat, Anne, and the other guests followed. They burst through the building's front door and stopped short. Dolphin and Carinne ran up behind them.

They watched as a wall of water surged in from the ocean. It swirled around the listing ships and covered the exposed seafloor.

Then it slammed into the fort's sea wall. But it did not stop. It flooded over the wall, knocking guards off their feet, causing them to slide in the rushing water along the cobbled stone. There seemed no end to the powerful and sudden wave. It began to break ships free of their moorings and smashed them together. On what had been the dry shore, palm trees snapped and buildings were flooded. And still the water continued to rise.

They watched in horror as the black ocean water climbed over the fort's walls, filled its courtyard, and, at last, submerged its cells.

The devastation of the massive wave on the island of New Providence could not be measured. All structures not made of heavy stone or not high above sea level like Blake's estate were completely washed away. When the water finally receded enough for rescuers to get down to the fort, Commodore Blake, Declan Ross, and Cat were first among them. They ran through the fort's splintered gate, across the mud-strewn courtyard, and to the cells.

They saw a few empty cells as they ran. These were filled with muddy brown puddles and pieces of debris. But the cells that held prisoners were far worse. Not a single living soul in any cell. Many of Thorne's crew, who just a month earlier had run their hands through treasure enough to make them kings, were now left with strands of muddy seaweed draped across their pale fingers. Ross thought it ironic that one of the most powerful and feared pirates in the world, the scourge of the sea, would meet his end in this way . . . drowned like a common rat.

Blake, Ross, and Cat turned a corner, but knowing the way, Blake pulled ahead. He raced up a small flight of stairs to the upper level. As Ross and Cat tried to keep up, they could see the dark waterline high on the stone. It was far above the doors of the cells.

Ross and Cat took the stairs two at a time, trying to catch up. They raced along the walk just in time to see Blake stop and step awkwardly back from an open cell door. Cat's heart began to pound. He and Ross approached slowly and looked inside. But the cell that had held Bartholomew Thorne was empty.

Acknowledgments

Thank you, Mary Lu, for helping me weather the storms of life. This book, and all that I write, is as much yours as mine. Your love and sacrifice made it happen. 1C13. To my faithful crew: Kayla, Tommy, Bryce, and Rachel . . . you are the greatest treasure a father could ever hope to have. I love you and always will. Brian, Jeff, and Leslie: My imagination would never have been what it is today without your presence in my life. Mom and Dad: Thank you for always sparking my creativity and love of reading—and for providing me with a rich and anchor-stable home. To the Dovel family: Thank you for your endless generosity and for continuing to support my writing. You guys SO rock!

Bill and Lisa Russell, Dave and Heather Peters, Doug and Chris Smith, Todd Wahlne, Danny Sutton, Warren Cramutola, Chris and Alaina Haerbig, Dan and Courtney Cwiek, Janet Berbes, Chris and Dawn Harvey, Don and Valerie Counts, Mat and Serrina Davis, and Jeff and Leslie Leggett—you are most excellent friends. Michelle Black: You continue to be a special encouragement in my writing.

The brilliant students of Folly Quarter Middle School—Thank you for helping me develop *Isle of Swords*. Dr. Carl Perkins and Mrs. Julie Rout: Thank you for the time to share my books with others. To the 6th Grade Team . . . your talent and expertise inspire me daily. (Deer!) And to Susan Ryan, thanks for the cool pirate book!

Gregg Wooding: Thanks for standing in the gap so many times. All my friends at Thomas Nelson Children's Books & Education: Thank you for the opportunity to set sail on a new adventure. And Beverly and June for helping me make *Isle of Swords* worthy of being published.

My friends at the Christian Science Fiction and Fantasy Tour: Your actions are "like small stones that start an avalanche in the mountains." DiscoverSea Shipwreck Museum in Bethany Beach: There's no research like seeing and touching firsthand. I love your museum! The staff of Eldersburg Public Library: I love your quiet study room!

Fantasy 4 Fiction Tour friends, Bryan Davis, Sharon Hinck, and Christopher Hopper: Thanks for an incredible adventure. And oh yeah, Christopher, we need to get back to the Banshee! I hear they have a new sandwich with Jamaican jerk sauce. And finally, to my readers: I pray that this adventure is worthy of your time and hope that it'll lead you to greater adventures of your own.

Florida
New Providence
Bahama Island
Andros Island
British Fort
Cuba
Great Inagua
Cayman Islands
Hisp
Jamaica
80
85
CARIBBEAN
Sand
Honduras
85
Nicaragua
Costa Rica
Panama
Colombia